Firing

philosophies within contemporary ceramic practice

Firing

philosophies within contemporary ceramic practice

David Jones

The Crowood Press

First published in 2007 by
The Crowood Press Ltd
Ramsbury, Marlborough
Wiltshire SN8 2HR

www.crowood.com

British Library Cataloguing-in-Publication Data
A catalogue record for this book is available from the
British Library.

ISBN 978 1 86126 935 5

Acknowledgements
I would like to thank all the artists and potters whose assistance
and hard work has made this book finally possible. I am especially
grateful to them and their photographers for providing and giving
permission to reproduce their wonderful work. My thanks are also
due to my friends and collaborators, Rod Dorling and John Bell,
for their input in matters photographic and in terms of design.

My gratitude is also due to Arts Council England and to the
Research Committee at the University of Wolverhampton, without
whose support this venture would not have been possible; and also
to my colleagues and students, many of whom have contributed to
this work, and whose inspiration and enthusiasm to learn, by turning research questions into practice, has kept me going.

Dedication
To the Jones, Stimler and Bertz clans, who all understand that
through books we reach out into the future and across the past.

Typeset and designed by D & N Publishing
Lambourn Woodlands, Hungerford, Berkshire.

Printed and bound in India by Replika Press.

Unless otherwise stated all quotes and extracts originate from the
author's interviews and personal correspondence with the artists.

Items in **bold** are to be found in the glossary.

Contents

Foreword

Foreword by Janet Mansfield

Janet Mansfield OAM, D.LITT is an acclaimed woodfire potter; she is an acknowledged author and is also the editor of *Ceramics – Art and Perception* and President of the International Academy of Ceramics.

The act of firing, the process of applying heat to clay, has always been a source of wonder for ceramic artists. The resulting permanency of fired clay has meant that the nature of the materials themselves has changed and will remain so through millennia. This places a responsibility on all of us who commit our work to fire. We do so in good faith, working with clay as an art form that has relevance to our lives and our environment. The art of firing, as opposed to the act, is another broad subject, one that David Jones, in this book, has taken on enthusiastically, covering all known methods by using examples of serious contemporary ceramic artists. From the simple bonfire to the most sophisticated of methodologies, through test kilns to traditional large brick kilns, he explains the reasons why heat is important in the art of the ceramist.

Although firing one's clay pieces is only one of the processes that a potter or ceramic artist must master, without such knowledge nothing of lasting value remains. Heat must be obtained to fuse one's clay into some level of vitrification and that heat must be held until the sintering of the clay is completed. Depending on the clay body minerals, different temperatures are needed to permanently fuse the clay so that is unaffected by water or chemicals. Different clays will sinter at different temperatures and this will often involve a potter in experimentation if the clay is unknown. Thus firing becomes one of the important and satisfying aspects of the potter's art. Then there are different surfaces obtainable through firing: salt and soda vapour firing, lustre firing, specific firings for glazes, and woodfiring for ash and flame effects. In-situ firings for large sculptural works where forms are built over fireboxes and fired on the spot where they are to remain, or firing just for the spectacle of the moment, all have their place in the art of firing.

Firing: Philosophies within Contemporary Ceramic Practice, the title of the book, implies a comprehensive study of the processes of firing and the theory behind it. And such is the case. David Jones brings his experience as a practising artist to bear on all the aspects of the art of firing. Even more, he addresses the chemistry of heating clay materials to the different temperatures used by ceramists: low, medium and high, and he assesses the results obtained. He tackles the science of combustion and what happens in the ceramist's kiln and passes on knowledge that was once only the prerogative of master to student; and he is generous with his information.

This is not the first book by David Jones and he is well known as an artist and teacher. His reputation is international. I have found that he has unusual ways of approaching a subject. This is often counter to what one would expect. He engages our interest in unexpected ways by not accepting old myths but probing the truth and challenging us to do the same. As expected then, this new book will add to the knowledge of ceramic art and enable us to understand, in a special way, the breadth of possibilities through the firing of clay.

OPPOSITE PAGE:
Embers in the firebox. Petra Reynolds and Jeremy Steward.
(Photo: Rod Dorling)

1

Introduction

yet from those flames
No light; but rather darkness visible

John Milton, *Paradise Lost*, Book 1, Line 60

'Fire' and 'change' are two of the central tropes of ceramics. They are themes that have been used both to understand ceramics and to narrate our lives. To take formless mud and to fashion it is a way of creating that allows us to walk in the footsteps of our ancestors, who themselves must have felt that they were stepping in the tracks of gods. Ceramic can be considered just a hardened mud, a silt-like deposit that has been exposed to the heat of a bonfire; and yet ceramic artefacts are found long after all other traces of the human beings that made them have disappeared.

Fire has an ambiguous role in ceramics. It fixes the manipulated clay and prevents it from being refashioned into a new form (but it can also have a destructive power of transmutation and can leave an elegant form re-softened and distorted after it experiences the extremes of a prolonged firing). Fire thus removes clay from the world of mutability and takes it to permanence.

To observe the fashioning of clay into a recognizable form, to allow it to air-harden, and then to watch its dissolution into an amorphous state merely with the addition of water must have been an early, metaphoric glimpse of creation and final annihilation. And to arrest that eternal circle by cooking the clay in the heart of a fire might have represented an opportunity to escape the inevitable, to leave the quotidian and to gaze on the Eternal. It is an escape that itself involves transformation, and potters have the opportunity to engage in this atavistic experience every time that they fire a kiln. For

OPPOSITE PAGE:
David Jones Raku firing. (Photo: Rod Dorling)

RIGHT: *Bonfire firing at Gulgong in Australia. (Photo: David Jones)*

some makers this alchemical change, this exposure of their clay objects to extreme experience, is an intoxicating seduction. The marks left on the clay by the path of the flame tell of some aw(e)ful rite of passage; it is a kind of testing – both of clay and of potter. This way of firing feels never truer than when stoking an *anagama* (a simple tunnel of clay built in or on a hillside, first developed in the Far East). Days can be spent in smoky exhaustion, feeding the devouring monster with what seems like a forest of trees.

There are then other ceramicists who apparently have scant regard for this dimension of ceramics and its intimate relationship to the kiln, and choose instead to finish their work in an electric kiln, utilizing commercial glazes. Theirs is more a pleasure in design and control rather than the unpredictability of intense combustion and drifting kiln vapours.

The oppositions of fire and carefully executed design, of freedom and precision, of play and planning, of written word and direct, authentic speech (*langue* and *parole*) are themes at the heart of human endeavour and of an understanding of our nature. Firing can thus act as a metaphor for a philosophically questioned existence, as well as being the way of finishing the surface of a clay object.

Tradition: The Transmission and Utilization of Knowledge

to articulate the past … means to seize hold of a memory as it flashes up at a moment of danger. … That danger affects both the content of the tradition and its receivers. The same threat hangs over both … In every era the attempt must be made anew to wrest tradition away from a conformism that is about to overpower it.

(Benjamin, 1968: p.255)

Throughout history one can observe the development of the methodologies of firing, which build upon learned experience. This passing on of knowledge originally took place through the communication between potters, working side by side. Parents would show their children also, and experienced potters would demonstrate some of their secrets to friends and apprentices. But 'secrets' they were. The Pottery Craft Guilds of the Middle Ages called their knowledge their 'Mystery', and, as it was these secrets that gave one group of potters an advantage over another, it is easy to understand why this knowledge was guarded jealously. We also know that the knowledge of firing was greatly valued and sought after – the kidnapping raids mounted by the Japanese to capture the Korean potters and kiln experts in the Middle Ages are one example of this, and the extraordinary secrecy

surrounding European lustre firing also bears this out (Caiger-Smith, 1991).

In the past, a potter would usually only have been able to learn a single particular process and technique and thereby become a master of that; indeed, there is a lifetime's practice involved in developing most skills. Yet today we have the Internet and a plethora of books, documenting every niche of ceramic practice. The knowledge that was so hard-won by our ancestors is now freely available in the average library of a small town, or as a download to our computers. In our postmodern world it is possible to dip into techniques and processes at will. In art schools and at workshops, people experiment with a vast range of ceramic practice.

Certainly, in order to find one's own voice, it is very useful to wear a complete wardrobe of different hats – experimenting with a succession of techniques in order to find one that suits the best. Most potters, after they have identified a tradition or combination of modes of making and firing, would be best advised to focus for a period of time on that style in order to refine their understanding of the methodologies involved. Thus when one looks at the work of established potters it is possible to see individuals who have focused their attention in a very narrow beam to illuminate a very finely delimited area of making and firing. Every so often, a clay artist will step out of their established ritual of making and confront their work with a new way of firing. This can highlight the essential nature of their practice, as they move from one process to another. The culture of Western art has also created the phenomenon of 'The Artist': he or she who creates an idea, identifies a mode of firing best suited to its expression and works with a master firer who can best effect his or her intentions.

The Evolution of Firing Practices

In various parts of the world different firing practices have evolved, from what we assume were very similar beginnings in the form of bonfires. The traditions evolved further in the Far East than in the rest of the world, with the remarkable technological innovations that allowed potters in Korea, China and Japan to fire to yellow-white heat and to produce vitreous **stoneware** pots more than a thousand years ago. In Europe and the Near East, the development of high-firing kilns had to wait until the fourteenth century, with **salt**-glaze production in Germany. In the rest of Europe, and particularly around the Mediterranean, a tradition evolved of manufacturing only at red heat (with the consequent production of porous ceramics). The potters of the Americas, Africa and the Indian subcontinent have produced ceramic of great sophistication and ingenuity without developing a dominant high-fired practice.

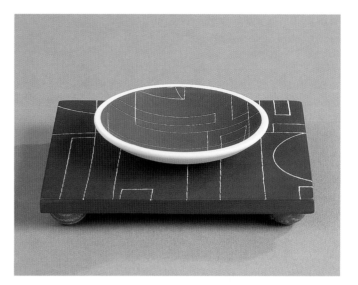

ABOVE: *Jane Perryman, burnished vessel, saggar-fired in sawdust. (Photo: Graham Murrell).*

ABOVE RIGHT: *Vicky Shaw, 'Composition', electric-fired.*

RIGHT: *Peter Lange, results of* mazdagama *firing.*

BELOW: *An ancient practice becomes contemporary performance: African women potters preparing for firing at Aberystwyth International Ceramic Festival, 2005.*

Contemporary ceramicists can now re-examine the past and exploit those practices that were once innovations in their own right. Of particular interest is the way in which a particular firing technique can determine a whole raft of thinking about clay and form. The use of traditional firing techniques in a modern idiom, rather than in the production of a time-honoured range of forms, shows how the once nearly extinct practices of the past can be rejuvenated and exploited to give expression to new artistic endeavours. This interplay of tradition and contemporary ideas gives a vitality to present-day ceramics that places it in the forefront of modern artistic expression and elevates it beyond much of today's fine-art practice that is so divorced from a relationship to the past.

If one looks at present-day ceramics then it is possible to see the great developments that have been afforded by the use of electricity as a fuel for heating a kiln. In museums, by contrast, there are many pots illustrating the traces left by a flame passing through the kiln, resulting in accidental marks left on the clay by the passage of fire. In Europe and the USA in the early twentieth century these marks and earthy **ash** glazes were revered as the goal of potters, and were held up in stark contrast to the apparent sterility of ceramic fired in an electric kiln in a factory. Value was placed on the notion of the kiln giving something to an object that was not a design feature placed in the piece at its inception but given later – a lucky accident, but one that can be planned for.

Firing in an electric kiln does not provide these benefits (or indeed problems, depending on how those chance events are perceived) but instead allows the artist's intentions to be realized with a much greater degree of accuracy, albeit one that

Markus Klausmann, saggar opened after firing.

is tempered with a potentially featureless coolness of surface. It took the urbanization of studio ceramicists to elicit the most creative use of electric firing in the latter half of the twentieth century. In Europe, the work of Hans Coper and Lucie Rie began to demonstrate the creative potential of a **neutral firing**. Just after the end of the Second World War Lucie Rie ordered what was the largest electric kiln purchased by a craft potter and she pioneered the use of glazes that could create beautiful surfaces in an electric kiln, that is, without using in-kiln **reduction** and its corresponding 'warming' of the glaze surface. She underlined the distinction between town-based potters using electricity and country potters using wood to fire. Outside of industrial applications an electric (or gas) kiln is often much smaller than a wood-burning kiln; hence it can be fired more frequently with tests and so a faster feedback can be achieved, allowing the faster development of the fired surface.

These qualities of extreme control though did not just arrive with the discovery of the use of electricity for firing in the nineteenth century. For instance, the court ceramics of

LEFT: *Elizabeth Klein, ceramic sculpture fired in an electric kiln.*

BELOW: *Catrin Mostyn Jones.*

ABOVE: Markus Klausmann, saggar-fired pot.

ABOVE RIGHT: David Jones Raku firing. (Photo: Rod Dorling)

RIGHT: Chris Faller, 'Archaeology of the Future', red clay terra sigillata *on slip-cast object with black enamel.*

China were fired in sealed clay boxes, called **saggars**, to protect the ware from the flame; potters in Greece more than 2,000 years ago also used extreme control of the firing process, alternating **oxidation** and **reduction** on very precise thicknesses of **slip** in order to orchestrate the red and black coloration on their pots.

This is, of course, not to say that there is anything necessarily haphazard about the firing of wood kilns. As a consequence of the time and effort taken to reach temperature in a wood-burning kiln they are often large and therefore the financial value of the contents of the kiln is great: thus, they need to be as successful as possible in their outcomes. In a small kiln greater risks can be taken with firing cycles and adjusting the variables of glaze composition – so an electric kiln can be a saviour from the demands of wood.

At the other extreme, and as a reaction to these efforts to control kiln and contents precisely, comes the recent interest in low-temperature firing methodologies in ceramics like **Raku**, **low-temperature salt** and **sawdust firing**. These processes emphasize accident and chance in the work and are orchestrated to enhance the form of the object, often without the use of glaze. These properties of firing owe much to the zeitgeist of abstract expressionism and improvisational jazz, in which 'happening' is an essential part of the process.

In Raku (as in high-temperature wood firing, and particularly with the snarling, glowing monsters that are *anagama* kilns) there is an almost heroic quality to the experience of tending the kiln. The traditional methods of high-temperature wood firing involve the endurance of days of firing, working in shifts, in smoke and exhaustion, in order to create the desired effects. In Raku, the image of the potter delving into the still red-hot kiln in order to extract a glowing pot again reinforces the notion of ceramic firing as combat and challenge – a testing of artist with and against the vagaries of combustion. A 'neutral' electric firing could not be more different: one closes the door, turns on the computer and returns when the firing has finished, quite

RIGHT: *Petra Reynolds' salting kiln.*

BELOW: *Anna Stina Naess, translucent porcelain cylinders, electric firing.*

Bonfire firing at Aberystwyth Ceramic Fair, half an hour later.
(Photo: David Jones)

unsupervised. (It is nonetheless important to examine the qualities of surface that are produced in this much gentler interaction with heat and to accord them an equal status with the extreme experiences of flame firing.)

The scale of work and the size of kilns are other factors that require consideration. In principle there is a relationship between the size of kiln a potter uses and the frequency of firing. There is also the aspect of the division of labour in ceramic processes. Early pottery production was undertaken on a small scale and one imagines that the maker was also the person in charge of firing. One can still see a very simple form of firing in the bonfires that are heaped over pots in some contemporary African societies, where the women who have made the work through the winter and spring come together to fire their work.

Later potters, as the making of utility items and decorative work became more of an industrial activity, saw an efficiency in separating out the roles of making and firing and specializing in the different areas of skill; once there is a specialist in charge of firing then the firing of more pieces at once creates an economy of effort, and the size of kiln grows exponentially, with one person or a team of experts firing the kiln. The massive climbing kilns of Korea, China and Japan would hold the products of a large number of potters and be fired by itinerant teams of firers who would travel the country taking charge of the kilns, which would be fired perhaps only once a year.

Art and Utility

The advent of factory-scale industrialization in the eighteenth century, and the manufacture of cheap plastic utensils in the twentieth century, destroyed much of the handmade pottery infrastructure by undercutting the prices. As a result, there was a near total decline in the production of handmade pottery in the West, and it only survived in less technologically developed countries because wages were so low that it remained more economical than importing.

The pottery traditions have been supported by two main factors: tourism and the repositioning of crafts in the art world. There is a great demand for souvenirs from holidays and there is also a new class of collectors in the West, who are prepared to pay for hand-crafted ceramics even though the price for utilitarian items far exceeds that from an industrial producer. Ceramics has also substantially become a part of the art market. Buyers are prepared to pay for the hand-crafted item – and to a large extent the hand of the potter is evident not merely in the selection and creation of clay bodies, but also in the manufacture of artefacts and finally in their firing.

What is searched for is evidence of skill and the synthesis of idea, hand, feeling and process in the formation of 'craft' objects. The forming skill is evident in the very direct tactile qualities of ceramics, but the skill of firing is existentially present also in terms of the softness, hardness and coloration, and particularly in the glaze surfaces fixed by fire. By and large the search for the individual characteristics of objects has largely rejected the uniformity of industrial processes, both of manufacture and of firing. However, there is still a healthy market for domestic pottery and uniformity of firing, and standardization of product is held in balance with the quality of minute variation within the range of the work.

The development of expressive uses of clay and its employment as a material in art and sculptural idioms has long favoured smaller kilns. They are easier tools to use, are suitable laboratories in the pursuit of new effects and their relative cheapness to buy (or build) makes them the pre-eminent choice for most potters.

Thus today we have come nearly full circle and the majority of potters work completely by themselves or in a very small workshop with fellow artists or assistants. There are exceptions to this, however. There are qualities that larger kilns confer, and recent years have seen a resurgence in firings where the kiln, and the duration of firing, is a major participant in the production of the final product. These kilns, which echo the firing qualities first achieved accidentally by Asian potters thousands of years ago, are now actively researched by contemporary practitioners who are designing new variants of climbing kilns in order to capture the effects seen in historic Chinese, Korean and Japanese pots.

The relationship of clay artists to industry has focused much of the new thinking. Recent years have seen the development of large-scale ceramics designed and built for industrial firing, particularly in association with brickworks. Factories that have a vital artist-in-residence programme, like Arabia in Finland, INAX, Kohler and so on, obviously encourage their artists to utilize their particular materials and firing methodologies.

Until the beginning of the twentieth century, firing methodologies moved largely in the direction of increasing degrees of refinement. Historically one can observe moves to cleaner and whiter clay bodies and purer uninflected surfaces, which occurred both in the development of Chinese ceramics and (in imitation) in the West, culminating in factory-based industrial production. Reaction to their aesthetic qualities then led to a rediscovery and reinvestigation of those craft practices of firing that had been superseded in the pursuit of 'perfection'.

For utilitarian applications simple plain glazes, providing smooth and hygienic surfaces, have also been most desired. One consequence was the development of a refined surface that could be interpreted as sterile and featureless – in other words, dull. This was first seized upon as the perfect ground for painting; ceramic was often perceived as superior to paper and canvas as firing gives the painting, on or under a stable glaze, a degree of permanence not available to light-sensitive pigments. (The fired 'paintings' of Renaissance Italy, in 'Majolica', give us a view of the brightness of the colours used at that time – long after the paintings have faded, changed irrevocably by light and atmosphere.)

The early practitioners of the craft pottery revival were committed to making utilitarian glazes, but with more 'character' than the scientifically produced factory glazes. These often imitated oriental glazes and accentuated the handmade quality of the pots produced. But even if the surfaces were designed to create a sensation of depth, they still had to be washed after use. It has only been in the last half century, with the grudging acceptance of clay as a valid material for making non-functional work, that enormous developments in clay surface and glaze have been undertaken – and many of the glazes used today exploit qualities that still appear under the heading of 'Glaze Faults' in older textbooks.

In recent years there has been a number of cycles of reaction, to brown pots and then to industrial surfaces; at present there exists a postmodern consensus that anything is possible.

LEFT: *Vigdis Oien, 'Inside Outside', brick sculpture, fired at Blockleys, UK. (Photo: Synlig)*

BELOW: *Thomas Thunig, three vases, wood-fired.*

Museums and the Persistence of 'the Fired'

Fired clay artefacts have long been employed as one of the chief markers along the pathway to the past. The major part of most archaeological collections is ceramic, which predates metal production by millennia and persists in the ground unique amongst ancient human products (except for cave paintings, bones and stone tools). Only gold objects are as inert, and last as long, but because of the preciousness of the material and its rarity there is very little gold work extant (as it was often re-melted and reused, in response to new ownership, fashion and culture).

Firing is therefore a direct link to knowledge about the past. Ceramic objects survive despite their brittleness, because they have no value as a recyclable material. The firing of clay has made permanent the skill and artistic vision of cultures that have long since disappeared, and in many instances it is the only record that we have of their existence. There is a form of intellectual knowledge, and an understanding of the social organization of a society, that can be decoded from these artefacts. For those of us working in clay now there is also the frozen haptic skill of the maker that acts as a record of human achievement – often surpassing contemporary production – and when the museum case is opened we can place our own hands where those of the potter rested thousands of years ago.

Of the many ancient clay artefacts that can be found in museum collections a large number of the complete and undamaged examples were recovered from graves. They were either pots used as receptacles for ashes, containing the remains of the funeral pyre of the deceased, now just a collection of charred bones, or were vessels containing food to accompany the spirit to the afterlife, or symbolic representations of the world that had been left behind. Other ceramics can be found in vast spoil heaps, either at kiln sites where wasters are broken and thrown or in the remains of domestic rubbish dumps. The organic material of such heaps decomposes and then all that remains are manmade (ceramic) hills, sometimes of nearly 100ft depth of shards – frequently the only physical traces of the ordinary peoples who lived, ate and died at that site. For the most part these heaps of shards are of simple low-fired domestic pottery – the everyday utensils of ordinary human beings – interspersed with roof tiles and bricks and the occasional fragment of decorated pottery. These objects do not merely represent an historical record to be consulted in a museum, but also they have been commandeered by contemporary artists and incorporated in their work in order to forge a personal link with a tradition. In this way these traces of the past become part of the grammar of their work, utilizing small fired shards as inclusions in order to communicate an idea of the continuity of the traditions of making and firing.

Neil Brownsword, 'Remnant 2000', re-fired ceramic from Stoke-on-Trent.

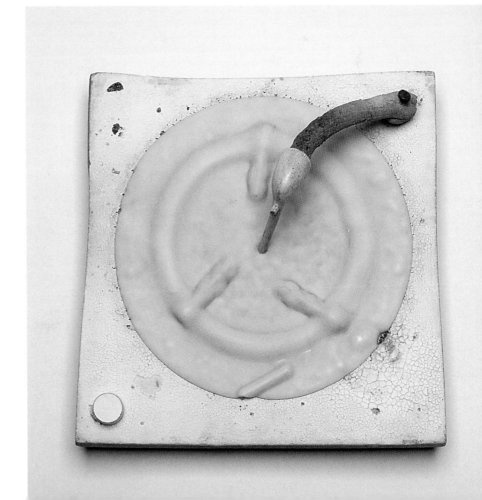

2

The Bonfire

Monk, the All is aflame. What All is aflame? The eye is aflame. Forms are aflame. Consciousness at the eye is aflame. Contact at the eye is aflame. And whatever there is that arises in dependence on contact at the eye – experienced as pleasure, pain or neither-pleasure-nor-pain – that too is aflame. Aflame with what? Aflame with the fire of passion, the fire of aversion, the fire of delusion. Aflame, I tell you, with birth, aging and death, with sorrows, lamentations, pains, distresses, and despairs.

The Fire Sermon by The Buddha (trans. Bhikku Thanissaro)

ABOVE: *John Roloff, 'Oculus', 2m diameter (steel, propane, refractory mats, lava).*

OPPOSITE PAGE: *Bonfire. (Photo: Rod Dorling)*

The Origins of Fire

Fire is the oldest tool employed by human beings. It existed long before our ancestors appeared on the Earth and our own history is very much bound up with learning about its uses and about containing its power.

There are three essential ingredients necessary for combustion – heat, fuel and oxygen. Heat has existed since the Earth's inception. Oxygen appeared in large quantities about 2 billion years after the formation of the Earth, as a result of photosynthesis by small plants in the oceans. However, sufficient biomass for combustion only appeared on land in the last 400 million years; thus before that time fire as such did not exist. After that time it became almost impossible for it not to happen and there were spontaneous outbreaks of fire as brushwood accumulated in the forests, and was ignited by lightning strike, or volcanic action. Human beings capable of exploiting fire appeared only 500,000 years ago (fire would have been an essential 'commodity' to protect, for defence and for the preparation of food).

Much of the early period of vegetative colonization of the Earth resulted in non-combustion and anaerobic conditions in large swamps; the carbon fixed by the photosynthesizing plants did not return to the air as carbon dioxide, and instead was buried under sedimentary deposits, to become the coal seams and the oil and gas fields that are

LEFT: *Wali Hawes, 'Fire Tree' at Réunion.*

BELOW LEFT: *Iris Bertz, basket in willow. (Photo: David Jones)*

BELOW: *Iris Bertz and David Jones, basket in willow lined with clay. (Photo: David Jones)*

BOTTOM LEFT: *Iris Bertz and David Jones, basket form firing. (Photo: David Jones)*

BOTTOM RIGHT: *Iris Bertz and David Jones, clay basket form, Raku fired. (Photo: David Jones)*

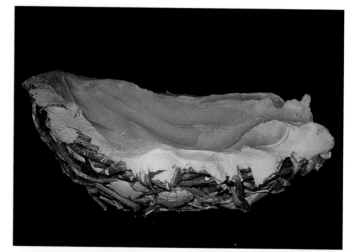

exploited today. (The history of the last 200 years is the story of accelerated industrialization, powered by the exhumation and plunder of ancient carbon deposits, and their burning for energy.)

Fire is a force that not only has been harnessed by humans but has also developed in close association with us, shaping not merely our science and technology but also our imagination, and even our physical form. For example, the use of fire in cooking liberated our early ancestors from the need to have such large jaw muscles for biting food: by breaking down the fibres in cooking, and allowing them to eat a much wider range of foodstuffs, one consequence of cooking was that the space occupied by muscle in the skull could be replaced by brain. Thus, more and more cunning uses of the technology of fire could be developed, one of which is the control of fire and its utilization in kilns.

The cooking of food functions both practically, intellectually and ritually as a paradigm for the cooking of any other matter – wood, ore, metal, clay and stone can all be changed into forms that have specific uses. Of course there was a great crossover between firing technologies and the smelting of ores and metal production also influenced ceramics, as potters began to realize that the ores used in the production of metals could be utilized as **glaze**.

Use of the Bonfire for Ceramics

'I am Prometheus, giver of fire to mortals.'

(Aeschulus in *Prometheus Bound*)

The firing of ceramic in a bonfire is the simplest of meth-odologies, yet one which can lead to the most complex and unpredictable of surfaces. The architecture of a bonfire is quite imprecise – by definition it is a pile of burnable matter and of indeterminate size.

At some point in time our ancestors 'discovered fire' – whether from a volcano or from a lightning strike – and saw the advantage for the tribe in retaining the burning phenomenon and carrying it with the group on their wanderings. The speculation is that fire would have served the dual roles of protection from dangerous animals and would have also extended their diet by making food more digestible, through cooking, thus increasing the possible geographical range of these nomadic peoples. For aeons they were unable to generate fire and so had to transport it; this would have been no easy achievement. A burning ember to be fed continually with new combustible materials would have been very difficult to tend and also hard to carry.

That transportation would have been effected in a container – a piece of bark, or later in time a woven container, a basket. It is a short step from this concept to actually lining the container with mud or clay in order to prevent the combustible materials from burning through. The fire would have been rejuvenated within the basket and then a larger fire built over it. At some point the heat would have become sufficient to change the clay into permanent ceramic and someone would have noticed the hardened lining, which was in effect a clay vessel, in the embers of the fire and realized its potential in the carrying, storage and preservation of food. (It is interesting to note that many early pots have a basket pattern imprinted on them, recapitulating this early development.)

Today, there is nothing very sophisticated to us about the use of fire in many areas of life to effect change on materials by subjecting them to heat. The change effected on clay by the heat of a bonfire is a very simple, observable phenomenon. Yet this was a development that seemingly took millennia to be incorporated into human culture after the emergence of our hominid ancestors in the fossil record. From another perspective, the discovery of fire and its uses represents arguably the most major technological advance effected by humankind, enabling our dispersal across the globe – and ceramics is its earliest and most permanent outcome.

Fire as Metaphor

Myths of fire abound and its transforming power is such that it is symbolically central to our understanding of our place in the world. Creation myths often centre on fire, and also on stories of cleansing. It is this background, both technical and mythic, that informs our attitude to kilns today.

Burial

The death of tribal members in these ancient societies was often ritualized. Burial and cremation would both be completed with the burial of pottery items to accompany the deceased on their journey through death. It is hard to resist the assumption that a parallel was noticed, and enshrined, between the change effected on clay by firing and on a dead body by the conflagration that engulfs a funeral pyre, making the ashes and pots ideal companions in that final internment. The cremated remains were often placed in a pot and such pots, or the entire body, were often sealed

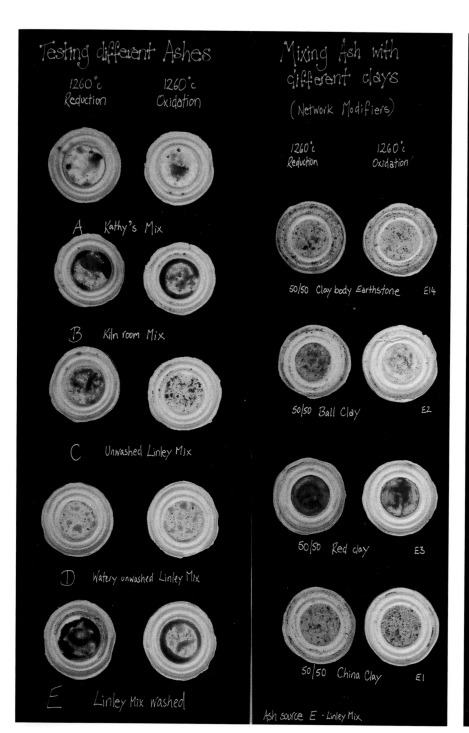

Testing different Ashes

1260°c Reduction   1260°c Oxidation

A   Kathy's Mix

B   Kiln room Mix

C   Unwashed Linley Mix

D   Watery unwashed Linley Mix

E   Linley Mix washed

Mixing Ash with different clays

(Network Modifiers)

1260°c Reduction   1260°c Oxidation

50/50 Clay body Earthstone   E14

50/50 Ball Clay   E2

50/50 Red clay   E3

50/50 China Clay   E1

Ash source E · Linley Mix

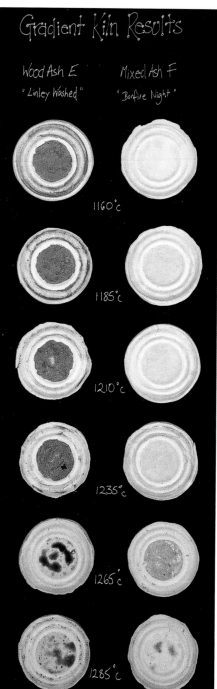

Gradient Kiln Results

Wood Ash E "Linley Washed"   Mixed Ash F "Bonfire Night"

1160°c

1185°c

1210°c

1235°c

1265°c

1285°c

Test 16 – Adding Human ash to base glaze

Base glaze   10%   20%   30%   40%   50%

ABOVE LEFT: *Ruth Gibson, comparative wood ash tests, 1260°C, oxidation and reduction.*

ABOVE RIGHT: *Ruth Gibson, Linley wood ash test fired in a gradient kiln.*

LEFT: *Emma Fenelon, human ash glaze test, adding cremains to base glaze line-blend.*

into a tomb with other vessels containing food for that next journey.

High-fired ceramic is close to stone in its chemistry and is not too greatly affected by the acids present from burial in the ground, but even bonfire-fired ceramic is relatively inert and will survive fairly well in moist soil; and in the dry desert conditions of the Near East, near perfect preservation of soft fabric ceramic from almost ten thousand years ago has occurred. Pots from even further back in history come from the Japanese mainland, and are not the everyday pots of utility but the extemporization of Jomon potters improvising in a quite flamboyant way upon the simple theme of containment.

The objects buried can sometimes be seen to have had a dual function – they had a strictly necessary, everyday role in the life of the living but, once their owner had died, then such useful artefacts were sacrificed with the dead as a necessary accompaniment for their next journey. This combination of utilitarian and ritual uses of clay objects is central to our understanding of them and is a source of our continuing fascination with them spanning into the third millennium.

Ritual of Fire and Clay

Many of these early ceramic findings demonstrate the importance of ritual in the life of the makers. Either the objects were created for a specific function in burial, or their previous life as functional utensils in the world of the living is re-ascribed and the new function as grave goods supersedes the previous one.

Current practice in the West does not seem to cater for the use of ceramics in our dealings with the dead – but it is quite easy to see the re-ascription of meaning that is directed at objects placed within a glass case in a museum collection, or indeed in the assortment of mugs that can be found on many a sideboard in people's homes. These are apparently useful utensils that have been bought, not in order to be used, but to be admired, either as attractive objects in their own right, or as nostalgic objects that refer us back to an earlier time when 'the handmade' had an important place in everyone's lives.

In the past there have been many ceramic traditions that have expressed themselves through their use of ceramics in funerary wares. The range of these is many and various. Some are vessels for the containment of the body – for example coffins such as those made in Syria, Crete and Rhodes. Other smaller vessels were made to contain cremated remains – for instance the 'Beaker Pots' of northern Europe and the Egyptian Canopic jars. Within this geographical spread there exists a multiplicity of form and decoration that testifies to the ingenuity of potters in their creation.

There are also created figures that are believed to stand in for humans who, formerly, would have been sacrificed at a burial in order to confirm the power of the dead after this life (for example, servants or other members of a household). There are whole armies made from clay buried with the Chinese emperors; in Japan, Haniwa figures symbolically guarded the graves of the aristocracy. There are also many examples of African figurines that are placed to guard sites of burial, encapsulating the relationship of fire–transformation–death as a continuation of this life, but in another form. Pots belonging to the deceased are also often ceremonially broken on the grave of the dead.

The figurative representation of humans in clay is an obvious form of symbolism and one can easily understand how it is possible for the clay to be used to represent real beings. Additionally, the analogy of the pot and the human body is well documented in many cultures: vessels are described as having a body, a bottom, a belly, a neck, a lip, a mouth, a shoulder, a waist and a foot. They are further anthropomorphized through firing, when they are imbued with spirit. They are regarded by many cultures as if beings that are alive. Comparisons can be made with the creation of man in the Bible: 'The Lord God formed man of the dust of the ground, and breathed into his nostrils the breath of life; and man became a living soul'(Genesis 2:7).

Furthermore, there are the objects that are used as we might use flowers, as *momento mori*, in order to remember the dead and our own deaths. For instance, in Athens nearly 2,000 years ago jars were sold at the gates of the cemetery and placed within the tombs of those who were to be commemorated.

The ritual aspect of firing has long been part of people's lives. Even in cultures where potters were socially segregated from the rest of the town or village, everyone in the community would have been aware of the practice of firing. Like the metal smiths who worked in later ages the potters were often separated and occupied their own areas – because of the magic associated with their work. To the medieval guilds these secrets were known as the craftsman's 'mystery'. The place of firing in anthropological contexts gives a hint of how these qualities of pot and firing might have been perceived in other earlier cultures.

Fire as Tool and Symbol

The earliest-dated ceramics – that is, objects made from clay and that have been chemically changed to a hard, permanent material – are the Vestonice figurines from central Europe, pre-dating the archaeological finds of pots. They were apparently a symbolic use of the manipulated earth that was thrown into the fire as part of a ritual. Their firing and hardening was a (unnecessary) by-product of the ceremony (but a fortuitous accident for archaeologists, who have found piles of these figurines from the remains of fires

Jan Mycklebust, three wire-cut bowls. Porcelain with celadon glaze, reduction fired 2006. (Photo: Graham Murrell)

in caves, often shattered but sometimes with examples that survived intact). Certainly we have no evidence that this earliest example of ceramics was used as a foundation on which to build any new knowledge, as for the next few millennia there is no evidence in the archaeological record of any other fired clay. Thus it is that figurative sculpture, in its ritual use, is the earliest proper example of firing.

Sometimes the take-up of available technology does not occur. For example in African communities where the use of charcoal for smelting metal in a kiln occurs, it might be assumed that this technology would be transferred to pottery firing. This does not always happen, as has been noted by the anthropologist Nigel Barley. For instance, within the Dowayo communities of Cameroon there are social–symbolic pressures to 'maintain parallels with the open threshing floor where millet is processed' (Barley, 1994, p.44), and so the pots are fired in a bonfire in the open.

There are also prohibitions associated with firing, the commonest being that a woman is not allowed to fire pots while menstruating (Barley, 1994). A further taboo brings the stark opposites of fire and water into relief, for a woman cannot drink or wash herself while the pots are firing, for fear of damaging the pots or bringing 'corruption' to them. There are also protocols determining the time of year that pots can be fired; it is believed that the rains can be affected, or the pots destroyed, if the wrong months are chosen for firing.

Barley (1994, p.24) points out that 'Rotation is implicit in all pots. Fast wheels require moister, finer clay which in turn cannot be fired at low temperatures and has not the thermal tolerance of low fired pots. Potting wheels tend therefore to be associated with the building of kilns but not vice versa.' Thus we can see the associated developments of mechanized production techniques with the need for more sophisticated structures within which to fire them, because throwing on the wheel brings new demands in terms of hardening, which can only be achieved at higher temperatures.

In less technologically developed societies, anthropologists have observed that there is a very strong link between firing and sex. Nigel Barley writes of the people from a tribe in West Africa: 'An uninitiated Bemba girl is scorned as *citongo*, "an unfired pot", [this involves] the semantics of "hot" as a word that encompasses danger and excitement and the use of heat as a means of enforcing moral sanctions about sexuality. It is almost inevitable that potting will enter into this' (Barley, 1994, p.106). He goes on to mention another African tribe, the Thonga of South Africa: 'At the birth of the first child the relatives visit the mother, clap and dance as they sing, "I praise my cooking pot which did not crack"'.

Contemporary Uses of Bonfire Qualities

Many of the qualities that we observe in the firing of pots in a bonfire, those that occur as accidental and disorganized markings on the resultant pieces, have come to be appropriated as significant gestures in contemporary ceramic production. Thus we find much made of the basic language of smoke or fire-**flashing** on pots brought out of a bonfire; such features are now organized and planned for by clay artists today. These marks on ceramic come about as the result of the often quite complex chemistry associated with burning and the effects that combustion has on the chemical constituents of clay. These outcomes are to do with both the make-up of the clay and the materials in the bonfire.

Fire as Technology

The processes and transformations that occur in a bonfire are both simple and mysterious. There is an inevitability about the range and consequences of fire; there is nothing that is not affected by heat. Clay is one of the most notable materials that is metamorphosed in this way. The initial change in clay is from a muddy substance that can be manipulated in the hands – assuming any form that the mind (and the hand) decides – to a hard substance that can be carved like a soft stone. This is a transformation that happens at ordinary ambient temperature – even in cold, damp environments – and requires no assistance from a fire, except to speed up the process.

When clay is subjected to fire a number of *physical* changes occur, and these changes have had great significance in cultural development. First, any water that had not already evaporated from the body in drying is driven off, and if the clay is still too damp for the speed of evaporation then damage can occur. The vapour produced when heating the water (trapped in the pores in the clay) occupies a much greater volume than liquid water, and if that steam is produced too quickly within a thick clay wall then the outer face will be blown off, as the gas cannot exit fast enough through the capillary pores. However, even when the clay is completely dry and no more steam is being created, it has not actually undergone a fundamental change; the potter can put the desiccated clay into water and it will reconstitute to form a mud again.

It is only when the temperature of the clay rises above 600°C that the reversible reaction of clay and water is arrested and further water (this time chemically combined) is driven off. Now a change has occurred that means that formed ceramic placed in water will not slake down, but will maintain whatever shape has been imposed. The temperature required for this transformation is achieved in a hot bonfire – either one in which light combustibles generate a lot of heat very rapidly, or from the prolonged accumulation of heat from slower-burning materials.

Bonfire firing can therefore be fast or slow. In contemporary firings in Africa the pots can reach high red-hot temperatures in only thirty minutes and can be finished by rolling in plant juices, to seal the pores of the clay – all within an hour. Such a firing is where a furious heat is produced by burning fine brushwood. In these circumstances the clay must be dry, very thin-walled and 'open' (that is, have a fair proportion of sand or pre-fired coarse grog material mixed in), otherwise the clay will crack and shatter. All these inclusions can alter the coloration of the ceramic. Sometimes sand that has a much higher iron content than the clay (and thus reddens the body) is added. Alternatively shells can whiten and organic fillers like chaff can increase local reduction (*see* Chapter 3 for an explanation of the process of reduction).

Ashraf Hanna, burnished clay vessel, 26cm.

Ecological Implications of Firing

In recent years, the environmental implications of the burning of fossil fuels have been realized even by the political establishment. As users of fire we have to question our very use of the Earth's precious resources for non-essential outcomes. In reality, contemporary studio-based firers produce very little pollution, and use minimal materials.

The issues of responsibility for the effect of humans on the Earth and our use of combustion are considered by many of the contributors to this book, but it has become a focus particularly for John Roloff (*see* pages 180–3) and the three collaborators: Andre Singer Thomson, Valerie Otani and Elizabeth Stanek (*see* pages 193–5).

3

The Chemistry of the Bonfire
~
Theories of Combustion

Contemporary science has almost completely neglected the truly primordial problem that the descriptions of the phenomenon of fire in chemistry textbooks have become shorter and shorter. There are, indeed, a good many modern books on chemistry in which it is impossible to find any mention of flame or fire. Fire is no longer a reality for science.

(Bachelard, *The Psychoanalysis of Fire*, p.2)

At the root of ceramics lies one of the earliest cultural discoveries of mankind: the transforming power of fire. It is evident from the fossil record that humans have used fire for aeons to cook, to warm themselves and to protect themselves. The ritual and sacred aspect of fire derives from these essential functions. The explanation of fire and its effects in terms of chemistry is a very recent phenomenon, that reached a climax only in the last two or three centuries. It follows that potters, like other human beings, have managed perfectly well, for millennia, without the complex explanations provided by chemistry. This very simple chemistry, and the elucidations it provides, represents a very particular understanding of the world and our place in it. An explanation in terms of chemistry substitutes one sort of 'magic' with another, but can also lead to new developments through new understanding, in terms of how flame and glaze work together.

OPPOSITE PAGE:
Flame. (Photo: Rod Dorling)

Fuels and their Formation

When we burn wood, dung, coal, oil or gas then we release an energy trapped by biochemical reactions. All of these materials are plant-based; wood and animal dung are very recently produced and the others are millions of years old. Coal, gas and oil are the, so-called, fossil fuels that are the end product of millions of years of decomposition and compression of the great forests that covered the Earth before the time of the dinosaurs, and were buried deep under the surface within the Earth's crust by subsequent sedimentation. Here, due to the extreme forces exerted on them by the pressure of the layers above, they became materials that remained stable for millions of years, until they were extracted by human action through mining.

All of these fuels depend on the chemistry of the carbon atom. Carbon is the most remarkable **element**, such that it has an entire discipline of chemistry devoted to it – not only can it form a multitude of complex molecules but it is also the basis of all living entities. It is unusual in that it can form chains of atoms not merely with other atoms but also with other carbon atoms. It forms long carbon-to-carbon links, with each longer strand being different in character to the others while retaining 'family resemblances'.

This linking of carbon atoms to each other and to hydrogen and oxygen atoms occurs, most significantly, in the biochemical process known as photosynthesis. Plants gather the constituent liquids and gases and synthesize them in special structures called mitochondria in their leaves. The carbon dioxide gas comes from the air and the water is drawn up through the roots from the ground. Sunlight is also 'absorbed' by the leaves, and, in the presence of the green pigment chlorophyll, is used to synthesize long chains of carbon atoms, to break up the water molecule into its constituent atoms of hydrogen and oxygen, and to graft these onto the carbon chains. All this linking takes energy (sunlight); if these links are subsequently broken then that

energy is released, which occurs in the process known as combustion, **oxidation** or burning.

Oxidation/Burning

Burning occurs when the fuel has been transformed to a gaseous state; that is, when the surface area of the combustible is maximized. The long molecules in fuels such as wood and dung (the animal-processed material) disassociate; that is they break down, with the heat released by the fire, into gases that are referred to by chemists as hydrocarbons. In a kind of chain-reaction the solids are vaporized into the flames as a gas and they burn (react with

John Leach, wood-fired kiln and wood store. (Photo: Rod Dorling)

Movement of Molecules

Matter normally moves from solid to liquid to gas, but sometimes it goes just from solid to gas (for example, wood = wood gases + ash). The particles that make up a solid move faster as they are heated and become less and less constrained, and eventually the solid melts and becomes a liquid; if one continues heating then the particles move faster still until they leave the constraints of the liquid state and the liquid becomes a gas. A gas is the most reactive state of a material, as the particles are freely available to oxygen and are not hemmed in by other molecules of the substance itself.

---

oxygen), thereby creating more heat for similar reactions to continue.

Chemically the release within a fire of this stored energy in plant form can by explained by the process of oxidation. The chains of carbon atoms are broken, and individual carbon atoms react with two atoms of oxygen to produce a molecule of carbon dioxide. The hydrogen reacts with oxygen to produce water. Oxidation/burning is a fierce reaction: a fire starts when a spark has sufficient energy to release further energy by breaking the carbon–carbon bond. This leads to the vaporization of further hydrocarbons from the fuel, the release of more energy, and the breaking of still more chemical bonds, providing more opportunities for reaction – and so the fire continues to burn. When there is sufficient oxygen present the product is carbon dioxide; where there is a starvation of oxygen to the flames then carbon monoxide is the product and reduction takes place (*see* page 30). (It is worth noting that our atmosphere is potentially an explosive mix of gases, but the oxygen is held in check by the proportions of the other gases present.)

There are a variety of factors that determine whether a fire burns and these are important considerations for us when dealing with the conditions for a successful ceramic firing. I shall endeavour to cover the general issues here (even though some may appear to be self-evident!). Our experience tells us that that for an effective fire wood must be broken into small pieces and must be dry; as it is heated wood gases are given off and they burn. Thus the preconditions for a good firing are:

1. Surface Area

WOOD. Our experience of fires tells us that if there is a large lump of wood – and if there are insufficient embers to create enough heat for volatilization of the hydrocarbons – then the fire goes out.

DUNG. This is the undigested cellulose that has passed through the body of a herbivore. When dry it burns easily and slowly, as the fibres have been broken into small parts by digestion in the ruminants' gut and its density prevents it burning too fast – this makes it an ideal fuel.

OIL. This is a liquid at room temperature and has a low surface area based on the size of its container. Oil must be atomized into droplets to increase surface area before efficient combustion can take place.

COAL. Although it is a solid and has a low surface area, once coal starts burning it produces a lot of combustible vapour that has a high calorific value (that is, it produces a lot of heat for a given volume of material).

GAS. This already has a very high surface area and is therefore a very efficient, and instantaneous, heating source. Potters purchase gas either conveyed by pipe to the studio, or in a compressed, liquefied form in reinforced, refillable metal cylinders that are coded (*red* for propane and *blue* for butane). Propane is the more usual choice as it does not tend to freeze as readily as butane.

2. Presence of Water

If the fuel is damp then the fire does not burn. This is due to the fact that the water needs to be evaporated, as water does not combust. The energy required to turn water into vapour is great – indeed, greater than the amount of heat contributed to the fire by the flame, and so it is extinguished. (The heat required to turn the water into a gas is known as the *latent heat of vaporization*.)

3. Availability of Oxygen (Air)

If there is insufficient air (which is 20 per cent oxygen) getting to the flames then, eventually, the fire will be extinguished. The process that ceramicists refer to as reduction (*see* page 30) occurs if the oxygen supply is merely reduced.

Latent Heat

'Latent heat' is a term used to describe the energy required to turn a solid or a liquid at a given temperature into a gas. For example, ice requires energy to become water and then, at 100°C, more energy is required to turn boiling water into steam so that it will dissipate.

This can affect the metal **salts** in the clay and glazes as carbon monoxide and carbon soot are produced. If the ceramic is hot enough to be reactive (above 700°C) then it changes the metal oxides in the glaze by removing some of their oxygen and thereby creating different colours – chiefly from iron and copper. In this scenario, as the carbon is insufficiently combusted the burning is inefficient, and because less chemical bonds are broken there is less energy released and thus there is a much diminished heating effect.

Once the kiln is hot enough then the solids and liquids turn to vapour. Thus wood, coal, oil and dung become a gas and in this form they combine with oxygen to burn as hydrocarbons. Wood and coal gases can be composed of many different lengths of carbon chain. The hydrocarbons butane and propane are depicted diagrammatically as follows:

```
    H   H   H   H                      H   H   H
    |   |   |   |                      |   |   |
H — C — C — C — C — H          H — C — C — C — H
    |   |   |   |                      |   |   |
    H   H   H   H                      H   H   H

        Butane                             Propane
```

where C = carbon atom; H = hydrogen atom;
— = chemical bond.

When we purchase the refined gases propane and butane they are held under compression in liquid form, as this occupies far less space. When the pressure is released, by opening the valve on the bottle, the gas can volatilize becoming a gas again and be burnt. In practice, when firing a large kiln bottles are often linked so that the gas does not freeze in the bottles as it vaporizes. (This is another example of the latent heat of vaporization: as the liquid gas takes considerable energy (in the form of heat) to become a vapour, it can lead, on a cool day, to the formation of a layer of ice on the outside of the gas cylinder and the slowing down of the vaporization process, and consequently of the speed of firing.)

When the hydrocarbon gas burns it reacts with oxygen. When sufficient oxygen is present the products that accompany the release of energy are carbon dioxide and water:

$C_3H_8 + 5O_2 = 3CO_2 + 4H_2O$ + energy
Propane + oxygen = carbon dioxide + water + heat + light

The energy is released as heat and light (the colour of the flame).

When insufficient oxygen is present for complete burning then, instead of all combustion products becoming carbon dioxide and water, carbon monoxide (CO) and hydrogen (H_2) can also be produced. Carbon monoxide allows the available oxygen to be shared out amongst a greater number of carbon atoms. It has two significant qualities for us to be aware of as potters: its role in reduction and its toxicity.

Reduction

Sometimes the packing of material in a bonfire is very dense and so air cannot easily penetrate the pile; once the heap has reached a high temperature then smothered hydrocarbons cannot burn fully. Where there is insufficient oxygen the deadly, colourless gas carbon monoxide is produced, which is highly reactive. It will take the oxygen that it requires to become the more stable carbon dioxide from wherever it can:

$2CO + O_2 = 2CO_2$

The only place available in the confines of the heart of a fire is from the clay, and in particular the glazes on the ware. At these temperatures the excess of the wood or gas disassociates into simple hydrocarbons; in the complete absence of oxygen with which to combust, it produces highly reactive and penetrative carbon vapour. The presence of very hot carbon monoxide (*see* page 33 for an explanation of the associated dangers) and hot carbonaceous smoke can lead to the process that we refer to as reduction.

In a kiln, if the temperature of the ware is high enough, then any introduction of wood or gas that exceeds the volume of oxygen available for it to burn will create yellow flames in the kiln and black smoke from the chimney. At red heat the carbon vapour will be **absorbed** into the pores in the ceramic (colouring it black – and if the wall of the fired ceramic is broken it will be blackish throughout); this is a feature that we associate with bonfire, sawdust, Raku and saggar firing.

As a kiln reaches still higher temperatures, above red heat, and approaches the vitrification of the ceramic (at 1200–1400°C), the carbon vapour (smoke) can, additionally, be **adsorbed** (held as a thin surface film) onto the surface of the ceramic. It is very reactive in the process of reduction and chemically tries to acquire oxygen from wherever it can, to create carbon dioxide. (The main result is to turn iron-bearing glazes greenish and copper glazes reddish.) This can happen even if the reduction process is started later and there is no body reduction.

It is evident that reduction is almost impossible to avoid in a fuel-burning kiln, where the ware is in contact with the flame or fuel. It happens naturally in the stoking cycle of a wood-fired kiln each time more wood is added: the sticks choke the supply of air and so there are more hydrocarbons released into the kiln as volatiles, which compete for the available oxygen, resulting, periodically, in periods of

Fritz Rossmann, vessel with celadon glaze (with 1 per cent iron oxide), fired in reduction.

reduction. In a gas-fired kiln the **damper** is closed to choke the draw of air into the burners, and the (primary) air supply to the burners can also be closed.

Iron and Copper Oxides in Reduction

Irrespective of the form in which the metals are introduced into the glaze, after heating they exist as oxides. The desirable consequences of reduction come from its effect on the oxides of iron and copper. Both metals can produce stable oxides that bond with one or more atoms of oxygen, depending on how much oxygen is available.

Iron oxide is present in practically all clays and is sensitive to atmospheric conditions. We have all seen iron rust in damp, oxygen-rich conditions, when it goes reddish brown – this rust is the red form of iron oxide (Fe_2O_3). In oxygen-deficient conditions – like, for instance, a stagnant pond (a common last home for supermarket trolleys!) – iron will oxidize to a black oxide (FeO). These oxides, when dissolved in the molten glaze, give characteristic colours to it. The red iron oxide produces browns, oranges and reddish hues; the black iron oxide gives greens and blues (in much lower concentrations).

The chemical reactions that occur are:

	Iron	
	Oxidation	Reduction
	$Fe_2O_3 + CO$	$> 2FeO + CO_2$
Effects on clay:	brown	grey
Effects on glaze:	amber/brown/	blue/green/
	black	brown/black

It is also significant to note that Fe_2O_3 and FeO behave quite differently in the melt. The reddish, higher oxygen form is akin to the amphoteric oxide alumina (Al_2O_3) and it will resist the glaze and body melting. After reduction, it is present as FeO and it behaves like cobalt oxide (CoO) and it hastens melting. This increase in fluxing action is depicted in the formula:

$$Fe_2O_3 + CO > 2FeO + CO_2$$

When reduced iron is re-oxidized, in clay body fired to red heat, it can go a new colour along a spectrum from white to orange to grey to black. The burning back of smoked areas will reintroduce a new range of colour as blacks and greys appear and disappear again, leaving a mottled surface depicting the passage of flame.

Copper will produce a black oxide (Cu^{2+}) in the presence of sufficient oxygen (and greens and blues in the glaze) or a red oxide (Cu^{1+}) in the presence of insufficient oxygen (and (elusive) reds in the glaze).

	Copper	
	$2CuO + CO$	$> Cu_2O + CO_2$
Effects on glaze:	green/blue	red

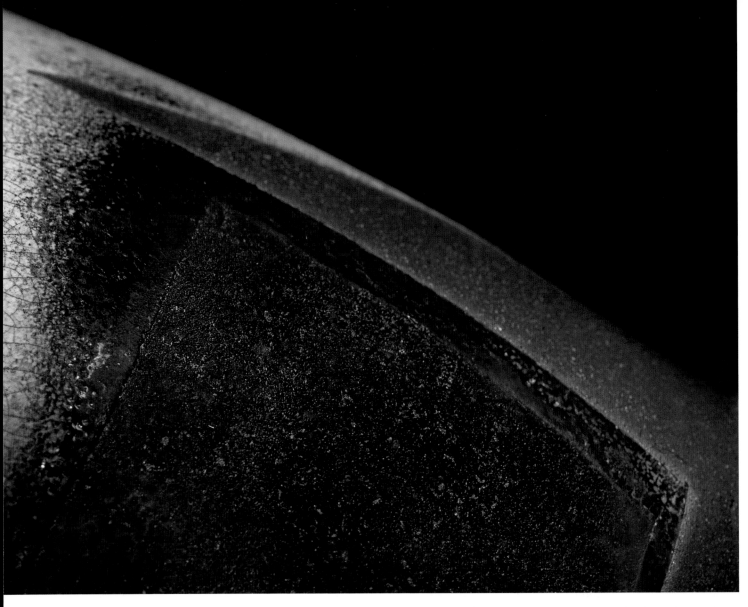

David Jones, Raku pot fired in reduction. Copper in glaze, flashing from bronze to reds to purples. (Photo: Rod Dorling)

Low-Temperature Reduction

By its very nature, a bonfire is an imprecise tool. It is well suited to the firing of **earthenware** pots, which are still porous when finished and they often owe some of their decorative individuality to the marks of fire left on their surface. Pots fired in a bonfire will come out blackened. This observation of simple firing strategies has been developed and refined in contemporary ceramic expression. Reduction is directed, and the sooty carbon produced is absorbed into the still-porous body of the pot to create a pattern of marking that cannot be planned, as such, but reveals the passage of burning through a combustible material like dung, wood, straw or sawdust. The less dense the packing of the material around the ceramic then the better the sawdust will combust and the less black the final product will become. Today various artists have used this accidental technique for orchestrating a series of marks on their fired works.

Ben Brierley, 'wood-fired platter', 58cm.

Regina Heinz, 'Space Map',
electric fired, 32 × 28 × 10cm.

High-Temperature Reduction

The temperatures reached in a bonfire cannot match those achieved in a heat-retaining stoneware kiln. The development of glaze and the consequent need to fire to quite precise temperatures lead to the development of more sophisticated kilns. The invention of a kiln, with the burning of wood in a separate area, created the situation where the development of glaze-type surfaces was possible. It was possible to achieve much higher temperatures in the tunnel-like *anagama* kilns of China, Japan and Korea than in the up-draught kilns utilized in Europe and the Near East. Ash fusion on the surface of the ware provided a decorative finish, and an additional sealing of the clay.

There is generally a search for two effects: the reduction of the glaze or the reduction of both glaze and body. These are qualities produced in a kiln where flames impinge on the clay surface. For clay body reduction the process of restricting oxygen to the burners or sufficient air in the fire box and airflow in the kiln starts early, just around bisque-firing temperature (approximately 950°C). This is a low enough temperature for the body still to be reactive, as it has not yet had a chance to sinter and fuse, and a high enough temperature to be well above the **flashpoint** of the gas so that it does not create an explosive mixture with air in the kiln, should the flame go out. A reduction firing (just to affect glaze) needs only start at 1100°C, when the glaze is beginning to melt. In reduction the fuel is not combusting efficiently, as the carbon is not reacting with the full amount of oxygen that it could; it thereby releases less energy and as a result when reduction takes place there is often a drop in temperature. Thus periods of reduction must alternate with periods of full combustion (oxidation) for the final temperature of the kiln to be achieved (between 1250°C and 1350°C). When a period of oxidation is used to terminate a firing it can lead to a brightening of the glaze.

Toxicity

It is crucial to remember that in the confines of a kiln shed the production of carbon monoxide can be deadly. Carbon monoxide is extremely toxic; its inhalation can lead to death or brain damage in as little as a quarter of an hour. It binds with the red pigment in our blood (the haemoglobin, which carries oxygen around the body) to form a stable compound that does not easily disassociate. With the oxygen transporter in the blood out of action the brain gets no fuel for its vital processes and the result is death. Sitting in an unventilated kiln room while firing a kiln under reduction conditions can have similar effects to the pumping of exhaust gases from an engine into the car. Consequently one must ensure adequate ventilation to all rooms containing a fuel-burning kiln, and ideally install extraction equipment.

Wood Firing and Glaze Melting

When the flame impinges directly on the surface of the pot there are chemical changes that occur as the clay becomes ceramic. If there is not perfect and total combustion then, additionally, the products of combustion (soot) can be trapped in the still-porous body, blackening the material. If

this burns out later the clay can still be left in a state of reduction, with a corresponding colour change having occurred. Even within a bonfire temperatures can be attained that are sufficient to melt the clay, and so there are many surfaces and textures that result from open firing.

Iron-bearing clays in particular are affected by reduction and are more susceptible to melting; a palette of colours from orange to purple can be achieved. This marking can be further directed in a pit firing or a saggar by including fire-sensitive materials such as sawdust, seaweed, salt, copper, and so on, which can encourage the marks that are left by the passage of the flames.

As the temperature of the firing rises then fine ash that has been transported through the fire or through the kiln can deposit on the pots and become reactive; it starts to melt onto the clay surface as a **glaze**. Plant ash contains the inorganic (non-carbonaceous) salts utilized and stored by the plant during its life (where they play an essential role in various biochemical processes). These trace elements still exist in the fuel. They comprise the major part of the **fly ash** and are metal salts that work as fluxes; they fuse with the silica and alumina in the clay to make a glaze. At stoneware temperature in a wood-fired kiln there can be a very heavy coating of ash, which often appears as a greenish glaze due to iron contamination. (The iron either comes with the ash or dissolves out of the clay body.) This fly ash starts as a thin matt deposit and can build up into a thick, shiny coating during a long wood firing.

The Physics and Chemistry of Firing

When clay is heated it undergoes a number of changes – both physical (reversible) and chemical (permanent) changes. The first changes in the firing are mainly physical: the water with which the clay has been lubricated (which makes it workable) is driven off. Much of this evaporation occurs as the ambient air takes up the water vapour and removes it from the ware. The speed of drying of the clay depends on the humidity of the surrounding air and the rate at which it is exchanged; we know from our observations in the studio that cool, damp air does not allow a pot to dry as quickly as on a hot, dry, windy summer's day. (Michael Cardew observes in *Pioneer Pottery* (1969) that the pots made and fired in the wet season by the African potters had a much greater tendency to crack in the firing than those that had dried more completely in the dry season.)

Dale Huffmann, vase, wood-fired in anagama.

Silica Phases, Conversions and Inversions

The changes that occur in firing are complex and as potters, in practice, we only need a simple set of instructional dos and don'ts. Therefore if the chemistry appears frightening, skip this section and refer to the conclusions. (However, one day you might want an explanation of why these events happen and for that reason this section is waiting for you!) The chemist's explanation looks at the composition of clay bodies and provides an account of what is happening in scientific terminology. Silica is not merely a major constituent of glazes and clay bodies, but we may also note that it composes almost 60 per cent of the mass of the Earth's crust. Pure silica is found, mainly, as quartz rock crystal, sand and flint. As part of the clay molecule, silica comprises nearly half of the formula by weight. There is normally an even greater proportion of silica in a clay body, as very often sand and fine-ground silica are part of its composition, either occurring naturally or mixed in later for texture and temper. Silica has a melting point of 1713°C (a temperature far beyond the scope of a ceramic kiln, which would have melted far sooner); yet the sintering of silica makes the clay particles fuse together as the heat agitates the molecules and they coalesce. Silica is a crystalline material that can exist in a number of forms, each of which can have a different structure as a result of changes in temperature, known as phases.

For the purposes of understanding firing we need to be aware of the following different physical forms that silica can take, whilst remaining chemically the same:

■ quartz;
■ crystoballite; and
■ tridymite.

Silica has a crystalline structure. When it is heated it changes from one phase to another; this means that the crystal structure rearranges itself and in effect becomes larger.

The significant quartz phase inversion is at 573°C. At this temperature any unbound silica in the body undergoes a physical change known as the Alpha–Beta (α–β) quartz inversion. In the so-called Beta phase the silica molecule twists and becomes approximately 1 per cent larger than it was before in the Alpha phase. If there is a lot of silica in the body, then this can cause a severe problem if the outside is, say, at 600°C and the interior only 500°C. This would mean that the outside would expand (to the Beta quartz phase) and the inside stay where it is (at the Alpha quartz phase), and these stresses will generate a crack. These problems become even greater in the cooling cycle, as more free silica is present.

The significant crystoballite phase inversion is at 226°C. Since crystoballite is a form that is created by prolonged heating in the kiln, then if the kiln door is opened at around 250°C, so-called dunting cracks (caused by rapid cooling) can occur.

The significant tridymite phase is progressive over the range 280–220°C. It is a much more gradual change than the other inversions and can in fact smooth them over and, to some extent, cancel out some of the problems of dunting cracks.

Firing: Stage by Stage

0–100°C. Even when a pot is dried in a hot, dry room there is still moisture left in the clay when it is ready to fire. This water must be driven off slowly as it can only escape from the clay through the minute capillaries that are formed between the tiny clay particles. The water is driven off as vapour; this gaseous form of water occupies a much greater volume than it did as a liquid. If the clay is heated too quickly, therefore, the volume of steam suddenly generated is too large to escape easily. If the clay is tight – that is, has very fine clay particles and no coarse matter in its composition – then there is a good chance of the pot exploding or a piece of the fabric being blown off as the steam expands. It is important to note that coarse materials in the clay body – grogs and sand – can allow for easier dissipation of the steam by creating channels to the surface.

100–200°C. The boiling point of water is 100°C. When this temperature is reached, the physically combined water turns extremely rapidly from liquid to vapour and consequently it suddenly occupies a much greater volume. The wall thickness of the clay will have a significant bearing on the firing cycle. Heat is communicated to the outside wall of the pot, by **radiation** from electric kiln **elements** or by **convection** of the firing gases, and this heat is then carried into the interior of the wall by **conduction** from particle to particle. In physical terms the heat energy manifests itself as a vibration of atoms within the particles – the hotter they are then the faster they vibrate (until in fact they are so agitated that they leave their structured solid state and become a liquid). Because the heat is passed on from particle to particle then it follows that the thicker the wall, the slower it is for the heat to penetrate; so if the rate of heating is too rapid then the exterior can become much hotter than the interior, with the result that it expands and cracking can occur.

200–600°C. Nothing very remarkable happens in the kiln as the temperature rises, for all the physically combined water has been driven off. Indeed, if one stopped the firing at this point then with the addition of water one could reconstitute the clay by slaking down the pot and returning the fabric to usable clay (with a reduced plasticity). There is not really any

problem at this stage with the quartz inversion as there is not a significant quantity formed in the body.

APPROXIMATELY 600°C (DULL RED HEAT). As the temperature rises then water is driven off again. This time it is not the physically combined water but the chemically combined water that is given off as steam. This temperature is easily attained in a bonfire and it represents a permanent change to the material as it transforms from clay to ceramic. After this temperature, putting the (now bisque-fired) piece into water does not result in a pile of mud; the form of the piece is unaffected. As with the physically combined water it is important not to accelerate through this transition too quickly as the steam produced, if not allowed to dissipate slowly, can cause the ceramic to explode.

600–1000°C. Once no more steam is being expelled from the kiln then it can be fired to the required temperature as fast as is desired. With a bonfire that final top temperature

LEFT: Peter Klube, zinc-barium crystalline glaze.

BELOW: Joanna Howells, 'Wine Cooler' (detail), celadon glaze.

cannot be attained with precision and can vary between firings.

1000°C (BISQUE-FIRING TEMPERATURE). This is a common temperature at which to stop a firing, as the ceramic is now sufficiently hard to be safely handled and yet still sufficiently porous to absorb glaze.

1100°C. Some iron-rich dark clays and some white clays (high in calcium and magnesium) start to melt.

1250°C. By this temperature most stoneware clays have sintered and the particles have fused together to make an impervious ceramic. This is a common temperature to which to fire stoneware glazes. They have the benefit both of a fused hard body and a glassy coat.

The faster the cooling the less chance crystals have to grow, so this is important to bear in mind with certain glazes. For example, in order to generate small crystals and consequently a higher level of shine in some **temmokus**, the kiln is crash-cooled from the top temperature. At other times one wants to encourage crystal growth and development (say, in macro-crystalline glazes) and so the cooling is prolonged by the introduction of heat to the kiln as it cools down, maintaining the fluid state of the glaze for a longer period of time.

600°C. Around this temperature there is a danger from the quartz inversion causing cracking in the body, so it is important to protect the ware from draughts.

600–150°C. At this stage one can find that cracks occur, particularly on cooling, as there is often a draught through a very narrow gap that focuses cold air and cooling very locally. After a prolonged high-temperature firing there is a fusing of the silica molecules and therefore more crystalline silica to undergo these phase transitions at 226°C.

Again, there is the problem of cracking, caused by the crystoballite inversion.

Health and Safety: Carbon Monoxide

The burning of a blue flame from gaps in the brickwork of a kiln is most likely to be toxic carbon monoxide burning and is thus an indicator warning the potter of a deadly situation in the kiln shed!

Peter Beard, sculpture fired in an electric kiln.

4

Kilns
~
Theories and Practice of Heat Retention

Technology today is the campfire around which we tell our stories.

Laurie Anderson (Performance Artist)

Introduction to Kilns

Early kilns ignored deep, inaccessible sources of energy and concentrated on those available on the Earth's surface – wood, dung and peat. Indeed, our potting ancestors would still recognize the current practice of ceramics as continuous with their own if they looked at fuel-burning kilns. However, an electric kiln, a metal box that gets hot due to resistance in the elements, is nearly as mysterious as the combustion that drives my computer – yet the same laws drive them both. A kiln is but an enclosure that contains heat and prevents it from escaping, while at the same time preventing draughts and sudden changes of temperature. If a bonfire is deemed inadequate to cook the clay then a variety of mechanisms can be employed to improve the situation.

A kiln is a wall that surrounds, contains and controls the fire. At its simplest, a kiln can be made from materials that a potter might have to hand: stones (which are inclined to explode) or the best material (one that is readily available), which is the pots themselves, cracked and broken from previous firings. These are stacked around the bonfire and provide a surprisingly good screen against fluctuations in temperature created by the wind. In particular they shield the wares on their cooling cycle and help to prevent dunting cracks. Bisque-fired clay is the best material for making such a wall and, as it retains some of the heat of the firing, it slows the cooling as the absorbed heat radiates slowly off the walls. It acts as a **heat sink**, and because it slows the rate of cooling it enables the ceramic to pass through the quartz inversion phases in a controlled manner, which is another way that it helps to reduce cracking.

The next advance in terms of developing a kiln is to make the line of shards around the outside of the fire continuous, by mortaring them in place with a sandy clay slip; this retains much more heat and produces more even temperatures. The next stage is to build a continuous wall, or to create modules (bricks). To increase the insulation properties one must utilize the best insulator that is available and that is air – static air. To get air into the ceramic one must either pump it in – a technique that has been used only in the last half-century (in the production of low-density ceramic bricks and **ceramic fibre**) – or create air gaps in the clay by mixing in a combustible material that will create spaces as it burns out. Simple kilns everywhere in the world are built using bricks that have been made from a mix of clay, crushed refractory pot (grog) and straw or dung.

OPPOSITE PAGE:
Petra Reynolds and Jeremy Steward firing. (Photo : Rod Dorling)

Kilns: A Historical Background

The most basic kilns are those where the flame and the pots are protected from the weather by an enclosure of pre-fired broken pot shards. For firing, the pots are placed on the ground, on top of a pile of brushwood and dried dung, and more combustible material is piled over. Once the fire is alight the shards are placed around the fire to diminish draughts and thereby protect the ware from heating and cooling too rapidly – which, along with the problems of creating steam from firing damp clay too quickly, is the most common cause of damage in the firing of ceramics.

In the development of kilns it is a short step from use of a protected bonfire to the creation of a special, more permanent enclosure for the pots and thence to a separate firebox for burning the fuel. In a kiln flames are lead from the firebox into the kiln chamber and through the clay pieces. The simplest kind of structure is where the fire is positioned directly underneath the kiln chamber and the heat rises vertically upwards through the stack of pots. This is referred to as an updraught kiln, and historically has been the main type of kiln used throughout the world.

Only in the Far East (in China, Korea and Japan) were other types of kiln initially developed to employ different methods of flame deflection through the kiln. Only in those countries were high enough temperatures achieved to go beyond red heat and to change the porous ceramic into a vitrified, sealed clay body. These kilns are referred to as downdraught and cross-draught kilns; the ware is protected by a **bag wall** from the direct impingement of the fire. It is not clear why the superior qualities of stoneware were not realized in the Near East or Europe, but this is quite possibly just another technological development in which for so long the West lagged behind the East. The construction of such kilns is quite simple and, at its most basic, firing to stoneware temperatures is largely about superior heat retention and prolonged firing with a highly energetic fuel (such as burning a very large volume of wood). However, for a long time potters and their patrons in Europe were quite content with the qualities of low-temperature (earthenware) firing.

Ceramic was always a low-status material and was ranked below silver and gold and base metals in the hierarchy of materials for tableware. The poor had wood and earthenware. Yet, in every culture, there has always been a tradition of fine ceramic for the higher classes. Unlike in China, no one in Europe had discovered the white burning clays necessary for **porcelain** production. It took until the geological surveys conducted by Wedgwood and Böttger in the eighteenth century for the large reserves in south-western England and Germany to be discovered and exploited.

About seven hundred years ago traders on the Silk Road from Europe through the Near East to China brought fine stoneware and porcelain to Europe. This was a time that coincided with the emergence of the middle classes in Europe, the beginning of the breakdown of feudalism and therefore an increased market for status artefacts. There was also a dearth of precious metal with which to make them, even though precious metal plate was regularly melted

Connie Bertz, vases, electric-fired kiln.

down to make fashionable objects for that generation. Suddenly the desire for porcelain became a craze, and many of the local potters tried to imitate the fine white surfaces in order to cash-in on the demand. For some time they used their existing technologies and in different ways tried to create a white clay, as it was obviously very difficult to discover the secrets of high-temperature firing from China. Great cargoes of porcelain were brought to Europe to feed the desire for tea drinking. (Ostensibly the ceramics were originally brought as ballast in the tea chests; very soon the demand for vessels for this new, fashionable drink stimulated supply from Chinese kilns for ware specifically for the European market.)

The Eastern kilns were not so very complex, but the methodology of kiln firing utilized allowed them to construct enormous structures that were fired infrequently and with very standardized results. The firing required such a level of expertise that there were teams of kiln-firers who would travel from one site to another supervising the firing of the kilns, perhaps as seldom as once or twice per year.

As the pressures toward economy of scale grew with larger-volume kilns, so the single chamber started to be subdivided into a succession of smaller chambers where more localized and more easily controlled atmospheres and temperatures could be achieved that did not have the vast overall temperature range of the single-chambered kiln. Thus began the development of the *noborigama*, or multi-chambered kiln, in the East. The chambers are fired one after another by side-stoking (feeding in from the side) up the slope of the kiln. They can be packed with different glazes or clay bodies; as each chamber finishes then the next can be fired using the wasted heat from the chamber before, precisely, with wood stoked from the side. Most often the last chamber would be a **bisque firing** and would just be achieved with the waste heat of the former chambers, thus saving fuel.

Gas Kilns

Reduction firing with a gas kiln is now common practice in most ceramics departments and studios. In a gas-fired kiln we wish to imitate the reduction effects on the ceramic achieved in a traditional fuel-burning kiln. Reduction is achieved by restricting the amount of air that enters with the gas (known as the primary air) by altering the amount of air coming in at the burners. It is also facilitated by putting a damper across the flue (in the exit or chimney), which reduces the draw of the kiln.

In a gas firing the reducing flame is a soft, licking flame that is yellow in colour, due to the particles of uncombusted carbon (the fully oxidizing flame is blue at the burner).

The pots emerge quite transformed by the firing; the clay as well as the glazes can undergo dramatic change. The reduction can also encourage a body–glaze interface to develop, where the two materials become a new compound. Clay body reduction commences (before the body is made impervious by the liquefying of the glaze over the clay) just at a high red heat – approximately 950°C (that is, beyond the flashpoint of the gas to avoid an explosion). Glaze reduction can be commenced when the glaze is molten, at approximately 1100°C.

Electric Kilns

The great advantage of electricity is sometimes seen as its greatest drawback in the art of ceramics. It is a clean fuel (for the end-user), created by energy generated elsewhere by the burning of fuel in a power station or by nuclear/wind/water energy. Thus in an electric kiln there is no flame or vapour circulation; instead of the heating effect occurring via convection the heat is communicated to the ware by radiation. The heat is generated in spiral-wound elements supported in the floor, walls and ceiling. The resistance of the elements to the passage of electricity through them results in a heating effect, which causes them to glow from red-hot to white-hot. (The metal reacts with the oxygen in the air, forming a protective oxide layer that does not melt because it is very refractory – its melting point is over 2000°C.)

The Element

Confusingly, the word 'element' is used by both chemists and ceramicists. The chemist defines an element as the simplest, pure and indivisible material capable of participating in a chemical reaction. A potter will use the word element to refer to the electrical heating device within a kiln.

One can use either a kiln with elements made from the special metal alloy known as Kanthal, or silicon carbide rods. In order to achieve reduction an oxygen-hungry atmosphere needs to be created. There are a number of ways to do this that all follow the same basic principle: that of introducing a hydrocarbon into the atmosphere through the kiln spyholes. It can be achieved by pushing thin sticks through the holes (carbon dioxide and ash will be produced) or mothballs (naphthalene will vaporize to achieve the desired results and leave no ash).

Chemically there are problems that need to be understood. If a reduction atmosphere is created in the kiln with Kanthal elements then the carbon monoxide reacts with the aluminium oxide layer on the elements and removes it. This starts to thin and weaken the elements; thus any reduction firing should be followed by an oxidizing firing in order to re-establish the oxide coating on the elements. Successive reduction firings can significantly shorten the life of the elements.

Instead of Kanthal elements some electric kilns specifically designed for reduction have elements made from silicon carbide. Silicon carbide conducts electricity like a metal and it is not affected by the atmosphere of reduction. It is either fashioned into rods that sit directly in the kiln, or tubes that act as a protection for normal Kanthal elements. As they age, silicon carbide elements break down to carbon and silica, which do not conduct electricity and so work progressively less efficiently.

Health and Safety: Reduction Firing in an Electric Kiln

In addition to the introduction of hydrocarbons via the insertion of combustible material through the spyholes, it is also possible to use bottled gas. However, if the temperature drops below the flashpoint of the gas, say 1000°C, or is not high enough to combust it, then an explosive mixture could be produced with air and destroy the kiln. Since electric kilns are not normally as well vented as gas kilns it is also likely that you will be emitting toxic carbon monoxide into the kiln room – so good air extraction is imperative before you try this.

Firing in an electric kiln is often, inaccurately, called an oxidation firing, where in fact it would be more accurate to name it a neutral firing, as it is neither reducing nor oxidizing, as there is no fuel to combust. Without reduction there is normally less interaction between glaze and clay body, and since there is no movement of flame through the chamber the surfaces produced on the ware are more uniform from one piece to the next.

Neutral/oxidized firings are a challenge that many town potters have faced for the last half-century and many who fire using electricity treat these apparent limitations as a creative restriction and have devised spectacular glazes for the electric kiln, such that its repertory is as rich as that for the fuel kilns – but perhaps without its nuances of accident. Although the firing does not necessarily lead to the softening of the glaze colour that one sees with reduction, particularly with wood firing, it can permit a strong, even strident palette of colour and effect. The surfaces created by Peter Beard, Regina Heinz and Catrin Mostyn Jones are testament to overcoming the apparent limitations created by the absence of a flame firing.

Traditional Kiln Construction

There are no great secrets to kiln building. There are some general principles to follow, however, born of the distillation of careful study of historic kilns. In this book I am concentrating on drawing out the general principles and I wish to focus on the thinking that motivates choices.

There now exists a plethora of excellent handbooks that give structural diagrams for the building of all types and scales of kiln. All over the developed world kilns can be found that are vastly more efficient than the early examples on which they are based, using high-tech materials that have been developed for mass production. In order to create the 'best' results in our studios, in pursuit of more expressionistic (often informed by more 'primitive') ambitions, we use a combination of both old and new technology and thinking.

Key Principles

The following are some key principles, albeit some of them very obvious, of firing a fuel-burning kiln:

- A kiln is a system for retaining and conserving heat and it is necessary to distribute heat as evenly as possible.
- So long as more heat enters the kiln than is lost then the temperature will rise.
- There is a fire at one end, and an exit flue at the other. A potter needs to control and contain the heat, and plan to direct the flow of hot gases within its volume.
- It is important to ensure that the kiln has sufficient draw, to pull the heat through the kiln.
- Hot air rises, but the flame can be made to circulate through the pack by forcing it to exit through the floor.
- The materials from which the kiln is constructed must withstand the highest temperatures experienced. Check with the manufacturers and choose a brick or fibre rated at temperatures well above that at which you intend to fire.
- You may need to make a decision regarding the use of energy-hungry, durable bricks or lightweight, friable, but economical, modern refractories.
- There needs to be a balance between low-heat mass materials (which conserve fuel and thereby the costs of firing) and heat retention in order to avoid dunting cracks.
- Use as few dense (hot-face) bricks as possible, as they require much more heating.
- Although insulating bricks are more expensive, their use will not result in such high fuel bills.

- By increasing the efficiency of the burning, minimizing the heat loss and improving the circulation of heat around the kiln, one can maximize the efficiency of the whole structure.
- The greater the amount of wood consumed in a kiln, the greater the coating of fly ash deposited on the pots.
- Any materials introduced into the kiln, like salt and soda, will be dispersed according to the patterns of flow.
- A damper needs to be included in the plans, to regulate reduction.
- It is always easier to narrow the chimney than to make a brick structure wider, so when constructing a new kiln it is best to make the chimney a little wider than seems necessary and to constrict it later if required. In a wood kiln the rule of thumb is to make the area of the chimney one-fifth to one-tenth of the area of the grate, and slightly more than equal to the area of the inlet flues.
- In a kiln where the firebox is some distance from the chimney, pre-heating can encourage the drawing through of the flame: start by setting a fire in the base of the chimney and heating the brick structure of the chimney before the firing proper commences. Then when the main fire is started in the firebox the flames will be pulled, albeit softly and lazily, through the pack by the hot air rising from the chimney (it is particularly important not to hurry the firing if one is firing raw, not bisque-fired, pots).

Key Questions to Ask Yourself

In order to identify the kiln you wish to build or buy, you need to know the following:

- how much fuel you are prepared to use/waste, with regards to both the cost and the environment;
- the purpose of your kiln (commercial, creative, exploratory);
- the temperature at which you wish to fire;
- the ideal fuel, weighed up against the types of fuel available;
- the degree of mechanical control of firing desired versus the degree of hands-on connection to firing;
- the size of the kiln versus the frequency of firing;
- whether to buy a designed kiln or self-build;
- the cost of materials;
- health and safety aspects; and
- environmental issues relating to the site.

John Leach kiln firing, light reduction. (Photo: Rod Dorling)

John Leach kiln firing, heavy reduction. (Photo: Rod Dorling)

LEFT: Framework of willow to be clad in clay, built by Ros Ingram and students from the University of Wolverhampton. (Photo: Peter Higgs)

BELOW: Ben Brierley, wood lath structure for forming a kiln.

Building Materials

Materials for building kilns are much more sophisticated now than in the past, but if you are not intending to use the kiln for commercial production then you can discover an enormous amount about the behaviour of clay and heat by using scrap materials such as reused house bricks, slop clay over paper and wood structures, which burn out, or dismantled commercial operations. The simplest kiln is a hollow structure created by pasting clay over an existing combustible structure (a willow frame, for instance, will burn out in the firing).

The most efficient insulator is a vacuum; the next best available insulator is the air. Bricks can be designed to trap air within the pores in their structure. To minimize clay mass in the kiln walls the simplest method is to mix something with the clay bricks that will burn out when the kiln is fired. Sawdust, straw, chaff or dung are ideal materials – and the lower the density of the fired brick, the higher its insulation qualities. White clays are mostly very refractory (having a high melting point) and can be used to trap air; they are also less likely to melt, with the extreme heat experienced in firing, than most red clays.

The next rule of thumb is that the less clay there is in the structure to heat up then the less fuel is 'wasted'. One must always bear in mind that if there is little thermal mass in the structure to heat up then it will also not retain heat and so it will cool down quickly – so a balance must be kept between the thermal mass of the kiln walls and the resistance of the ware to rapid cooling. Fused clay is denser and conducts heat very much better than unvitrified porous clays, and is therefore also to be avoided as much heat can be lost by using too many such hard bricks. Nowadays sophisticated bricks are made by blowing air through a slop of clay.

The most advanced materials are ceramic fibres. (These were devised to create the protective tiles to protect the reentry of the Apollo rockets.) They are very light and easy to use, and can be compressed into board or woven into blanket and bent and adapted to fit any structure. They are made by extruding clay into a vacuum to produce a very open

RIGHT: *Ian Jones, kiln firing.*

BELOW: *Ben Brierley, kiln building with the second brick layer in place and the chimney nearing completion.*

texture of clay and air. They become slightly harder and more brittle with use, so they are less practical for reuse. They are the material of choice for Raku (low-temperature) kilns and for the new sculpture kilns (*refer to* Chapter 17 for the discussion of John Roloff's work).

Bricks as a module are incredibly easy to use. As they are based around a right angle it is important to start from a level base and to use a plumb line or spirit level to ensure rectilinearity, and a removable former to generate a curve or an arch (*see* Chapter 9 for work of Ben Brierley and Dale Huffman).

Brick Recipe

1 part clay (the best clay for this purpose is the most 'open' and refractory. Such clays can be identified by their coarse, gritty texture and light colour)

1 part sand

2 parts damp cut straw (or herbivore dung, which is much easier to mix in as it will crumble if allowed to dry)

Mix and press into wood moulds. Allow to dry.

Once they have dried completely one can use these 'raw' bricks straight away to build with – but obviously only the faces that enclose the fire will become ceramic. Thus often one builds a clamp kiln, which is used solely for firing the bricks (slowly) before use.

Making Your Own Bricks

One can easily experiment with making bricks – but the idea is to get as much combustible material into the clay as possible while retaining as much strength as possible. The more clay there is in the bricks of the kiln structure then the more energy one has to expend in heating up that structure – however, if the bricks are too porous then they will collapse, under their own weight, as they are stacked.

5

Assessing the Progress of Firing
~
Measurement of Temperature or Heat-Work

ABOVE: *Melted conepack and draw-rings out of a wood kiln. (Photo: David Jones)*

RIGHT: *Emma Harmes sculpture, porcelain, gas fired. (Photo: Rod Dorling)*

OPPOSITE PAGE: *John Leach's kiln. Bricked-up door. (Photo: Rod Dorling)*

The general rule is that the greater the amount of **heat-work** the harder and less porous the ceramic product. It was the final use of the piece that dictated these requirements in the past. Although history appears to tell a story of advances in technology, which give the appearance of progress, it is in fact the case that simple low-fired ceramic perfectly well serves its use as a cooking vessel over a hot flame because of its open and unvitrified nature, or for storage, once having been sealed with gums and wax. These fabrics are also rather

friable (prone to crumbling), so a compromise had to be reached between durability in handling and the softness of the ceramic.

With increasing heat-work the clay particles sinter (melt) and join together, until at high temperatures the body becomes a continuous material and then (if over-fired) it liquefies, bubbles and melts.

Heat-Work and the Effects of Firing

'Heat-work' is the word used to describe the measurement of the changes that have been effected on clay or a glaze. It is a function of a combination of effects: temperature; duration of the firing; kiln atmosphere; and volatiles in the kiln. As it is rather an inhospitable environment, we are unable to physically get inside the kiln to examine the transformations that are taking place. Instead there have been a number of inventions that allow us to access this essential information. The simplest is to place test pieces strategically in the space and to remove them and examine them away from the heat. This way of sampling the ongoing products of firing has been used for thousands of years and has only been superseded, in certain circumstances, in recent history.

Draw-Rings

The main way that we extract information from within the conflagration is using 'draw-rings' – so-called because they are little circles of clay that are easy to 'draw' (pick) out of the kiln on a wet stick or an iron rod. These are drawn out of the kiln and quenched in water, and give an excellent indication of what is happening on the other side of the insulating wall sheltering the potter from the fantastically high temperatures in the kiln. (Nonetheless, some interpretation is required, as compensation must be made for the artificially fast cooling to which the test piece has been subjected; this is an adjustment that comes with close observation and experience.)

A draw-ring is a simply made circle of clay (from the same body clay from which the pots are made). They are lined up, behind a removable brick in the kiln wall, so that once the first one is removed the next is revealed. These samples are taken systematically until the firing is deemed over; it is always good practice to have at least one left in case the firing takes longer than expected. So that one can be consistent in comparing knowledge gained from successive firings it is always a good idea to position the rings in the same geographic site in the kiln. The draw ring can be the repository of so much information: the degree of vitrification, the

hardness of the ceramic, the build-up of ash, the build-up of salt and soda glaze, the maturing of the glaze, the build-up of lustre, and so on.

In-Kiln Heat Measurement

Cones

Draw-rings represent an intermittent monitoring of the conditions of the kiln and the firing, as we can only know what has happened to the ring once it has been removed from the kiln and cooled. As ceramics became increasingly industrialized in the West there was an concomitant need for continuous assessment of what was taking place in the kiln, and for firings that were as far as possible a direct imitation of the last (successful) firing for standardization of product.

Cones were devised as a more sophisticated method of testing that, similarly, is physically in the kiln and can be observed from outside. Pyrometric cones are manufactured to standardized recipes, being composed of ground-up mixtures of glaze materials. In their capacity as a glaze they would mature later in the firing, but as a cone they start flowing (in a predictable manner) earlier in the firing. Nowadays we use industrially manufactured cone-shaped lumps of these materials, which are completely standardized in terms of ingredients, size and shape. Thus each time they are placed in a kiln they are in the same position and are chemically identical to the cones that were used on the last occasion; they therefore offer a standardized record of firing.

This technique reached its final fruition in the researches of a German chemist, Hermann Seger, and the pyrometric cones are named after him. We now use three-sided pyramids (cones) of these standardized, purified materials placed at an angle to the vertical – when they have bent a certain amount of heat-work has been completed. A fired cone represents exactly the same effects on the pieces in the kiln as happened when an identical cone bent last time and overrules local variations like the speed of firing, changes in supply of wood, wind conditions, and so on.

The cone is placed in a pack of three with guide cones either side placed in a wad of refractory clay, each at an angle (so that they will melt with the cone number uppermost), thoroughly dried (so that it will not explode!) and in an easily visible spot in the kiln (opposite a spyhole). Thus the kiln structure determines that the cone pack is always placed in the same place in the kiln. The first guide cone softens as it responds to the heat-work done, indicating the nearing of the completion of the firing; when it starts to bend it gives us a 20°C warning of the end of the firing. It starts to bend and then collapse as the main cone starts to soften; when that has reached the pre-determined angle of droop (based on the experience of the previous firings) the kiln firing is stopped. So the main cone can be nearly flat or have just the tip starting to bend; the careful observation of the last firing will dictate the precise moment. The third cone is there as an insurance to confirm that the firing did not accidentally proceed for too long.

Pyrometric Bars

The cone technology has also been developed to create an automatic kiln shut-off mechanism: a horizontal bar of pyrometric material is laid across sensors and when it melts it shuts down the kiln.

Thermocouple

The thermocouple is a temperature-measuring device protected in a porcelain sheath. It is a bi-metallic strip where two dissimilar metals are joined at the tip; when exposed to heat they create a small difference in voltage that changes in relationship to the temperature and is calibrated on a scale known as a pyrometer. The 'pyro' can also be linked to control devices near the kiln that will **soak** it, or control rise and fall of temperature. Most electric kilns are controlled nowadays with a pyrometer, but as is evident from the discussion so far the temperature in the kiln is only half the story and for a more accurate picture it is always worthwhile, if not essential, to employ cones to ascertain the heat-work done.

A firing that is to 1150°C and soaked – that is, maintained at that temperature for eleven days like the Bizen firings at Imbe in Japan – can easily have the same effect on the vitrification of the clay as a quick firing to 1280°C. (The potters do these prolonged firings because the colour effects achieved at lower temperatures are much brighter than the stony effects achieved at stoneware temperatures.)

Optical Pyrometer

An optical pyrometer measures the temperature of a kiln by correlating the colour of the kiln interior with temperature. The hotter the kiln becomes the shorter the wavelength of the radiated light: from red to orange to yellow to white to blue.

I believe it is only in situations where heat-work done is not that significant – in a bisque or a Raku firing – where one would not use a pack of cones. Raku is a special case in point as one can lift the lid and directly inspect the degree of melt of the glaze – thereby dispensing with the need for either pyrometer or cones.

RIGHT: David Jones, Raku kiln showing red heat. (Photo: Rod Dorling)

BELOW: David Jones vitrified porcelain, electric kiln firing, 1260°. (Photo: Rod Dorling)

6

The Twentieth-Century Background to Firing in the West

The Arts and Crafts Movement

The twentieth century witnessed great technological advances in the development of materials and techniques for firing ceramics. This built on the previous period of industrialization, with the division of labour and concomitant alienation of ceramic workers in the Industrial Revolution. Alongside the increased specialization in the workplace and immensely greater efficiency in terms of volume of production came a lowering of the price of pottery, which enabled the poor to afford well-finished, hygienic china.

The early followers of the nineteenth-century 'Arts and Crafts Movement', championed by C.R. Ashbee and William Morris, led an aesthetic assault on the 'soulless' quality of commercial tableware; this lead to a re-examination of the qualities embodied in small-scale production. Although the Arts and Crafts pottery movement endeavoured to compete with the factories in terms of cost this would always be a lost battle; but its search for 'humanity' in the conditions of work, and in the product, lead to a radical re-evaluation of firing practices over subsequent generations.

The early pioneers of the Arts and Crafts Movement were the first to react to these qualities; they were initially content to use existing kiln methodologies and to adapt them to their needs, and they then looked to other exemplars for inspiration. For instance, the Bloomsbury group produced painted ceramics and William de Morgan produced tiles inspired by Turkish and Moorish ceramics, with both very much within the European matrix of ceramic expression. They initiated a reaction to, and rejection of, urban values and proposed a return to village guild-manufacturing practices; this ideal of a bucolic world born in the cities of the Industrial Revolution was to prove a fundamental influence in the thinking of potters at the beginning of the last century. However, the idea of firing, as a medium for decoration or of expression, was not a dominant force in their thinking.

In Britain the small-scale operations of craft workshops had all but been eclipsed by low-cost mass production by the end of the nineteenth century; this was a situation matched in a number of other countries of mainland Europe. The work in the ceramic factories, where the employees were seen merely as an extension to a machine, was largely dehumanizing; their financial remuneration was small, by comparison with the profits made by the owners of these establishments; and their life expectancy was very low. In Britain there was a reaction by potters, artists and designers (many of a socialist or Fabian political persuasion) against the alienation of the factories represented by Stoke-on-Trent. They proclaimed a desire to create objects that would enhance their owners' lives, in small-scale, labour-friendly workshops. Their focus was on a refined beauty in utility.

OPPOSITE PAGE:
John Leach kiln, reduction back-pressure. (Photo: Rod Dorling)

Bernard Leach and Firing

There are aspects of Bernard Leach's writing and practice that make him both a revolutionary and a reactionary figure in the discussion of the firing of ceramics. Leach was as much a significant writer and educator (through his books) as he was a potter of international significance. Born at the end of the nineteenth century, he made a moral and ethical case for a quite different way of making ceramics that was based on what he had distilled from his observations of, and idealization of, practice in Japan. He rejected the divisions of labour and dehumanizing, alienating modes of manufacture found in factory mass-production and focused instead on a Romantic idea, which became an ideal, of medieval Japanese ceramic production: where the potter was in charge of practically every aspect of the work. It was a myth, of course, gazing back to a rosy view of feudal life, and enshrined in a patriarchal politics, but it was an idea(l) that won the hearts of his many students and followers and dovetailed with the prevailing Arts and Crafts view.

At the end of the nineteenth century China, Korea and Japan (all pre-industrialized countries) were still repositories of extraordinary ceramic knowledge and sophistication in terms of kiln design and firing techniques. They had utilized a quite different temperature range than that explored in the West (with a few exceptions). Although it was oriental porcelain that was the model for the bone china imitations produced in Stoke, the clays used in the West were far less plastic and allowed for a less expressive product, as bone china was not suited to hand working, having evolved for mass-production using plaster of Paris moulds.

Leach originally went to Japan to teach etching and drawing. His narrative was that, as the guest of a small group of upper-class young men, one evening he experienced a Raku firing performed by an artisan potter for their participation and enjoyment. As a result Leach transferred his interests to ceramics. Leach was flattered that he had been adopted by the last in a ceramics dynasty, making Tea Ceremony wares as Kenzan VII. His teacher, Kenzan VI, gave Leach glaze recipes and also kiln-building and firing instructions, which he reproduced in *A Potter's Book*.

It has been quoted that, 'When the old master died, Leach became, in effect, Kenzan VII. "I exhibited a few pots with my paintings. All the pots were sold. So I said, 'What ho!'"' (*Time*, 27 February 1950). Leach became a potter.

Leach's 'language of firing' formed the dominant narrative of British studio ceramics for the first part of the last century, reverencing the Song dynasty (960–1279) period of pottery manufacture in China. The materials were crude ores and crushed stones, with rocks and ash as glaze materials, and the firing was simple and fuelled by wood. It was modified by his understanding of Japanese peasant pottery production and firing techniques and prevailed until

potters started visiting Japan themselves and saw celebrated examples of the 'marks of the fire' on the body of the pots. This 'Leach tradition' was quite the antithesis of the production techniques and qualities pursued in industrial manufacture; it prevailed as a dominant aesthetic in the Anglo-Saxon countries until the 1960s and 1970s when an Art School-led revolution (inspired by the Bauhaus émigrés) started to use industrial practices in a creative manner and another revolution in ceramics led to a renewed interest in low-fire methodologies.

Leach set up his pottery in the artist colony of St Ives and built a wood-burning kiln – although Cornwall is noted for its lack of trees! He wrote *A Potter's Book* in 1940 (Leach, 1977), the first 'primer' for craft potters; it deals with his findings concerning high-temperature Japanese glaze and kiln design, and his idiosyncratic fusion of the oriental with the British slipware tradition. The book is a record of the way in which the craft pottery movement was consumed by things oriental. He created an idea leading to an ideal (that was espoused by many of the next generation of potters) of a 'good life', being at one with the work, in a state of harmony with process and material. This counter-cultural movement led, through the proselytizing of Bernard Leach, to the 'little brown mug' phenomenon of the 1960s and 1970s, when handmade pottery (often of a quite lumpen nature) was seen as a highly desirable commodity and one could sell almost anything in Britain and the USA with a temmoku glaze! Nowadays there is a less sentimental reaction, but there exists nonetheless a tension between people who see only the drabness of ash deposits and stony glazes and those who perceive the subtlety and warmth of wood firing. (Beauty truly is in the mind of the beholder!)

Leach was one of the first commentators to notice, and to extol, the special qualities associated with high-temperature wood firing. I believe that this lead to him elevating the products of stoneware reduction firing to the top of the canon of ceramics; in any case there seems to have been little interest in the more extreme firing practices in Japan or the low-temperature firings of the indigenous communities of the Americas, Africa, the Near East and the Mediterranean. Partly this may be because these oriental effects were so different to those achieved at the lower temperatures associated with earthenware and by the hated ceramics industry.

The introduction of these oriental ways of thinking led to a truly radical revolutionizing of Western studio ceramics in a similar manner to the upheaval seen in painting and sculpture with Gaugin and Picasso after their exposure to the rawness and nuances of oriental and African artefacts. However, the fine artists modified their subject matter and the formal ways in which it might be portrayed, and didn't change the media with which they painted, the nature of their brushes or the ways in which they held their chisels, and so on – whereas the potters used new methodologies of fire to attain a new means of expression.

With the exception of the German salt-glaze tradition, stoneware (particularly reduction-fired stoneware) remained virtually unexplored in the West. Yet by the mid 1950s the alien and very foreign qualities of high-temperature wood-fuelled reduction firing had become part of the mainstream of contemporary ceramics; indeed, any deviation away from this orthodoxy was regarded as a betrayal by the self-appointed guardians of the 'Leach Tradition'! Yet the eventual subversion of the quasi-religion embodied in *A Potter's Book* lay within its own pages. Not merely did Leach have enormous respect for the British vernacular tradition of slip-ware, for its energy, joy and humour to act as a counterbalance to the high seriousness of Sung dynasty ceramics, but he commenced the book with his own account of an introduction to Raku.

This account of a fundamentally different ceramic tradition was read and transformed by the young American Paul Soldner; this is another of the strange mythologies of contemporary firing that I have retold in *Raku – Investigations into Fire* (Jones, 1999). Raku encompasses a complex set of philosophies involving accident, an aesthetic of imperfection and 'the ugly'.

A Recent History of Firing

Soldner, in America, read the account that Leach gave of the highly ritualized process involving the removal of the red-hot pot from the kiln and fast-cooling it in water. Soldner tried this and rapidly became bored with a firing technique that had served the Japanese well for over three hundred years (and Leach himself for decades). Soldner interspersed secondary reduction in leaves or sawdust, by rolling or burying the piece in combustibles on its removal from the kiln; this is now a practice that occurs at least once a year in every potter's group and ceramics department. (Raku is a family name and yet has been adopted for this special range of ceramic practice.)

In the 1960s and 1970s Raku stood as a freewheelin', improvisatory jazz-like counterpoint to the austere and restrained palette of reduction-fired stoneware. Raku was an escape from the restrictions of Bauhaus control and the refinement of stoneware and porcelain, and opened up the arena for extreme firing experiences.

In mainland Europe a different aesthetic prevailed, one that was informed by the teachings of the Bauhaus school, being less anachronistic and more forward-looking than the movement in Britain. To a limited extent the factories welcomed artists and designers, providing them with studios on the premises, which enabled the continental potters to retain a more involved link with industry. Despite the continuity of many small-scale ceramic workshops on the continent, there was not the same radical outward-looking phenomenon like that started by Leach, and developed by his acolytes, throughout the first part of the last century that turned to the Far East for inspiration. On the continent of Europe a very sophisticated aesthetic has evolved, taking the best of industrial firing and employing it to create art.

After the Second World War the Bauhaus émigrés fleeing the Nazi persecution of the Jews and of progressive education settled in Britain and the USA. Their influence helped to forge a quite new direction for the teaching of ceramics in art schools; it generated an aesthetic of design and clarity that was quite at variance with the philosophy of arcane magic based on fire that was the inheritance of the Leach legacy.

More recent developments have seen ceramics emancipate itself from being solely a means of making functional objects, and emerge also as a medium for expression and for making artistic statements. From this position we can see potters and artists looking specifically at the qualities that firing gives as an expressive destination, whether the object is for utility, a decorative piece or meant as an expression of ideas. It interesting to ponder the way in which contemporary clay artists have also made that observation that there are qualities that were part of a process – occurring accidentally as surface patterning – which are now searched out as an intended consequence of researches into early firing practices. It is these aspects of imitation and re-use of prior results which has come to dominate much of contemporary firing philosophy.

Self-evidently, objects produced in a factory look like objects made under the constraints of mass-production; they have a uniformity that comes from repetition and standardization of processes. The use of moulds instead of the human hand and the employment of specialist kiln firemen and massive-volume kilns helped to produce a much more predictable range of surfaces. Yet it is a vocabulary that has proven to be very easily translated by minimalist artists, who are searching for modules in order to make their artistic statement. This new, very restrained work has progressed alongside the more extreme burnt surfaces of, say, *anagama* firers. And one can now see examples of the development of bodies of work that utilize multiple pieces drawn from expressive fire in contemporary work (the work, for instance, of Sebastian Blackie on page 174).

New Developments

In the last half of the twentieth century urban studio-based potters, many educated in the art schools, were experimenting with electric firings, often inspired by the precision and control derived from the ceramics industry so hated by Leach. They also exploited the bright palette of commercially

Peter Beard. Ceramic sculpture, electric fired.

available industrial colours and they tried new chemicals to achieve effects in their town-based studios. For instance, the use of an excess of barium (an oxide closely related to calcium) in a glaze, allowed for a much brighter range of colour than the brown stoniness normally associated with stoneware, and its matting qualities gave a roughness quite different from the shiny brightness of earthenware.

Thus the 'Craft Pottery Movement' in Britain and then later in America was not merely a response to the uniform blandness of the objects made, but also to the alienating conditions of labour endured in the 'Dark Satanic Mills'; it both embraced new technological opportunities whilst at the same time looking back to historic (and technically superseded) practices. The search for perfection, evidenced in the wares of the Industrial Revolution, saw clay homogenized to make it possible to slip-cast and then fired, protected from the fumes and flames of the burning wood or coal, in ceramic boxes called saggars. This guarding against

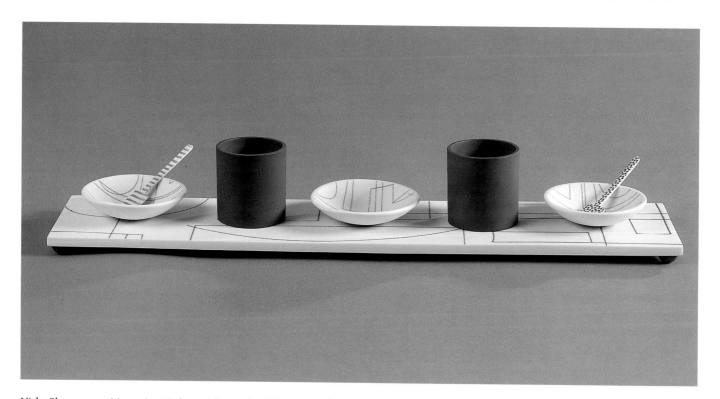

Vicky Shaw composition using Wedgwood Jasper clay body, electric fired.

Gwen Heeney constructing 'Fossil Pit'.

flame lead to a purer and less inflected surface with minimal variation (when compared with earlier modes of firing). The downside of this development led to a deracinated quality of ceramic, with no individual variation in glaze and body colour. When coal was later superseded by electricity and gas it was possible to make a quite even, characterless surface that satisfied the middle-class desire for a white ceramic that emulated the porcelains owned by the aristocratic classes.

As the century progressed a number of themes emerged as narratives in firing. Certainly not all potters now see the qualities of industrial, neutral firing as being antipathetic to their work, and they embrace the cool, uninflected surfaces as a pure fixing of their ideas. Such potters work in their own studios, or actually in the factories themselves, and employ a whole host of techniques to realize their own expression, thereby using the factory's firing cycles to their own benefit. The factory involving the employment of the creative designer has, of course, actually been very attractive to many who do not wish to get intimately involved with the dirt and sweat of a five-day wood firing. Electricity is so convenient to use as a fuel to power a kiln in a town (where most of us live) and many clay artists have embraced the philosophy of design: drawing, planning and executing ideas of form and decoration that are not unduly disturbed by firing. (Fifty hours of painstaking painting on clay is unlikely to be improved by accidental flashing or ash deposits.) In this way the work, including the firing, is closer to painting as the colours are prepared in advance and come out of the firing in a quite predictable way.

Two of my colleagues at the University of Wolverhampton work creatively in very close relationships with factories, yet in quite different areas. Vicky Shaw uses industrial bodies and electric firings, working closely with Wedgwood and Rosenthal to execute precise relationships of vessel and stand. Gwen Heeney works at the other extreme of scale and has created vast sculptures more than 100ft long made up of clay blocks and unfired bricks that she carves before returning them to the factory to fire. As the pioneers of the last century demonstrated, it is far from necessary to be restricted by electricity-powered firing.

7

Eating, Drinking, Cooking, Firing

We can speculate that it was a major advance toward human beings becoming the dominant species on Earth that the receptacle fashioned from river mud and used to carry fire by an itinerant band of hunters, and fired by accident, was seen to be also a useful storage container, which could then be used to cook food on that fire. It was a major step because the range of foodstuffs from which they could obtain nutrients was vastly increased; heating denatures many toxins and storage allows the consumption of out-of-season food, thereby extending the possible range of their travels.

A Cross-Cultural Experience

There is a strong kinship between food, its cooking and preparation, and ceramics. This is also reflected in language. In many cultures there is an overlap between the words for kiln and cooking place. The etymology of the English word kiln comes through the Latin and Italian word *cucina*, which also gives us 'kitchen' and 'cooking'. The word for oven is identical to the word for kiln in many languages (for example, *four* in French, *horno* in Spanish, *forno* in Italian, *Ofen* in German, etc.). We can trace the route back through language itself; one can hear the words 'fire' and 'furnace', 'oven' and 'cooking' within this etymological maze and find traces back to the common heritage of firing and cookery.

Nowhere has this synergy been noticed more clearly than in *The Raw and the Cooked* by Claude Levi-Strauss (Levi-Strauss, 1969). The cooking of food is a cultural acquisition

and represents a different stage in social evolution, and depends on many more complex relationships than a mere hunter-gatherer existence.

The line between 'town' and 'country' ceramics is nowhere more clearly drawn than in the division between the emotional 'warmth' of country, wood-fired ceramics and the 'cool' white ware of the industrial bone china producers. The 'toasted' colours of a 'natural' kiln complement the hues of cooked and raw foods; white and the colours of the electric firing offer contrast. With the white ware there is almost a demand for artifice; it acts a *tabula rasa* (a blank slate), a canvas or plinth for the execution of another idea. We potters might say that the firing hasn't given much to the outcome in the surface of the pot (all the images of nouvelle cuisine, tastefully arranged on black or white vessels spring to mind).

The pictures in the cookery books of the 1980s show a revolution in taste, reacting against the 'little brown mug syndrome' of the 1970s in Europe and the English-speaking world. (This seems in retrospect to have been an unreflective acceptance, by the buying public, of anything to do with the 'idea' of handmade pottery, ideally with a 'natural' coloured glaze, irrespective of its aesthetic qualities.) These receptacles were ideal to serve a wholesome stew, but proved inadequate when trying to deliver an idea of wealth and an aspirational lifestyle. The 1980s revolution in cooking, and the resultant plethora of cookery articles and programmes, required images of food on vessels geared to magazines and television. These features dealt with more and more elaborate designs, created with a minimum of (progressively more expensive) ingredients, on harsh white porcelain, which supplanted the 'wholesome' fare dished up on the temmoku-glazed platters of a previous decade.

Maybe it is just that this period is in too great a proximity to our own times, but I feel that there is a healthier balance now, where there are decent full portions as well as a real interest in presentation and more interesting food combinations (compared with the segregated foodiness of hempen vegetarianism and the clinical presentation of one beautifully placed lettuce leaf on a plate). With this view in mind it is worth considering the various contributions that the firing of ceramics can make to food, cooking and presentation.

Working in Harmony with Food and Drink

One of the forces propelling contemporary thinking about firing is how food and drink works in both visual and haptic (relating to the experience of touch on both hands and lips) ways with ceramics. For example, how the colours, textures and form of the fired clay object complements and enhances the taste and smell experience. There are a number of salutary experiments to perform to start to understand the complexity of the relationship.

To take the cup of tea as an example, we need to consider the differences between drinking it from a handled cup or handled mug; or in an oriental tea bowl with the finger tips on the rounded surface of the bowl or the hands clutched closely around a Japanese tea bowl. The distancing effect of the handle and the use of hard-fired ceramics with a bright shiny glaze set a paradigm for tea consumption and etiquette amongst the European upper classes from the eighteenth

RIGHT: *Mrs Takahashi demonstrating a Tea Ceremony.*

BELOW: *Dale Huffmann, tea bowls,* anagama wood firing.

century onwards. If one contrasts this extreme with another that was developing concurrently in Japan, where the formality of the *Cha-no-Yu* (Tea Ceremony) was being employed to create another sort of social cohesion, then one can only marvel at the way that two such elaborate manifestations should have been propelled by an interest in a beverage produced from the leaf of one species and its utensils (Jones, 1999).

Variations in Firing and in the Experience of Drinking

In the context of the nineteenth-century Western aesthetic of classical beauty, Raku bowls (made and fired for the Japanese cognoscenti) appear crude in the extreme by comparison with their European counterparts, created by the great factories in Meissen, Sevres and Stoke, which used Chinese bowls as their inspiration. Yet the aesthetic that lies behind Raku production is in many ways more complex than that which guided Western production. To drink from these two utterly dissimilar types of vessels is to experience the qualities of firing in a new way. The Japanese pots are made from rough clay and fired, and coated with a thick mid-temperature or earthenware glaze surface.

The way that high-fired ceramics rapidly communicates heat through its thin walls offers a significant contrast to the better insulating thick pots of Japan. Thin porcelain or bone china meets the lip as a hard, alien substance, yet the fineness of the porcelain sets off the colour of the tea and its contrasting hardness is a delight on the lips. The white cups, used in the drawing rooms of Georgian England, determined a way of holding the handle in a tense pinch between finger and thumb; the cup, supported on a saucer, is held away from the body. By contrast the Japanese tea bowl, low-fired from earthenware clay, feels 'soft'; without a handle it

Joanna Howells, 'Pyramid Selling', celadon-glazed reduction-fired cup sculpture.

ABOVE: *Charles Bound, tea bowl,* anagama *firing.*

LEFT: *Kushi Grazzini, salt-glazed tea bowls.*

must be cradled in the hands. It is not hard to see why the form of the tea bowl or *unomi* has become a touchstone for contemporary ceramicists as it requires the user to adopt a similar relationship to that adopted by the potter in its making, an event only intervened by the firing.

The firing represents a disjuncture in the handing of vessel from potter to user – a hot transition of change. The drinker puts his hands in the same place and attitude as the potter, and enters the intimate dialogue between maker and user. Thus whatever qualities are created by the firing act as a mediating skin between the form that the potter made and the drinker. A thick, glassy coat feels smoother and distances the user from the 'base clay'. A thin spraying of glaze, the touch of fly-ash or the delicate alighting of salt glaze on the shoulder of an otherwise bare pot gives a quite other sensation, of closeness and intimacy.

I think that the fly ash qualities of *anagama*-type firing and salt- and soda-glazing are particularly interesting disciplines as they allow the uneven development of glaze build-up where the ash, salt or soda falls. Thus the pot has thick areas of glaze (where it faces the flame or the salting ports) and thin, sometimes nearly bare areas (away from that particular direction). When holding the pot we can reconstruct the pack of the kiln and that orientation of the ware within it. We can choose to place an area heavy with glaze against our lips or drink from the 'dry' side of the cup. We can learn from the Japanese Tea Ceremony a consciousness about the visual and haptic orientation of the drinking vessel to our mouths, directing us to where the drinker is to choose to sip from a pot with an undulating and uneven rim.

Qualities of Non-Functional Ceramics

It is through use that we are forced into the most intimate contact with ceramics. When clay artists make non-functional work – that which has a decorative or a sculptural role in a space – it is often those very qualities of fired surface that they are trying to emulate or evoke, and to encourage the audience to interact with the pieces in a way analogous to that of the new owner of a drinking vessel. Indeed, surfaces for non-functional ceramics are often developed that are even more seductive in their contrasting of glazes, slips and bare clay than can be entertained in a functional vessel. (Their price, of course, often reflects the much greater amount of time devoted to making a single piece, and often brings with it the expectation that the purchaser will pay much more attention to it than to a humble pot.)

Sometimes those qualities are purely visual; sometimes the expectation is that the audience will interact with the work and discover the nuances of tactile surface as well as appearance. There are also auditory qualities – high-fired ceramic will ring like a metal bell. Thick, low-fired pots have a dull, non-resonant sound; and Raku-fired pots often bring a deep smell of smoke to the gallery as the water in the pores of the clay is evaporated by the powerful spot-lamps. Ironically it can be those very pieces that are dealt with in a highly receptive way, in our culture, that come closer to the attentiveness of the Japanese tea master using a tea bowl rather than the everyday mug that gets used in an unreflective manner – yet we feel that the mug can also 'speak' to us unconsciously, its day-to-day use bringing an enjoyment even when we are in an unobservant state.

One of the ironies of the 1970s handmade pottery aesthetic was that the public would buy plates and bowls with quite rough, matt glazes while ignoring those with a good, functional, shiny glaze, in their romantic rejection of industrial associations. The sound of cutlery on a dolomite matt glaze is one of the abiding horrors of that time, a dysfunctional feature whose matt glaze was deliberately developed in order to attract the purchaser. It is also possible for a fired surface to be developed to repel the audience, an experience that touches on Freud's concept of the *unheimlich* (interestingly one of the most alluring surfaces visually is also the most unpleasant to touch – namely dry barium glazes).

8

Glaze and Firing

The metaphoric load carried by ceramics used to be clear. They were decoded according to their function, and understood through their utility. Pots were fired according to the knowledge, experience and understanding of their tradition by the makers in the area. The choices of styles of firing were limited and the surfaces a combination of accident and design, brought about through necessity. Thus funerary urns would be like cooking pots or storage vessels, but we imagine that they would have been imbued with a greater weight of cultural expectation as a result of their destination in the earth. Indeed the idea that our ancestors were returning fired earth to the ground, itself, must have carried a symbolic weight. The finesse and attention accorded to each piece would surely have been gauged according to whether the pot was to be for immediate and disposable use – the equivalent of our disposable polystyrene containers – or for internment and intended to survive for millennia in an afterlife. Nowadays the cost of a cup, reflecting the investment of time in the creation of a useful artefact by a (artist-) maker, can also make us examine that metaphoric load.

Clive Bowen

The line between the purely functional and the purely aesthetic is a fluid continuum. Glazes that have been developed as a utilitarian surface can be reassigned to non-functional objects, and vice versa. Indeed, in much contemporary ceramics one can see the exploitation of many familiar fired

surfaces in a new guise. Many of these modes of firing were superseded by advances in glaze technology, but contemporary artists and potters have recognized the intrinsic merit of those surfaces and have employed them both for their own sakes and also for the references that they bring with them to archaic modes of production and the opportunity to create specific resonances with the past.

ABOVE: *Clive Bowen, large covered pot, wood-fired earthenware.*

RIGHT: *Clive Bowen, kiln.*

OPPOSITE PAGE: *Petra Reynolds and Jeremy Steward firing.*
(Photo: Rod Dorling)

Shannon Garson, two bowls, electric-fired.

Thus one can consider the work of Clive Bowen and his use of wood-fired lead-glazed earthenware. Whenever lead-glazed earthenware is mentioned there seems little doubt that its romantic associations are very significant. It is described as 'honey' and 'warm'. The work exudes homeliness; we associate lead-glazed slipware with our idea of the style of the seventeenth- and eighteenth-century farmhouse (while it is often sold to the most sophisticated of urban audiences, many of whom are many generations separated from their rural pasts).

When people purchase Bowen's products, actually they are purchasing the work of a very sophisticated maker, trained as a painter, who has taken the vocabulary of shape and pattern and created a completely new set of improvisations within it – much like the consummate jazz musician Charlie Parker, whom he reveres. The sense of abandon and the casual letting-free of a flurry of notes is palpable when standing amongst his pots. He works at a prodigious rate – it gives a fluency and spontaneity to the work that is reminiscent of the musician. Hit a bum note in a concert and you just pass on; I feel that in Bowen's work there is an ease that says, 'if it is not so good this time then I can make another next time' – his is not an art of overworking.

When one selects out of hundreds of pots Bowen says that it 'becomes accidentally good'. When so many people ask potters how they can bear to part with their work it seems ironic that we just accept that Charlie Parker and John Coltrane left their art to float on the wind, the concert only living on in the minds and bodies of the audience. The instruments that Bowen brings to his performance are his throwing, decoration skills and the soft-wood flame on lead-glazed firing provided by the beehive kiln. In our interview, Clive remarked that he really likes the smell and sound of wood firing; it is like music. He self-deprecatingly added that it is easier to make a good pot if you wood fire – in an electric kiln there is nothing given.

He works out of, rather than within, the British slipware tradition – a medieval directness informing an abstract expressionist sensibility. The sophisticate living the rural idyll. Bernard Leach in his own work had combined traditional Japanese pottery with English slipware – two strands of ceramic history in a fusion that long preceded postmodernism. Bowen unpicked the strands and discarded the faux Japanese, rejecting painting using a calligraphy brush, and has stayed with his own informed, very direct English style. These include marks in wet slip and fluid glaze that are enhanced by the fire, and become an ideal complement to the presentation of food.

Fritz Rossmann, two celadon-glazed bowls, reduction-fired.

Shannon Garson

Shannon makes delicate porcelain decorated with fragile drawings of flowers. It is carefully fired in an electric kiln using a shiny glaze that allows the painting centre stage and saves it from running. She describes a world of intimacy and solicitude that can be reclaimed by beautiful ceramics. She repositions functional ceramics, away from the horrors of the twenty-first century and the exploitative art world and turns the focus toward the home and the changes that accompany a pot when it is purchased, brought into the domestic arena and used:

> Domestic pots have gone hand in hand with human civilization.... The privilege of using handmade pots is that they contain the idea of human endeavour, a link with other people not with factories or corporations.... Potting enriches the life of the maker and ... pots enrich the life of the user.... 'Nana's milk jug' or favourite teacup becomes a part of the love and rituals of communication in these relationships. Bridges can be mended (or broken!) over a cup of tea, asking someone over for a meal or up for a cup of coffee is an entrenched part of the courting ritual. Later down the track there is nothing

like the satisfying crash of a piece of china smashing against a wall to illustrate your point. What other form of art is so intimately involved in the minutiae of life? ... Where handmade pots are invited to tea the artist, or rather the idea of the artist, is also invited ... handmade pots now travel far and wide disseminating their strange mixture of signs and symbols miles from where the clay was first mined.

Celadon Glaze

One of the most pleasing traditional solutions to the problem of an aesthetic and utilitarian surface for the serving of food is the use of the traditional Chinese glaze known as **celadon**. It was probably first used in Korea and has recently reached new heights of refinement in Japan. Two European exponents of this surface who have stretched the boundaries of the firing of this glaze are Fritz Rossmann and Joanna Howells. They are both internationally acknowledged makers of tableware, who have used their skills to question more deeply the nature of the fired object.

Celadon is a glaze that flows, runs and pools; it is so viscous that it can collect in heavy droplets under a ridge or on an edge. Without running completely off the pot, it can hang like a teardrop of glass, frozen, or like old, molten, melting snow. It can be applied so thickly that it hangs suspended, slipping off the pot within the kiln; it is caught by cooling the kiln just before the glaze runs fluid (which would stick pot and kiln structure together).

Celadon glaze demands its own language of clay form and detail, and the German potter Fritz Rossmann has developed a vocabulary of soft clay marks that can be accentuated by this tight-fitting glaze. There are lines, spirals, holes, depressions and cuts (both hard-edged and soft). The grammar is completed and complemented in the kiln by the melting of this rocky powder of glaze as it breaks over these lines, white where a sharp edge of porcelain cuts through and light blue or green across modelled edges.

Fritz Rossmann

Sometimes it is only necessary to gaze out of the studio window to understand the motivation of a potter. I have known Rossmann for many years; we have spoken about inspirations and histories and traditions – but it is the dominating view from the studio window that informs my understanding of the work. One can observe green, yellow-green, blue-green, grey-green, even red-green; then all the shades of muted blue away to the ends of the view. Sitting there I felt

like an amnesiac Inuit who had just lost their fabled hundred words for snow,* unable as I was to find words to describe the nuances of light and shade in the treescapes outside. Spring and early summer had brought this dominant visual stimulus to the Westerwald in Germany; it assailed the eyes, with an expanse of green, without remission. And, just as nature plays a multitude of games with the colour of leaves and trees, so Rossmann gently modulates and modifies the same vocabulary of light wavelength, through subtle manipulation of glaze formulae.

It is interesting to talk to Fritz about the historical heritage of his technique. Far from venerating the Chinese pots in European collections, he felt that many 'were the colour of a tank'. They were not clean colours; rather they were a dirty brownish, camouflage green. A visit to the Imperial collection that was the possession of the Chinese emperors before the Revolution (now housed in Taipei) proved a revelation as, instead of the predominance of greens, he saw the much cooler spectrum of Song dynasty palace wares for the first time, with their bluer and 'cleaner' coloration.

He has developed three main celadon glazes and one clear. By manipulating and overlaying these various glazes a very rich palette is developed. The range of variables that allow a successful firing have to be carefully constrained, so he always likes to unpack the kiln before packing the next

Fritz Rossmann, celadon-glazed vessel, reduction-fired.

Heavy-Crackle Celadon Glaze	
Nepheline syenite	66
Whiting	10
Dolomite	10
China clay	10
Zinc oxide	2
Barium carbonate	2
Red Clay 10 or iron oxide	0.5

For other effects substitute the nepheline syenite with potash, or soda feldspars.

Black Engobe	
White stoneware clay	40
China clay	40
Feldspar	20
Frit	10
Black stain	6

Firing: from 1060°C to 1280°C, heavy reduction in a gas kiln. Soak for 10 minutes at 1280°C in a clean, oxidizing flame.

*This claim first appears in the work of the anthropologist Franz Boaz who, in *The Handbook of North American Indians* (1911), remarks that the Eskimo language has many words for snow. (This was later exaggerated to nearly 100, much disputed, but I like the idea.) On the same line there is another 'myth', which is even closer to my theme, that some African languages associated with the jungle have a large number of words for the colour green.

load in order to confirm the thickness of application and the position on the kiln.

On a visit to his studio Rossman reflects on the green of the forest that surrounds him, telling me that 'Early spring is the best time when the leaves are new – soft and light in colour.' The rain outside that leaves rivulets of droplets on the vast old factory windows are reminiscent of the frozen poolings of glaze that gather above the feet of the bowls. Gaze becomes glaze. The myth of the naming of 'celadon glaze' after the hero of the same name in the romance *L'Astree* (1610) by the French writer Honore d'Urfe is one of those strange tales that fill ceramic books. Celadon was the lover of the heroine Astree, he is a sentimentalized version of the green man (idealized in the way of the nymphs and shepherds, beloved of Marie Antoinette over a century later). He was presented as a young man in green, and his dress became all the rage in Europe. It was just about this time that Chinese wares made their debut in Paris and won acclaim. People compared its colour to Celadon's suit and started to call the porcelain 'celadon', a name which has stuck and spread to other countries. (But of course for Fritz the return to an association with the trees is most appropriate – and an Eric Rohmer movie called *Les amours d' Astree et Celadon* has recently been released, so the name of a green glaze has been gracing billboards outside art cinemas across Europe.)

I have rarely felt nature to be intrusive, but here, perched on the edge, one's ears are filled with the sounds of rain and birds and wind – but it is all soft. And all that rain and sun forces more greenness from the ground. From the pots Rossmann has extended the dialogue with celadons, subtly varying the proportions of iron (and its sources) and changing from one feldspar to another. This can extend the language metaphor into even greater complexity as the eventual range of dialects multiplies. On closer examination it can be simplified and explained through the wide range adjustments of other variables: of firing temperature; position in the kiln; length of firing cycle; starting point of reduction; and how heavily the kiln is reduced. This complex of variables is compounded by the thickness, mode of application, double dipping and subsidiary use of **engobes**. All to make green.

Fritz Rossmann, celadon-glazed beakers, reduction-fired.

Joanna Howells

Joanna Howells is a potter whose work has always deliberately dealt with function and, more recently, with referential ideas about use and consumption. Rather than mark the work with a hard tool Joanna Howells has developed a vocabulary of mark that is dependent on softness. To say that hers is a feminized counterpoint to Fritz's sharper forms would be no exaggeration. She uses wet slip on the new thrown forms and combs and coaxes it to create gentle

swirls and spirals. Another trope involves a gently impressed texture over which the glaze slides when it is molten.

Her work involves a dialogue between the history of the useful and the domestic (that which has traditionally been regarded as women's work) and that world as seen from a contemporary post-feminist perspective. She has made the whole gamut of fired ceramics from mugs to serving dishes, from teapots to bowls; these are treated in a quite un-ironic fashion as manufactured handmade pots of the finest quality. But a recent direction has involved taking a new set of present-day icons and subjecting them to the same gentle scrutiny.

It is a research born of asking the question: what happens if we take an ugly, or un-aesthetic, form and treat it in the same reverential way that we would a classically proportioned vessel? Tetra-Paks and takeaway containers certainly don't enter our consciousness as beautiful items. They are referenced by imitation: the thrown object is altered and 'becomes' a Tetra-Pak. When it is coated with a celadon glaze, something happens. It is not transformed into a thing of beauty, but we are forced to see it in a new light – it causes us to read it both as the familiar container to be disposed of in a landfill site and also as the carrier of a meaning that comes to us from one thousand years of ceramic history.

Bound up with this regard for the dislocation of historical context is her reading of the act of firing as a mystical mode of purification. We are also reminded of Andy Warhol's Campbell's Soup Cans and the common and unironic use of celadon – a thousand-year-old glaze. The firing has often been seen as a metaphoric site for the testing not merely of the ceramic but also of the potter. There is something of the self that is subjected to the incinerating conditions of the kiln. She locates that testing in a feminized context by alluding to the idea of the female and transformation exerted through firing of her work, using the history of cooking and music as metaphor to enable her to talk about the meaning of fire:

In ages earlier than our own, which were more keenly aware of symbolic correspondences, their feeling for this origin of clay in the earth, symbol for the most concrete objective reality, which was passed through fire, symbol for celestial transmutation, certainly contributed a great deal to people's feeling for ceramic art.

(Rawson, 1984, p.23)

Joanna Howells says:

To what extent have these symbolic correspondences changed or shifted from earliest times to our own? Or perhaps more accurately, how have these correspondences been augmented over time so that new symbolic layers accrue while others recede without entirely disappearing?

Ceramics is an intriguing mixture of art and technique, the pragmatic and the poetic. A maker can become prosaically absorbed in details during a firing – has the kiln reached temperature, are there any cold spots, is the atmosphere even? and so on. However, there often comes a point when the power being harnessed takes over and the alchemy of the event takes the upper hand. The kiln becomes a roaring beast that has to be coaxed, tended, placated. A transformation is taking place, which transcends the purely technical and scientific analysis of heat acting on material and flux.

Fire is indispensable to humanity. It provides us with warmth and creative but also destructive power. Our sustenance depends on cooking. Claude Levi-Strauss in *The Raw and The Cooked*, his study of the myths of South American Indians, shows how for them a meal – 'real' food (p.336) – had to consist of cooked food, and his analysis shows that in these myths it is clear that raw = natural, cooked = culture.

The role of fire is that it transforms on a scale from 'nature' and 'rawness', which are destined to decay, to socializing and purifying, which protect from decay. Cooking moves objects higher up the scale of the raw/cooked axis and is characteristic of culture as opposed to the 'low', the 'raw' and the earth.

In addition there is a remarkable prevalence of customs of symbolically 'cooking' persons, which ranges from remote tribes to regions of France. Levi-Strauss (p.336) suggests:

the individuals who are 'cooked' are those deeply involved in a physiological process: the newborn child, or the pubescent girl. The conjunction of a member of the social group with nature must be achieved through the intervention of rituals involving cooking or fire. Cooking is normally an intermediate stage between a raw product of nature and the human consumer. Thus the rituals involving fire have the effect of making sure that a person is at one and the same time *cooked and socialized*.

Many makers of 'domestic' pottery either love cooking or eating – usually both. Takeshi Yasuda writes about the importance for him of food and the relationship it has to his work. What seems like a charming error when visitors to my studio ask me, 'How are the pots cooked?' or 'Where is your oven?' shows that 'firing' is really only potters' jargon for cooking. This reveals that the underlying relationship between ceramics and food, beyond the practical level of container and contained, is the change and transformation wrought by fire on materials. It is thought that the earliest potters were the women, and they are still generally the preparers of food, and it does seem as if much of pottery is very like cooking. Potters blend materials to make glazes, we get our hands dirty and wet, we knead clay like bread. The element that fuses the raw mixture together, that does the real act of transformation is the fire, and the kiln the crucible.

The ordeal by fire that my medium of porcelain undergoes is the most extreme of all types of pottery since the fabric of the clay itself (as well as the glaze) melts, so any weakness in the form is exposed and will cause it to collapse. The fact that ceramic pieces are exposed to the extreme heat of the kiln inevitably endows them with a metaphor of endurance since some of them do not survive.

At the same time, in the image of ordeal by fire, ceramic objects contain symbols of the purification rituals that stretch back to the earliest dawn of humankind. Ordeal by fire appears ubiquitously in myth throughout history (and in practice through much of it), and is not confined to what we might define as 'primitive' society. It was surely no coincidence that witches and heretics throughout history have been executed by burning. The burning of Joan of Arc – The Maid of Orleans – would have added another symbol of purity to the remaining legend of her virginity.

An Enlightenment version of the ordeal is contained in Mozart's *The Magic Flute*. Tamino and Pamina together undergo a series of trials, by fire, water, air and earth, which are purificatory ordeals (Brophy, 1990, p.182). Although eighteenth-century and Masonic thinking relegated women to roles in need of guidance or rescue by men, Mozart

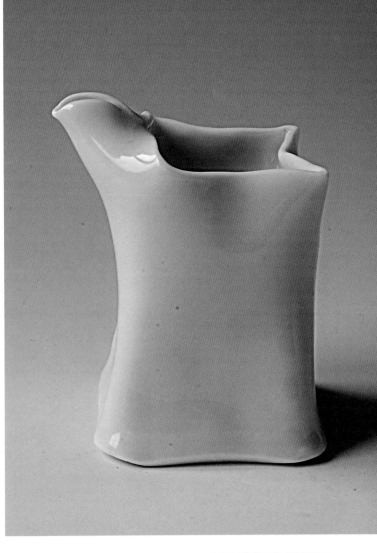

RIGHT: *Joanna Howells, 'Soy Joy', celadon glaze, gas-fired.*

BELOW: *Joanna Howells, 'Joanna Paks', celadon glaze, gas-fired.*

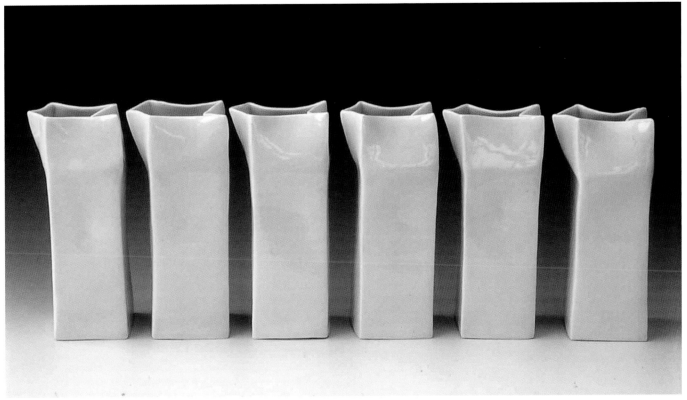

ABOVE: *Joanna Howells, 'Egg Tray', unglazed porcelain, with coloured grog inclusions, gas-fired.*

BELOW: *Joanna Howells, 'Covered Dish', celadon glaze, gas-fired.*

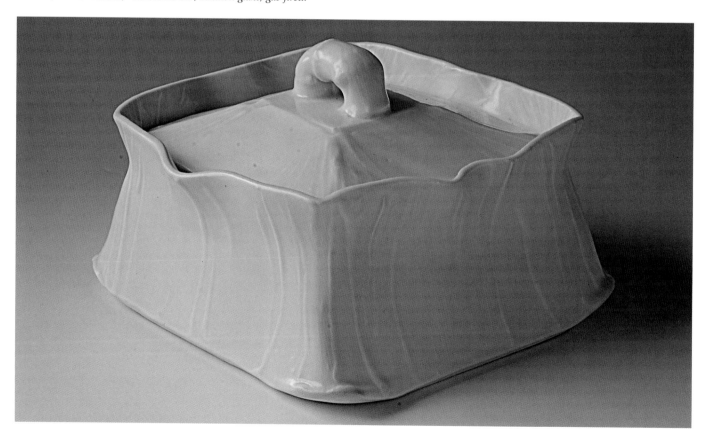

manages to transform Pamina from an inert thing into a feminine initiate herself, by undergoing the trials alongside Tamino. He thus subverts Sarastro's reasoning earlier in the opera, 'that woman needs a man to guide her, since without one every woman strays from her path and misses her function' (Brophy, 1990, p.162) – turning *The Magic Flute* into a promotion of equality for the sexes after all.

By surviving the trial by fire, ceramic pieces reference to an entire history of symbolic associations to purity. Every age has its myths and rituals, although it is hard for us to see our own. Levi-Strauss' contention is that there is no fundamental break between the primitive mind and contemporary attitudes: 'I aim to show not how men think in myths, but how myths operate in men's minds without their being aware of the fact' (Levi-Strauss, 1969, p.12).

In our secular age in the West we like to think that we have done away with many or most of our myths and rituals, and yet each age seems to have its need for symbols, particularly symbols of purity and wholesomeness. An obsession of our own age is a concern with the cleanliness and purity of food. There are regular scare stories in the media about contaminated, adulterated or highly processed foods, while the organic brand is simultaneously elevated to highly desirable status.

The matter is complicated by the necessary distinction between the entire process leading to the existence of organically grown food and the hijacking of the label for branding purposes by the food retailing giants. While the former caters to our physical need for foods free from harmful impurities and a system of growing that is in harmony with the environment, the latter exploits our psychological need to consume our food with a good conscience.

It is interesting to compare our ideas on the purity and wholesomeness of food with those of, say, the Victorians, when the appearance of purity in the forms of triple-refined white sugar or white bread could only be achieved for the masses by industrialized processes. In the 1850s processed or refined foods were considered purer and therefore healthier *because* they were the products of the latest industrial processes and far removed from the 'backward', 'primitive' and 'bacteria-ridden' fields and farmyards from where they originated.

Conversely, we are now more inclined to tolerate the 'clean dirt' of the pesticide-free farmyard than the complex processing of food in the antiseptic environments of food factories. Thus we see how certain symbolic correspondences can alter radically through time.

This is not – or not yet – the case for ceramics, and it is hard to foresee any such similar shift in the way we think and feel about pottery. Ceramics already symbolize the mystery of purification that we inherit from the ancients, and porcelain contains the most extreme form of this in that its ordeal is the most extreme. Taking the analogy of the nature/culture spectrum, porcelain, because of the extreme of fire that it undergoes, acquires a symbol of the highest form of culture/society – for instance in imperial China. It still retains this aura even now. However, there is a second layer of purity that porcelain contains, in that its fired form represents the most complete transformation of the earthy material that is clay, into a translucent material of such whiteness and purity. White has, for many cultures, always been the colour most associated with the spiritual. Celadon glazes, being simple, unsullied and delicate, reinforce the purity of the clay and therefore, perhaps especially now, seem particularly suited to food and drink.

One of the magical/paradoxical things about pottery and, for me, porcelain in particular, is that it embodies a durability and contains the echoes of its tremendous endurance while still being fragile – these images are contradictory, but contribute to the unconscious appeal of these objects.

9

Marked by Fire:
~
Wood Fire
and *Anagama*

The *Anagama*

The simplest of the oriental climbing kilns was the one-chamber kiln or *anagama*, which has its roots in ancient and traditional ceramics in the Far East; it was a structure built like a tunnel on or in the ground. It climbed up the hillside; an approximate 1:6 slope is sufficient to draw the flame and the heat through the ware. It works on the principle of creating enough heat and heat-work to achieve the desired results. It will attain a higher temperature than a simple up-draught kiln; the firebox is coextensive with the chamber – there is no real division – and thus the kiln can be used as one vast firebox containing the ware. In an *anagama* the flame from the wood carries the ash through the chamber, pieces are placed for maximum contact with flame and ash, and wood is often thrown directly onto the ware to gain the maximum effect of heat, pressure and ash deposit. The position of the objects in the pack depends on the degree to which the work is affected by the special conditions of such a kiln.

The primary effect of these firings is that the ware is vitrified by the higher temperatures achieved, and the heat-work done over days of firing. The type of fuel, and position in the kiln, determines qualities of surface. Pots in the 'throat' of the kiln (the chimney exit) receive much less ash deposit than those near the front, and those buried in the firebox itself are subjected to the most extreme experience of burning. To achieve a higher temperature and more intense combustion the tunnel can have a chimney built onto it at the end.

The chimney affects the draw of the kiln, that is, the rate at which the flames are pulled through the kiln. The simple rule is that the higher and hotter the chimney, the more air will be drawn through. The flames penetrate the entire kiln; the air carries not merely heat created by the disintegrating hydrocarbons but it also bears the inorganic (non-carbonaceous) components of wood – namely metal salts that normally appear as ash in the fire pit. The **fly** ash that is carried through the kiln on the **flame path** reacts with the silica in the clay to create a matt or shiny coating – the glaze. The principle is that the more combusted gases are pulled into the kiln, the higher the quantity of calories that can be transmitted to the ware. Also, the longer the time that the flame circulates in a kiln, the more heat is transferred to the ware, which makes the kiln more efficient.

This kind of one-chamber kiln was originally a tunnel excavated through the ground. It is covered to protect it from the rain, particularly at the uphill end where water might flow in, and fired to a sufficient temperature to set the walls of the chamber by turning the clay in the ground to ceramic. The soil through which the kiln is dug needed to have a high clay content and then the walls of the tunnel will fire and become strong and stable for a long time. (It is obviously important that the kiln does not collapse on the packer or the firing pots.) However, if there is too much iron in the soil, or fluxing rocks or insufficient clay, then the kiln can melt with the heat and collapse (or not harden at all).

Nowadays, in our twenty-first century, when fire is regarded as impossibly dangerous, heating and light are provided by hidden forms of combustion (electricity).

Indeed fire is deemed now to be so alien, and even regarded as anti-social in the urban context, that many people living in modern homes in cities in the West never see the hearth fire that traditionally made the 'house' a 'home' (*see* Pyne, 2001). *Anagama* kilns and their firing imbue the work with an aura of the ancient; they give a sense of geological volcanic forces and the primitive, qualities that are rare in the most highly sophisticated technological countries on Earth. There is a great resurgence of interest in such methodologies in Britain, Australia and the USA, which is starting to deal with this sense of absence in our lives.

The *anagama* tradition can enter into the creative process, primarily as a conscious research and development exercise, but there is also a sense in which it can be unconsciously transformed and a new hybrid born.

others are touched with an exquisite delicacy as the flame brushes the surface of the ceramic over the duration of the firing. For urban dwellers in the twenty-first century it represents an opportunity to re-experience some of the hardship, excitement, collaboration and creative risk experienced by peoples living in earlier times. Firing such a kiln is a feat of endurance and the culmination of months of meticulous planning. Working in total concentration for five to ten days in shifts alters one's perception of ceramics, and of life, as the stoking of the kiln becomes an all-consuming occupation and form of meditation.

There is a growing band of individuals who work in this way, in small, informal regular groups of experts and

Contemporary *Anagama* Firing

Within the last twenty to thirty years this method of firing has achieved great popularity within the canon of contemporary ceramics. Some of the products are, as might be expected, rough and burnt, yet

ABOVE: *Kumano tea bowl, white slip and shino glaze.*

LEFT: *Kumano vase, white slip and shino glaze,* anagama-fired.

BELOW: *Kumano tea bowl, white slip and shino glaze,* anagama-fired.

enthusiasts; it is also becoming a feature of many workshops and symposia. The sense of escape from our own world is palpable, and the rewards are not merely the satisfaction of making and firing a product but also the experience of being in intimate contact with a very dangerous force and guiding it to try to achieve the most felicitous results. It is a form of cooperation with an elemental presence, a force of nature, to which individual consciousness is subsumed and a meditative state is achieved (or just total exhaustion).

Wood firers commit the product of many months' labour to their kiln. The outcome is always mixed – not all pieces are completely wonderful – and there are numerous failures in the process. Owen Rye has written:

> Woodfire aesthetics dictate that the best results are obtained in parts of the kiln that promise the greatest risk of damage. So while woodfire may, because of its traditional origins, appear to be at the conservative end of ceramics, it is always at the cutting edge of taking risks in the arts (Rye, 1992, p.40).

In *The Nature and Art of Workmanship* (Pye, 1995) David Pye has written philosophically of the role played by the 'workmanship of risk', as opposed to the 'workmanship of certainty' in which 'the quality of the result is not pre-determined'. My colleague Professor Keith Cummings has reflected on this duality and speaks of the 'identifiable personal signature' recognizable in a work of risk – a three-way relationship between craftsperson, material and tools (Cummings, 'Craft: Risk, Certainty and Opportunity', p.52). Applying this analysis to wood firers we can see that the relationship of the clay to the *anagama*, brought together by the potter, is what makes this triangular relationship so special (Pye, 1995, p.20).

Mostly when a piece of ceramic is purchased the private collector does not overstress themselves with worrying about the level of suffering endured by the artist – the criterion is the amount of pleasure that is derived through ownership of a piece. However, nowadays the narrative framework surrounding the art is growing in significance and art gallery and museum collections have sophisticated explications of the work, including personal biographies and the method by which it was produced, thus the story of its inception is actually a significant part of its meaning.

Potters who use *anagama* firing are amongst the most adventurous, and can also be seen to be the most traditional, of our clan. There are terrific risks involved in the process. Pieces can be made or marred by the experience. So much is given to the work by the fire that the object is rarely invested with much before the firing, thus the kiln is often loaded with fairly blank pots in order for it to wreak its magic on the clay, the potter directing the path of the flame through the pack in order to decorate the pots with marks of fire. There are of course exceptions to any rule, and there are potters, like Martin McWilliam, who devote many

hours both to making and refining a form and then also to risking all in an *anagama*. Like all other processes an *anagama* firing can be used to fire functional items, or purely for expressive ends.

Many *anagama* potters talk in mystical tones of clay and fire – it seems quite apparent that the fashioning of the material is not seen as such a significant activity by most of these practitioners. Time is generally invested in firing and its long preparation rather than in the creation of form. Many throw on the wheel in the loose, soft-clay manner beloved of the Japanese and exemplified by Kumano. Often the clay is unrefined (or the potter can even mix in feldspar lumps to simulate 'natural' clays). In its fashioning (normally on the wheel) it can tear and break. It encapsulates the ultimate sense of process. The firing can be so savage that hard forms often soften and melt. Glazes can be applied so thickly that the clay is quite hidden, only appearing on corners or on an edge, pooling over the bottom of the piece as the alkalis in the ash lower the temperature of the glaze melt still further. Or no glaze might be applied and the only decoration is the deposit on the ware; 'dragon fly' blobs of ash-formed glaze are treasured happenings.

The clay is often a bare canvas that acts as a document that charts the flow of flame and ash through the kiln. The skill of the artist then lies in: the orchestration of the kiln; its packing; the choice of types of clay and the wood varieties burnt; the possible addition of salt; the length of firing (and therefore the build-up of deposits on the ceramic); the temperature reached; and the heat-work achieved (which can melt the ashes to a glaze or leave the surfaces dry and crusty). To some extent these surfaces only refer to themselves and the possibilities offered by the kiln. They create a language that is hermetic – it seems isolated from any other kind of experience and it sometimes seems to be impossible to open up this narrative and interpret what it means.

Many of the items that are hallowed in such circles are made by unrecorded potters, whom Leach and Yanagi referred to as the 'Unknown Craftsman'. (Incidentally, in Bernard Leach's *A Potter's Book* there is no mention of this style of firing that many of us in the ceramics fraternity have come to see as synonymous with Japanese ceramic expression. The great kiln sites of Shigaraki and Tokoname and so on were passed over in favour of a much cleaner kind of firing, where wood was just the incidental fuel, rather than the fuel of choice.) Thus the biographies or thoughts of these potters can play no part in our search for the meaning of these works.

The theorist Roland Barthes creates an analogy between text (to him any human manifestation can be counted as a text) and another craft-based discipline – *text*iles. He states that a 'text is a tissue [or fabric] of quotations … [it derives from] innumerable centres of culture'. That is, rather than drawing on just one individual experience the essential meaning of a work depends on the reflections of the reader(s), rather than the intentions of the writer: 'a text's unity lies not in its origins ... [or its creator] ... but in its destination' (that is, its audience) (Barthes, 1989, p.37). For Barthes, every work (of literature) is 'eternally written here and now' with each rereading or, in our case, with each handling of the pot, because the 'origin' of meaning lies in 'language itself' and its impressions on the reader or handler. Many of our colleagues in the ceramic world are more than happy just to let the pot speak for itself – leaving much space for the critics and theorists to occupy the high ground and to establish canons of taste and hierarchies of makers.

Barthes' writing parallels the concept of the 'intentional fallacy', developed by Wimsatt and Beardsley, which sought to expose the problem that we the audience also want a major role in the interpretation of a text or pot – such that it can mean something quite different to the intention of the maker because we can read that interpretation into the piece. To counter this, a part of my purpose in writing this book has been to allow makers a voice and to hear their own private understanding of their work, which very often addresses an understanding based on process.

Janet Mansfield

Janet Mansfield is the author of many books in the field of firing and ceramics and editor of *Ceramics Art and Perception*. As such she is ideally placed to provide an overview to the resurgent fascination with extreme high fire as she discusses her own work:

> Ceramics as a discipline can take an artist in many different directions – just look at the thousands of years of history of ceramics and its expression across cultures to find pleasure in its possibilities. The aesthetic appreciation of ceramics is as individual as the people who make it.
>
> The ceramics that I make are wood-fired and salt-glazed. Days are spent in stacking and firing to obtain maximum controlled effects. Form is carefully considered, because that is where the individual artist makes a personal statement. Form has to be considered as part of the total intention as it dictates the type of stacking and firing, not the other way round.
>
> These firings have been taken to the extreme temperature of 1360°C over a period of some days, a high risk and dangerous experience where pieces move, ash flows and the clay melts into softness; this causes scars where the movement and the ash adheres pots to other pots nearby or to the supports on which they stand. To subject these earthen materials to such high temperatures places the works on the edge of their tolerance and therefore to their acceptance by either the maker or the collecting public. But the risk and this level of interaction of clay and fire excites me. My work is not the safe

ABOVE: *Janet Mansfield, 'Vase', wood-fired* anagama.

BELOW: *Janet Mansfield, 'Covered Jar', wood-fired* anagama.

Janet Mansfield, 'Vase', wood-fired anagama.

option but there are others who understand these boundaries of the potter's art. I enjoy making works that can be used, works that show individuality and the processes in their creation. And I hope others will find the same level of enjoyment using these pieces each day.

Charles Bound

Charles Bound has examined his own development as a potter and within that personal biography answers to his intense involvement with inclusions in clays and in firings of duration.

Wood firing began for me in a gas kiln. I began scattering ash directly onto pots, laying twigs on plates as lines of decoration, and combining both these methods over glazes. Because there was varied thickness in the scattered ash and the twigs sat proud of the surface they were on until burned, there entered an element beyond total control, what I understood to be the object of most glaze work.

A friend then invited me to fire his small fast-fire kiln. Out of it my work came, some distorted, most looking like high-fired bisque. It wasn't encouraging. Pre-applied ash seemed a better bet. I left most of the pots in his basement and carried on with the gas kiln. Then I helped another friend build an overly ambitious three-chambered kiln – more high-fired bisque, except the bag wall bricks which, when replaced with pots, began to show what could be interesting in a wood kiln: putting pots in a river of flame just as I had done with stones in a stream when growing up. The pots began to have gradations of surface, depth and colour where the flame slipped off them on its way along the kiln. Things from the wood began to stick to the pots in varying degrees of melt, giving rough, smooth, matt, shiny surfaces, often in quite small areas. The differential heat from upstream to downstream altered the shapes of some pots, moved others to stick

Charles Bound, anagama-fired *bowl.*

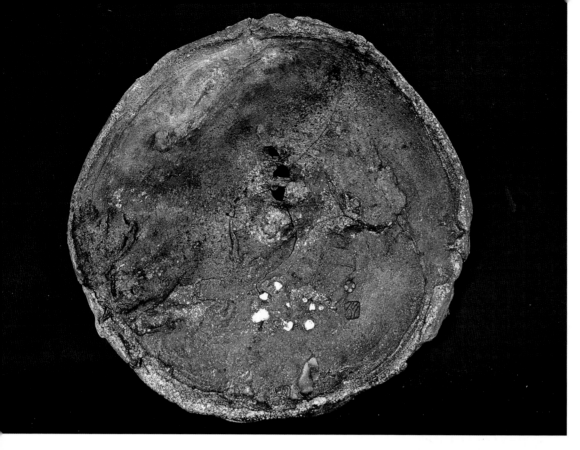

Charles Bound, anagama-*fired plate.*

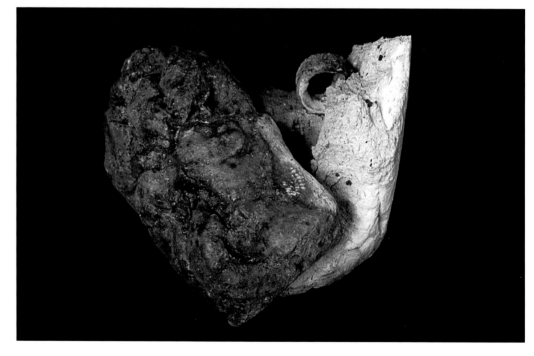

Charles Bound, anagama-*fired object.*

against each other or make shadows on the pots' sides where they blocked the flame's flow. There began from this process of more than heat and atmosphere to be a suggestion away from pots toward fired clay, bits of earth, pieces and lumps going through the firing.

When I was offered space on a farm I built a tunnel kiln and began seriously finding out what was going on and how I might use it. I began to see some of the satisfaction of working with a tool offering much but with its own way of doing so. Subsequently, the ten years I have been firing in a tunnel

kiln have been an ongoing negotiation between what goes into the kiln (what forms, clay, additions, packing arrangements), how the kiln fires and what I have learned to see in the results to be able to move on, holding at bay as best I can existent prejudices. In the process I have increased my capacity to see both what is possible in the kiln and how the results refer back to the environment where we live and work so that muted colours and simplified shapes have become more acceptable and encouraged. Being on a farm meant materials such as chaff, old bolts and straw got into the clay, and the process of helping occasionally on the farm offered insights on how to do things, solve problems and recognize how natural shapes incline to simplicity even when complex. This seeing has partly come from just ongoing involvement with clay and work but also because a wood-fired kiln is an active participant in the results.

The kiln offers things I would never have seen or considered had I greater technical expertise and control of the process and outcomes. So, I have gotten the taste for working with the clay as it presents itself and working into it rather than being primarily concerned with surface. As things come out of the kiln with fused sand from the floor attached, distorted, occasionally with bits spalled off, I also have begun to cultivate the wreckage that occurs in a wood kiln while at the same time trying to create a stillness in each piece from the complexity of the working and firing, often re-firing, occasionally grit blasting, and assembling or re-firing shards from a waste heap. The kiln has become a partner, its often seemed cussedness offering glimpses of possibilities by its nature, such as to have different parts of a piece in completely different atmospheres (part open, part buried in embers) or to stress the clay enough to provide cracks as opened lines that complete a pot (particularly large plates

fired upright on their rims). These glimpses, which broadly fall into categories I once assumed failures, offer consideration of directions to work in and develop; and occasionally something simple and beautiful comes out of the kiln: a found object, a bit of earth, that suggests to me much of what I've gradually come to recognize I'm investing my energy in. Occasionally a piece arrives that equally refers to being man-made and the materials it came from. And that is always immensely satisfying.

Ian Jones and Moraig McKenna

I have wanted to give an authentic voice to practitioners of many of these techniques and the Australian couple Ian Jones and Moraig McKenna have collaborated with me for

ABOVE: *Moraig McKenna, wood-fired vase. (Photo: Stuart Hay)*

RIGHT: *Ian Jones, anagama-fired vase. (Photo: Stuart Hay)*

a long time in interviews and emails to produce this account of their kiln and influences. It is important to have this kind of an analysis to elucidate the detailed planning and execution that informs each packing and firing. It is an intensely technical and practical account that acts as a portal to the understanding of their work:

Moraig McKenna and I fire a 9m-long *anagama*-style kiln. We have been firing together since 2002, and try to fire the kiln four times each winter. Firing a kiln of this type is a strong, visceral process with the power of the kiln, the astonishing heat from the stokehole at cone 13, the slow oily reduction flame moving through the kiln, the raking of the bed of charcoal in the side stoke and the overpowering exhaustion after days' sleep deprivation all combining to make it into some kind of primal experience.

Integral to the ceramics we make is the relationship between unglazed clay and the flame and ash of the wood firing. Each time wood is thrown into the kiln ash floats through the kiln, settling on the surfaces of the pots facing the firebox and melting. The flame writes a story on each pot, a record of its location in the kiln and of the firing process.

We fire the kiln for about five days, and recently have begun to do much of the firing process with just the two of us, although we rely on friends to help us during the final stages of the firing. The process of sharing firings with another potter as equal partners is an exciting development for me after twenty-two years of firing large wood kilns, leading to new insights. The firing cycle is now a mixture of both of our methods of firing, and is developing into a more predictable process, leading to some exciting results.

The kiln that we currently fire is a 9m-long tunnel kiln, 1.2m wide and about the same in height, which we built in 2001. The first firings in this kiln were of mixed success but recently we have corrected this by increasing the draught through the chimney, closing off the secondary air entering the firebox through the stokehole, and letting more primary air enter under the grate, and have gained a greater control

Ian Jones stoking kiln. (Photo: Ian Hodgson)

Ian Jones, kiln firing.
(Photo: Ian Hodgson)

over the temperature throughout the entire kiln chamber. This has kept the flame tip much closer to the chimney end of the chamber, and the middle section of the kiln is now the hottest area throughout most of the firing. At the end of the firing we allow more secondary air in through the stokehole door, and this brings the heat to the front of the kiln, bringing the temperature on the front shelves to cone 13.

We fire in a heavily reducing atmosphere, and each firing lasts for five days. Each firing uses about 12 tonnes of pine, and we collect the timber directly from the forest or use sawmill waste. Wood preparation is a major commitment in terms of time and labour. We fire in eight-hour shifts, and as long as the wood preparation is adequate, we can share most of these shifts between the two of us.

Loading and Firing the Kiln

Amongst the variables that dictate the quality of result from this type of kiln (clay, type of wood, stoking technique), the way that the wares are set into the kiln is perhaps the most difficult about which to learn but has a great influence on the final results. Pots need to be placed in the kiln in a manner so that the large quantities of ash deposited on the pots will not fuse them to the shelves. Every pot must be placed on wads of fire clay, and the marks left by the wads become a major decorative factor.

We think of this kiln as having five distinct zones, and for each zone we will use different clays and have different expectations of the results. The zones are:

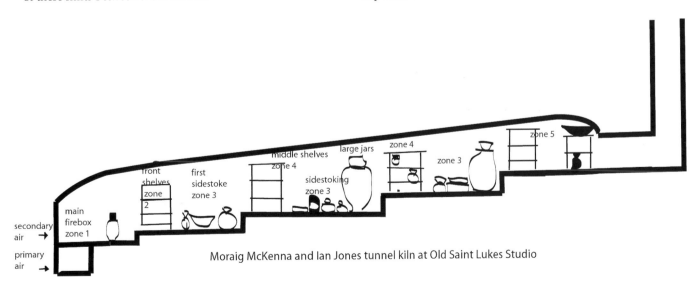

Moraig McKenna and Ian Jones tunnel kiln at Old Saint Lukes Studio

Ian Jones and Moraig McKenna: plan of kiln.

1. AROUND THE MAIN FIREBOX

In this area we use clays that can stand intense heat and expect to get a heavy coating of ash running down the surface of the pots. At times the pots in this area will be buried in the sea of charcoal that moves back from the firebox, and this charcoal can give the rough, black quality known as *koge* by Japanese potters. This is the highest-risk area in the kiln, but it also can produce the most dramatic surfaces on pots. In this area we set the pots using a very refractory fire clay mixed with rice hulls. The rice hulls make the mixture very friable after firing. Ian will often set pots such as tea bowls directly on the floor of the kiln in this zone and move them with a stainless steel poker at the end of the firing, lifting them onto the bed of coals to ensure that they don't stick to the floor during cooling. Moraig uses a porcelanous clay body in this zone to achieve glossy black surfaces and beaded green ash deposits.

2. THE FIRST BUNG OF SHELVES

This area produces works with heavy ash deposits, often with blue/grey coloration from carbon trapping. The pots here are all set on wads of clay, with careful consideration being given to the way the flames will move through the setting. Flames moving between two pots will focus the ash on a pot set directly behind them. The face away from the main firebox will get lots of flashing, giving reds and orange colours. This area produces lovely functional wares. In this zone we use fine, low-iron, highly fluxed clays that will develop heavily ashed surfaces.

3. THE SIDE STOKE AREAS

Ian strives to develop the reduction effect known to the Japanese potters as *sangiri* in these areas. *Sangiri* is the reduction effect developed by the strong reducing flame from charcoal piled around the works. The side-stoking areas are about 1m wide and they go right across the kiln. We mostly use a strongly iron-bearing clay and tumble pack the works in a layer up to 30cm deep using clay wadding with rice

Moraig McKenna, porcelain bottle, 17cm. (Photo: Stuart Hay)   *Ian Jones, natural ash-glazed vase, 22cm. (Photo: Stuart Hay)*

hulls and sea shells to separate the pots. When cone 9 goes down in the settings on either side of the tumble stack, long pieces of mill waste pine are gently lowered onto the tumble-stacked pots until a bed of charcoal covers the pots. This charcoal insulates the work from the full temperature of the chamber and allows colour to remain that would burn out at higher temperatures.

4. THE MIDDLE SHELF AREAS

We fire predominately functional work with a fine, low-iron stoneware clay in this safer and more predictable area. Many of the pots here will have a porcelain slip or raw glazes on the outside surfaces. We achieve a very pleasing quality of flashing here, and have recently been getting some exciting results with celadon-glazed porcelain. Most of the pots are set on clay wads but we have recently been setting flatware on a 5mm layer of rice hulls.

5. THE SHELVES CLOSE TO THE CHIMNEY

This area is fired under a lighter reduction atmosphere, and we fire pots made from a coarse stoneware clay decorated with white and blue-black slips and a clear glaze here.

TOP RIGHT: Ian Jones, stoneware pot with clear glaze, anagama-fired. (Photo: Stuart Hay)

RIGHT: Ian Jones, sangiri-effect vase, 17cm, anagama-fired. (Photo: Stuart Hay)

BELOW: Moraig McKenna, celadon-glazed baskets, stoneware and porcelain, anagama-fired, 22cm. (Photo: Stuart Hay)

Tradition, Influence and Ideas

Ian Jones writes:

My interest in wood-fired ceramics began when, as a student in 1974, I saw the jars from Tamba, Shigaraki, Tokoname and Echizen in *The Heritage of Japanese Ceramics* by Fujio Koyama [Koyama, 1973]. The glowing clay colours contrasting with the runs of the natural ash glaze of these pots have become the standard that I have hoped to attain. Japanese ceramics from the 'six ancient kilns' have had a strong influence on my work, but this has been contrasted with an interest in traditional functional ware from Europe and from the anglo-oriental tradition.

I love pots that are meant to be used, and I love seeing boards full of almost identical pots in the studio. One of the major interests for me as a potter is the variation in form that can give one of these nearly identical pots a balance, movement or intangible quality that excites me. I hoped initially to find some kind of synthesis of the competing influences from Japan and Europe, but over time have come to accept that my pots will proceed in parallel directions, brought together by the firing process in the tunnel kiln.

The dance of response between the effects of ash and flame in the firings and my work has been the guiding influence in my thirty-year career as a potter.

I was initially interested to pursue the question as to whether there were new distinct regional styles developing in the philosophy and practice of firing that could be clearly identified, or are we witnessing a globalization of styles and traditions? Ian commented that he had never consciously searched for a 'synthesis' of Japanese and European influences.

I'm not sure that I ever considered this as a search for an Australian voice or anything that reflected the environment that I live in, rather than as a search for a gelling of influences into a coherent and internally logical style of work. I don't see that after thirty years of potting this is likely to happen, and so I have accepted that I am going to have a couple of bodies of work that are tied together by the firing process. If I am

Ian Jones, 'Wall' stoneware, anagama *fired. It is the length of the kiln and thus a record of the different conditions of the fire.*

Moraig McKenna, 'Embodied surface', wood-fired porcelain and copper wire, 180 × 200 × 100cm. Fired exploration of the relationship between skin and wood-fired surface.

making pots that are meant to carry the heavy ash and charcoal effects of the main firebox, or making jugs and teapots to go in the shelves, I have to, in a sense, be a different potter, to think differently about the clay. When I make copper-green glazed (inspired by oribe glaze) pots, I am another potter in the sense that I am interested in different qualities of surface, a different way of working with the clay, and I throw using a rib much more than I usually do. I assume that I'm not alone in this changing of mental hats, but I am quite conscious of trying to think differently.

The cut and torn pieces are the pieces that I read as somehow representing geological forces of pressure and twisting. They started off as straight, faceted vases. I was excited by the quality of the torn clay when my faceting was done badly and I had to tear the clay away. The exploration was completely process-driven; I liked the quality of the torn surface and the way the ash reacted over this texture. Over time I started to read this surface as having qualities similar to layering in rock, and started to think about the forces of rock formation as I made these pieces. As I am working I play with words in my mind, pressure and twisting, fracture, disjunction, slippage. I don't know how other people read these pieces, and in a sense I don't care, as long as they see something of interest there.

Ian has asked questions about the nature of his kiln firing and about making a coherent statement that sums up his fascinations and interests as a 'process-led' potter. He developed a new series of sculptures that went beyond the normal 'restricted scale of vision' of the domestic to develop a monumental dimension. The 'Walls' speak of the colossal undertaking of an *anagama* firing and are the metaphoric conclusion of the process and could be read as a map of the interior of the kiln, each block fired in its appropriate position in the kiln.

Moraig writes of the way that wood firing enhances sensuous and delicate marks on the clay. She has researched a clay body that will resist much of the ash fall, and with its very low silica content will avoid the build-up of heavy glaze effect (glassiness is a product of the reaction between fluxes in the ash and silica in the clay). She speaks elegantly of that conflation of the clay body and the human body through firing:

In the making process I am interested in the response between my body and the clay and the way that clay captures marks of the making process, and wood-firing enhances the unglazed surface. I consider clay to be of great importance in the wood-firing process and researched a high-alumina

Nic Collins, fired kiln prior to unpacking.

porcelain clay body designed to produce good colour when fired with Australian hardwoods.

I find parallels between the wood-firing process and the way that human skin documents a lifetime's experiences through scars, wrinkles and blemishes. Our health and our emotional state are displayed through our skin.* Similarly, the colours, patterns and textures displayed on the surface of wood-fired work are a direct document of their creative process, completely dependent on the material they are made from and the conditions experienced by the work throughout the firing process. The clay body that I use is very fine and smooth, producing fleshy blushes of colour in reaction to the touch of the wood flame. In the same way that skin ages, layers of ash and experience accumulate over the duration of the firing and the work collects the scars of movement and contact with other objects.

Nic Collins

Nic Collins is a potter to whom place, site and its geology are all-important. He has worked for many years in proximity to some of the oldest (igneous) rocks in Britain – he was previously in the Dartmoor National Park and has now built his home and kilns just on its softer edge. The physical presence of the work and his uncompromising attitude to living, making and firing exude a sense of the rugged outsider.

The granite of Dartmoor was produced as the lava from prehistoric volcanoes crystallized and became solid. China clay is one of the final products of its subsequent erosion and that kaolin is mined today close by. Local quarries have also provided the stuff of some of his clay bodies. He visits them and collects small pockets of clay, feldspar and sand – sometimes only enough for one group of work before

---

*In forming these ideas I was influenced by the writings of James Elkins in his book *Pictures of the Body, Pain and Metamorphosis* (Stanford University Press, 1999).

ABOVE: Nic Collins,
anagama-fired pot
detail. (Photo: David
Jones)

RIGHT: Nic Collins,
anagama-fired pots.
(Photo: David Jones)

ABOVE: *Ben Brierley, kiln-firing day.*

RIGHT: *Ben Brierley, porcelain bottle, front of kiln on shelf, back view.*

BELOW: *Ben Brierley, porcelain bottle, front of kiln on shelf, front view.*

moving on to another geological stratum and its promise of new challenges.

His work with kilns is likewise a narrative involving risk. Some of his kilns are permanent structures, others are constructions that are built specifically to house one piece and are dismantled after firing and the traces of the kiln structure remain in the clay as a vestigial evidence of its presence. He uses building techniques that appear to be based on a traditional methodology but much of the time he is working spontaneously – using the materials at hand to create structures and unconsciously making many of the decisions made by our ancestors. Thus he has created his tunnel groundhog kiln using bent hazel branches pasted with clay and fired to provide an enclosure for the pots. His work is within a scheme of discovery that recapitulates ancient traditional practice without being in thrall to it.

Anagama and wood firers often make a virtue of not popping down to the local kiln suppliers and getting a metal box off the shelf. Instead they choose to build and construct their kilns in arduous circumstances; the story of their construction becomes part of the narrative of their ceramics. In a world where many people try to take the easiest route to a goal, their story often reads like the document of an explorer, struggling against the odds to achieve unknown results.

Ben Brierley

Ben Brierley is one of my graduate students from the University of Wolverhampton in the UK and he now works at Loughborough University; he has constructed a number of kilns in order to realize his intentions in firing work. His account is very evocative of the way that such a relationship can, literally, be built:

I know this kiln intimately, inside out, somehow intuitively I know how to stoke to coax another twenty degrees at the back. I know the signs that indicate that it needs more or less air. I know when the fire needs to be calmed with hard wood and logs to induce a slow, lazy flame and when it needs to rage through the pack using side-stoked pine slats. I know how the flame travels along the top of the arch depositing ash at the back of the kiln, or follows passageways lower in the pack touching and engulfing forms, finding the sweet spots. If I have to give up control I at least place that control with something I trust, and can at least influence to some small degree.

In building a kiln of this type to fire my work, a bond was built between the instrument of decoration and myself. I have never really been a maker that has enjoyed smothering a considered form with a potentially suffocating layer of glass, my aesthetic is much more to do with forms and the

clay body itself and how they respond to the fire and the atmospheres that are generated in the chamber and firebox. With hindsight the bond is as much due to the amount of effort that the building took – two months through the winter. Although covered, it was still cold, heavy work; many bricks had to be cut to fit specific spaces, expansion gaps figured out, and lots of problems overcome. The design is an amalgamation of what I consider to be the best bits of the other kilns I have fired; to some extent it was an unknown entity, however in many ways it also felt familiar. The form had to be sympathetic to the fire that would burn inside it. I knew what I wanted the kiln to achieve and the options that I wanted to have available to me when firing. At the end of it all it works a treat and gives me the surfaces that I had envisaged in the best scenarios.

When the making is done and the work to be fired is lined up on the shelves, and the wood has all been cut and stacked to facilitate three days and two nights of stoking, it is the end of the first stages of the overall process. The next stage, the placing of work in the chamber, is more fraught with potential pitfalls. This is the time I start to get a little anxious about the whole firing: the decisions that I make at this point will be the largest contributor to either having a good firing, a mediocre firing or, worst of all, a poor firing.

Confronted with an empty chamber I have to set the pots out one by one, positioning them carefully, in some areas tighter and in others more open. I sometimes use a torch to simulate the fire, identifying which areas of the work catch the light and which are in shade – it's crude but it helps. The kiln has to be packed from the back to the front, and this is where the relationship between placed pots comes into play. Every piece of work that is placed forward from the very back row will affect the work immediately around it and will also have an influence on the wider kiln pack. As the predicted flame paths have to be anticipated and utilized the pack becomes a construction of negative space, creating paths through which the ash and alkali-rich flames will pass, ultimately directing the generation of flame flashing and ash deposits, which are therefore as important in the overall process of firing as the positioning of the work itself. It is like assembling an engine without any instructions and following intuitive judgement, hoping that in the end all the components will work together. When I'm satisfied, I have to remove the pieces and then re-place them with their bases wadded to lift them off the floor or shelf. It is a slow job, working forward section by section.

The kiln has only two methods of control, and I use the term control loosely. It has air inlets below the stoking grate, which can be opened and closed, and it has two passive dampers (removable bricks) in the collection box at the base of the chimney to reduce the draw. These controls, such as they are, are used relatively frequently in response to the way the kiln changes throughout a firing. The kiln will require many different combinations of air intake and chimney draw

ABOVE: *Ben Brierley, porcelain shot cup fired at rear of kiln.*

BELOW: *Ben Brierley, porcelain shot cup fired on the front step in coals.*

to maintain the desired atmosphere and flame speed. It will change character at night and again during the day, whether it is warm and bright or overcast and wet. When firing I have to be in tune with these changes and be able to adjust the kiln correspondingly. It is this constant engagement with the firing process that I find so stimulating and, I consider, contributes to the character of the finished work.

I am always very anxious prior to a firing; will it go OK? Will my placing of the work utilize the flames and ash? Will the whole pack fall down? There is then three days of prolonged concentration, and the undertaking of hot work that requires rest to keep energy levels up but with an anxiety level that makes sleep difficult. When the firing is finished and the kiln sealed, there follows the unbearable wait until it is cool enough to unpack. There is a sense of relief and excitement that, although still anxious of the outcome, the hardest work is over.

The final finishing of the work after the firing does not occur until the kiln has cooled, the seal of the door is broken and the results are viewed. In the limited light allowed into the chamber through the door, the front of the kiln can be seen to be glistening with fly ash glaze and obvious 'stickers' (work fused to the kiln floor and front steps) can be seen for the first time, along with those pots that were last glimpsed through fourteen hundred degrees of white heat and flame teetering on the edge of the front step, with the thought that surely they will end up in the firebox. Some of them do, and if they manage to survive the stoking they can come out gloriously charred and distorted, telling unedited stories of the firing process. Tantalizing glimpses further in to the kiln increase excitement and speculation. Each piece is removed carefully – work at the front of the kiln usually needs a little persuasion with mallet and chisel as rivulets of fly ash glaze have endeavoured to make them part of the kiln. It is not until all the work is out that I can stand back and view the results.

The work has to be sorted out into that which is OK as it is and those pieces which need careful work with the angle grinder and wet-and-dry paper to remove fused wadding and to polish scars. It is the pieces that require grinding and more detailed attention that can be the most stunning, both aesthetically and as media for carrying the story of their process of being. It is a job that cannot be rushed; these are the pots that have been right at the front of the kiln, they have endured the most intense heat and atmosphere, the clay having been pushed to its limits. Pyro-plastic action has moved them in form, adding another degree of softness and character to the finished objects, the kiln imposing its own control.

The body may be charred with a course clinker adhering to it beneath which black, green, grey, blue, purple and maroon blushes give depths of surface that are not achievable in any other way. Ash, which has accumulated on surfaces (having been building and melting for three days and two nights), has now formed deep pools of iridescent glass with small crystals swimming in their depths, sometimes with hints of phosphorous blue. Sheets of glassy celadon green fly ash glaze covering forward-facing surfaces give way to quieter matter areas where the flame passed and didn't deposit but interacted with the clay, generating soft, warm reds, pinks and salmon hues. Dragonfly eye drips running off the edges of side-fired platters and bowls speak of the movements that have occurred, visible to me only as a white wall of flame and fleeting mirage shapes several days earlier. These are the surfaces and textures that I respond to; a vessel that has many faces, being different from every angle, tactile and vibrant.

My emotional connections with the work and my feeling of the work's integrity have been consolidated by the intense engagement of the firing. Demons have been rested. When all the work has been done I can finally stand back from the work, enjoy it and let go of it, placing it metaphorically (and hopefully physically) into another realm – that of other people's thoughts, emotions and interpretations, put up to be viewed by an audience. Some viewers will love it and some will hate it; however, that is for them to decide, and I hope they enjoy making the decision. I have 'keepers' that strike a particular chord with me, they will seed the build-up to the next firing, but in many ways the work is no longer mine; the pieces exist as objects in their own right and must fend for themselves.

Such an account paints a picture that entices some and leaves others content in their appreciation of their warm beds as the computer controller fires their work under perfect electric control. It is an image that imbues the work with a hard-won experience.

Dale Huffmann

Dale Huffmann articulates well the position of many potters who have visited (or hope to do research in) Japan:

Dale Huffmann vase, wood-fired.

Some Americans think my work is more Japanese while most Japanese find it more American. Some of my plates and bowls are geared to silverware and American ways of cooking and eating. Others have surfaces and styles that are clearly better for chopsticks. I am comfortable with both. Some of my cups are better suited to be *yunomi*, others have handles and are coffee mugs. I make work for the lower-ash areas of the kiln, which is glazed – the glaze is just moderated by the ash in the kiln. I make work for the higher-ash areas that benefit from a natural ash glaze, and I am starting to make work that spends much of the firing buried in the coals.

Owen Rye

Owen Rye is one of the world's leading exponents and thinkers about the strange 'art' of wood-fire. He has explored the nuances of technique and process over a long career, developing what we might, in the light of analyses by structuralist philosophers, refer to as a 'parole' – a dynamic and changing language of ceramics based on the evolution of new ways of firing. In addition he has also found time to eloquently express some of these discoveries in that more common language – that of writing. His thinking is profoundly informed by his work as an archaeologist in his desires to bring the past to light and to illuminate the present with his insights, his work still inspired by 'the mystery of past civilizations':

The art of the *anagama* involves a continuous process of uncertainty. With only a medieval Japanese model to follow, which is seemingly almost irrelevant to the modern-day art world and society, the *anagama* is, I believe, the most currently viable of the ancient traditions and means more than the concession to tradition that we make by respectfully retaining the Japanese name for this wood-fired tunnel kiln. To me, the art of the *anagama* means a total aesthetic art form incorporating materials, fire and intuition … [Rye talks of] the nexus between process and potential … [And asks that critics attempt to understand that] process determines what is possible and that no amount of inspiration will produce a work outside the limits of its technique.

The key to understanding process is integration: the way in which the selection of materials relates to the final texture and colour, the influence of the clay on form, the interrelationship of forming technique with the type of clay, and the way in which firing time, temperature and atmosphere interrelate with the materials and the form according to the types of fuel used. These are all determinative and inseparable aspects of the final work. The particular choices made in all of these elements of process are major contributors to individual style.

My preference is for light-coloured, open coarse clays that allow some eccentricity of form and the development of bright flashing colour. High-iron clays can give subtle colour changes but, as in life, everything loses its colour in the dark. My work is mainly vessels made on the potters' wheel. The wheel-made vessel allows interplay between the apparent familiarity of form and the unfamiliar and variable richness of surface. The best forms derive from a mixture of intent and

LEFT: *Owen Rye, vase,* anagama-*fired.*

BELOW: *Owen Rye, vase,* anagama-*fired.*

Owen Rye, *packing of kiln.*

Owen Rye, anagama *kiln after firing and before unpacking.*

accident. I look for qualities of form that proclaim the fluidity of clay, the softness derived from a somewhat erratic movement, slowed down and frozen. Subsequent processes influence form, particularly the method of packing the kiln where appropriately shaped vessels are stacked on each other. Finer details of surface finish are used on small-scale forms whereas unadorned form is more important at a larger scale where the viewer tends to stand at a distance.

The work is made in series, all related but each different, as a way of developing a particular form. Often the earlier, clumsier ones of the series, made before skills develop, are the ones that are ultimately the best. These combine well with the crudeness of the firing process; pieces of wood are thrown near and on the pots, moving them or partly burying them in ash, creating surface variations. Many vessels distort from the heat and the weight of others placed on them.

The surfaces of the pots produced in the *anagama* have a natural quality, evoking a feeling of an event beyond human control. It is the quality of the surface which above all gives this work its abstract character. Those potters who wish to emphasize applied marks on the surface of the clay will aim to achieve a thin layer of ash, and flashing colours. My aim is to emphasize the contrast between the man-made form and the natural surface, just as a Greek amphora raised from the depths of the Mediterranean is enhanced by an encrustation of layers of tiny skeletons. The endless complexity and layering of surface fascinates me: shiny wet transparent glass, dry heat-parched sand,

soft greys and greens, glowing pinks and oranges, craters and scars, bristling fused ash. This variation is often further emphasized by re-firing and by applying a further coating of glaze or slip, or modifying the surface in some other way to evoke a more elaborate suggestion of age and meaning.

After a piece has been removed from the kiln, decisions must be made as to how much evidence of the fire to leave, which areas to polish or to leave rough, feeling the difference between creating and destroying narrative, playing rough against smooth, wet against dry, dark against light and colour against grey.

It is an easy task to analyse works from the *anagama* in terms of colours, textures and forms and their interrelationship, but any art work is more than a collection of colours, textures and form. The nature of the *anagama* medium is not about clarity and certainty; rather, it is about uncertainty and mysteries not easily understood …

As potters involved in the aesthetic of *anagama* we are absorbed in a process of a different kind, a process of constant revision of our work and ideas. As clarity emerges, the work shifts to take on a new sense of ambiguity in a continuing search for that vital uncertainty. Philip Guston advocated maintaining a condition of continuity when he said: 'One is propelled to make what one has not yet made, nor seen made, what one does not yet know how to make.'* The art of *anagama* becomes truly the art of uncertainty.

Owen Rye

*Philip Guston in McKee, Renée (ed.) *Philip Guston: Paintings 1969–80* (Whitechapel Art Gallery, 1982)

10

Fire and Vapour:
~
Salt and Soda

Salt Firing

Fuel-burning kilns work on the principle of convection to convey heat to the ceramic ware. (Electric kilns work on the principle of radiation.) The convection currents also carry uncombusted fuel (which can lead to reduction) and ash (the alkaline, inorganic chemicals taken up by the plants in their lifetimes). These convection currents can also be used to transport other alkalis – namely the sodium ions that are introduced as common salt or sodium carbonate to vaporize once the kiln has achieved a high enough temperature. At high red heat (above 1100°C) salt or soda (sodium carbonate) are introduced – either sprayed as a concentrated solution dissolved in hot water or as dampened packages of salt wrapped in paper.

Common salt, sodium chloride (NaCl), is introduced damp into the kiln and it disassociates (breaks down) into its constituent ionic parts: sodium (Na^+) and chlorine (Cl^-); the chlorine is then released into the atmosphere as chlorine gas (Cl_2) and hydrogen chloride (HCl).

Chlorine Gas and Hydrogen Chloride

These are two poisonous gases that were used in the First World War. As it is unsociable and often against the law to release toxic clouds in built-up areas many potters now fire with soda (sodium carbonate, Na_2CO_3), whose by-product is carbon dioxide (CO_2).

OPPOSITE PAGE: Petra Reynolds and Jeremy Steward firing: pulling a draw ring to ascertain the state of the firing. (Photo: Rod Dorling)

RIGHT: Ruthanne Tudball spraying soda solution over the burners into the firebox.

The sodium ions from the salt or soda can be dispersed through the kiln by any flame-producing material. Wood already contains much potassium, which is closely related to sodium chemically. The presence of wood ash with the salt tends to 'warm' the colour palette by introducing brownish and reddish tints to the ceramic.

Normally salt is used in a firing to contribute a very thin glassy surface to the ceramic. It is the finest of possible glaze coverings and will coat the most delicate detail without obscuring it. My students frequently use light salt glaze over very delicate modelling or complex turned surfaces, in situations where a glaze would be like a thick overcoat that might hide everything.

One of the great advantages of salt-vapour firing is that it involves a single firing process – there is no need for an intermediate bisque firing, and the associated unloading and repacking of the kiln. Salt or soda is introduced to the kiln from the temperature at which it will vaporize easily (from 1100°C in the case of salt and from 1250°C for soda).

Common salt has a melting point of approximately 800°C and a boiling point just over 1400°C so it can be an active material within this temperature range.

It can be thrown, in dampened packets, which will give some intense areas of salting whilst leaving other areas with very little coverage, or tipped on a giant spoon (or angle iron, bamboo or similar) through special salting ports in the walls of the kiln over the burners. This gives a much more even distribution of salt vapour, as the salt is volatilized by the intense local heat of the burner flames (which exceed its boiling point). Soda is generally introduced in a super-saturated solution, made by dissolving soda in hot water, and sprayed in using an old plant sprayer.

Developed in the Rhineland, Germany in the thirteenth century as one of the cheapest materials for creating a glaze surface for domestic pottery, and also for sewer pipes, salt is now considered one of the most sophisticated surfaces for the finishing of contemporary ceramics. Some clays will produce an 'orange-peel effect' with salt vapour. It is probably because the silicates, with which the vapour reacts, are widely spaced in the clay surface; they serve as localized areas on which the glass develops. The salt accumulation is resisted by the alumina in (or painted onto) the clay and the adhesion of the droplets leads to greater accumulations of glaze – like droplets of water on a freshly waxed car. It is a perfect surface for utilitarian ceramics as it is very hard and inert and doesn't scratch easily or stain. There are many potters who have taken advantage of these qualities, firing with gas or wood.

LEFT: *Ruthanne Tudball, 'Iris Vase', soda-glazed, 22cm.*

BELOW: *Gwen Heeney introducing soda to the kiln at red heat.*

ABOVE: Martin McWilliam, 'F–F Mute', wood-fired stoneware showing masking from adjacent pots, 65 × 59 × 11cm.

BELOW: Martin McWilliam, 'B–F Fade', 27 × 93 × 9cm.

Martin McWilliam

Martin McWilliam works in Germany and makes a body of work of great complexity that *can* be analysed. These are objects that make great play with a postmodern sensibility. He uses the *anagama* firing to create a non-linear narrative, which can be decoded into time-related aspects of the life of the work.

The kiln load of ware is amassed over six months and fired in his single-chambered, wood-fired kiln. He uses an *anagama* by choice for his detailed and time-consuming ceramics, because through its utilization he has developed an original language of effect. In the kiln he packs the pieces tightly with pots touching one another. The *anagama* is treated as an enormous firebox, a very hot, enclosed bonfire with the burning wood and flames forced into intimate contact with the ware. He builds up an enormous bed of burning wood so that the objects are buried in embers. It works like a saggar firing: the close contact between fuel and clay forces them to conduct their dialogue, the smouldering carbon impregnating the still porous surface of the clay and then burning away again. Areas of dark **carbon trap** develop black ink-stain effects, and violets, and then burn away to give browns and greys, enhanced by pink flashes from the ash-bearing flame. The proximity of one piece to the next in the pack allows one pot to mask the next from the onslaught of flames and carbon trap, leaving blank areas on the surface. So when they are finally removed from the kiln they have a grammar, not merely of flame marks but also of an absence of mark, brought about through 'presence' where the effect of ash deposit flashing is masked by adjacent pots.

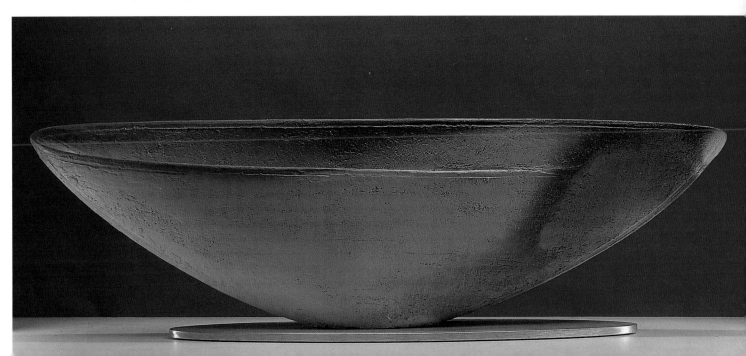

ABOVE & RIGHT: Martin McWilliam, kiln packing, illustrating the close proximity of pots.

McWilliam's work is hand-built from slabs and deals with the interplay between two and three dimensions and the illusion of a pot where one is not, for there is only the suggestion of a full-bodied piece there. As one can see from the profiles the pieces are incredibly slim and have that element of surprise and lack of depth, like the 'Flat Iron Building' in New York. The complexity of this game is enhanced for us by the knowledge that the whitish, shielded area on the work is itself created by a neighbouring, contiguous pot physically preventing the access of flame; thus the pot-like mark is actually produced by a pot on the surface of something that is only pretending to be a pot (when you get into such territory I can see why potters are wise and keep silent, allowing their pots to talk for them). It is a means of creating the kind of multivalent layering in a physical object that has a narrative structure built up out of a language of ceramic technique.

To begin with there is the object that embodies a reference to the vessel and to the 'idea of a pot' in its two-dimensional execution. The white patches where a pot stood close to the piece work like a photograph made by the firing on the piece – leaving a ghostly after-image like the human shadow burnt onto the wall in Hiroshima. Thus it is already establishing a realm for itself that is reminiscent of a photograph and hence it is already alluding to an idea of itself in a mode that is familiar to us – getting our knowledge of the (ceramic) world via pictures in magazines. Yet their palpable physicality counteracts that sensation and we are left in a world between dimensions, between physicality and idea.

Peter Meanley

Peter Meanley makes salt-glazed teapots, and to critically examine his making he has also completed a PhD focusing on these passions. He has been able to reflect on the historical, technical and aesthetic impulses that demonstrate how art is as viable a focus of, and also a means for, research – the equal to tools used in science and the humanities. His analysis has led him to a position where it is *the idea* of the functional teapot that is the target to which he shoots his

---

Technical Details

One of the features of salt glaze is the effect known as orange peel, where the soda–silica glaze created shows adhesion (that is, it sticks together, creating globules) rather than cohesion (where they flow evenly over the body of the pot). This is due to the alumina/silica balance in the clay – alumina resists the build-up of salt glaze and silica and soda (from the salt) forms the glaze. A body or slip with 70 per cent silica will have a much more fluid glass than one with 60 per cent.

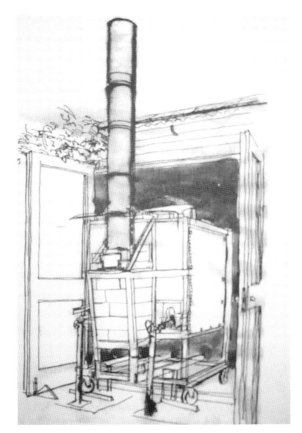

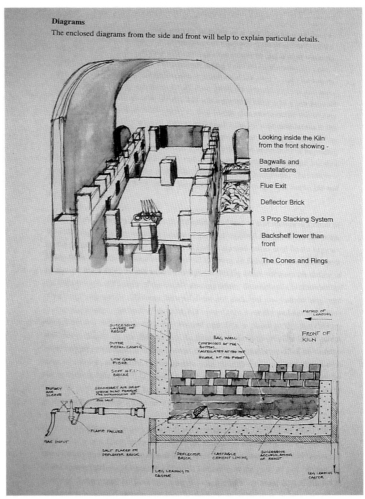

TOP LEFT: *Peter Meanley – drawing of adapted kiln.*

ABOVE: *Peter Meanley – internal structure of kiln.*

LEFT: *Peter Meanley, 'Invalid Feeder' teapot. (Photo: Peter McCaughan)*

BOTTOM LEFT: *Peter Meanley, 'Vegetable Cutter' teapot. (Photo: Peter McCaughan)*

BELOW: *Peter Meanley, 'Locomotive teapot'. (Photo: Peter McCaughan)*

inquisitive arrows. He explains, 'I am not specifically making teapots; more, I am trying to bring parts together in harmony with integrity and beauty. Some indeed resemble teapots; others do not. All are intended to contain, to be liftable, to pour and to be admired.'

For his research paper Meanley designed and built a small kiln that could be fired frequently. He did not expect it to survive long and its duration became an additional matter for speculation:

> My work has always had a particular relationship with the hand in terms of its size and also its necessity to be lifted, examined and possibly used. Examining objects is instinctive … Drawing enables me to search out the idea in the first instance … It is the particular relationship between handle and spout which is most important. The belly is the means by which the two can interplay and take different roles.

He cites historic pouring vessels from Persia and the Industrial Revolution amongst his influences, but also describes how tin cans, chair backs and British architecture conspire together to generate a fruitful dialogue. He notes that 'Bach's Goldberg Variations epitomizes a supreme example of an idea which starts in a very simple way and is repeated and repeated with constant variation.'

Peter Meanley used 'White Stoneware' clay from Potclays in the UK for his research; he has had a special body created by Scarva Pottery Supplies, eponymously known as 'Peter Meanley Body'. This has a composition of 65 per cent silica and contains 3 per cent of 40s/60s silver sand, which provides more dispersal of the 'orange peel' as it 'softens the "tight" forms'; it is very responsive to build-up of salt glaze.

By increasing the (resisting) alumina in the body the results will give less glassiness – so it is possible to effect a graduation from glassy, to globular break-up, through

Peter Meanley sketchbook: teapot variations.

Slip Recipes

For cone 11:

SMD ball clay	50
China clay (grolleg)	50

This would be an ideal place to start on a 'line blend' between the two materials. It is also important to test slip thickness for variations.

For cone 10 with 20 minute soak:

Hyplas 71	60–80
China clay (grolleg)	40–20

For colour:

Oxides are added to a base slip (100):

Brown

Base slip	100
Red clay	100

Chocolate brown

Base slip	100
Ilmenite	50

Fluid blue

Base slip	100
Cobalt oxide	1.5

Blue

Base slip	100
Cobalt oxide	1.5
Chrome oxide	1.5
Iron oxide	3
Manganese dioxide	6

Muted blue

Base slip	100
Cobalt oxide	1.5
Manganese dioxide	10

Note: Cobalt, manganese, ilmenite and rutile are vigorous fluxes. Additions of the amphoteric oxides red clay, red iron oxide, chromium oxide and so on will hold back the melt.

orange peel to a light flashing as the proportion of alumina in the mix is increased. This resistant quality, or enhanced glassiness, can also be effected by painting a slip on the surface of the clay. A siliceous ball clay and a refractory kaolin well represent the extremes for such a slip.

Salt-Glaze Firing

This small, quick-fire kiln was modified by coating the inside with a thick layer of a mix of kiln cement and alumina. One of the features of vapour glazing is the tendency of the ware to stick to surface, so it must be distanced from them using a 'wadding', which must easily separate from both the kiln batts and the underside of the pot.

Wadding Recipe

Alumina hydrate	8
China clay	2
Kyenite (100s)	1
Fireclay dust	1
Wholemeal flour	5

Mix dry in a large container with a lid. Remove quantities as necessary and add water. Reseal container. (The high level of flour means that it burns away, leaving a porous, crumbly texture that breaks away easily.)

Kiln Preparation

Prepare the kiln by carefully painting on a thin layer of salt-resist slip to protect the bricks and kiln batt supports.

Salt-Resist Slip

Alumina	2
China clay	1

Damage to the firebox due to the savage attack made on silica-based hard bricks by salt at high temperatures can be prevented with a thicker coating of:

High-alumina cement	1
Alumina hydrate	3

This never becomes hard and resists penetration by the corrosive vapours. Alternatively you could use 'Pyruma 1A', which forms a protective 'glaze'.

In order to create an even heat through the kiln a 'deflector brick' is placed in the flame path; it is directly underneath where the salt is introduced, embedded in the kiln wash, and it encourages the flame to travel over the bag wall.

Salting. Pumping in salt solution over the burner port. Petra Reynolds' kiln. (Photo: Rod Dorling)

Firing

- Fire for 10–12 hours to cone 10.
- Fire to cone 6 for the commencement of reduction.
- Fire to cone 3 for the introduction of the first salt, dropped onto the deflector brick: 100g dampened (approximately 10kg per cubic metre).
- Fire to cone 6 for the midway point of the introduction of the salt plus reduction achieved by restricting the outflow of gases by pushing in the damper.
- Fire to cones 9 and 10 for the climax.
- Fire till cone 10 is flat with 20 minutes' 'soak'.
- Remove 3 or 4 test rings to ascertain that the accumulation of salt glaze is as required.
- Oxidize the kiln for 10 minutes.
- **'Crash cool'** to 950°C to clear the atmosphere of salt vapour and achieve clarity of glaze (otherwise it can sometimes appear as if scum is on the surface).
- Close the kiln and wait for it to cool.

Use of Salt at Different Temperatures

One can see from the melting point of salt (approximately 800°C) that it becomes active from even below normal bisque-firing temperatures. Thus it is possible to utilize salt vapour at low temperatures as well as in high-firing stoneware.

Markus Klausmann

Markus Klausmann is a German potter whose work is inspired by his early training and his locale. He first apprenticed to be a toolmaker and the effects he uses for cutting clay (with sharp knives, axes and even a chainsaw) are reminiscent of this past training as well as the observations of the woodsmen in the Black Forest area where he lives. He makes both a range of sculptural vessels and domestic pottery with a type of finish that is reminiscent of Bizen ceramics in Japan. The temperature range employed by both is similar – approximately 1100°C.

In Bizen potteries the temperature is maintained in the kiln for ten days at this constant temperature by adding just one piece of wood on a very regular basis (approximately every ten minutes). The long-term heat-work vitrifies the pots and there are a range of markings on the surface of the ceramic (due to the fall of ash, the wrapping with straw, and masking with a refractory clay).

Klausmann uses ideas surrounding this firing technique. He encloses the clay with various volatiles in an almost-sealed clay box (a saggar) in his gas kiln. He first coats the clay in various iron-bearing slips that he has collected himself in Germany and in France, and then packs them tightly in sawdust in direct contact with packets of salt in a saggar. It is like a low-temperature wood/salt firing (and the temperature is critical for a successful outcome – too high and the ash will fuse to a glassy surface rather than the matt finish that has become his trademark).

Klausmann has done much research with sawdust from different woods; as each type of sawdust has a different composition (depending on species and geological environment) it provides different chemicals to the ceramic. This research mirrors that done half a century ago by Leach and his

Markus Klausmann, saggar-fired vessels.

students as they tested different wood ashes as the basis for stoneware glaze application. Klausmann once-fires in approximately one day – a considerable saving of time over the Japanese. However, whereas he fires small volumes of ceramic they are firing *anagamas* and *noborigamas*, with thousands of pots in a firing.

ABOVE: *Saggar packed ready for firing. Salt-soaked string and combustibles.*

RIGHT: *Markus Kausmann, saggar in kiln after firing.*

BELOW: *Markus Klausmann, image of opened saggar.*

11

Distanced from Fire:
~
Electric Kilns

Vicky Shaw

Vicky Shaw is a clay artist who seeks for the lightness and insubstantiality of clay, yet bases her work in the heavy ground of the everyday, using firing to achieve a delicate commentary on the nature of the domestic. Despite all the complications involved in perfecting her work, like any committed addict, she still fires it. She joined the ceramics department at the University of Wolverhampton on the same day as I, and many of our conversations over the past twenty years have involved discussions of the problems of firing as opposed to the delights that it might involve. She is not an artist who is seeking advantage from the kiln; instead she knows precisely what the kiln can provide and plans meticulously to achieve these results.

Shaw studied in Stoke on Trent and her thinking very much has that clarity of someone who designs for the industry: her carefully planned tests are laid out and she endeavours to reproduce these beautiful effects in her work. Her problems are that she is trying to fire some of the most difficult forms (for a studio potter), yet they appear to be to the contrary. They are the ultimate in simplicity – large flat slabs of porcelain and perfectly round bowls. The problem is that at the temperature of firing required for her colours the porcelain starts to vitrify and melt; thus any **plastic memory** associated with the manufacture of the piece is recalled by the clay body. A ripple or warp that has been accidentally placed in the raw clay in the manufacturing process, even if it has been perfectly resolved so that it is invisible when it goes into the kiln, can re-manifest itself. So

the rolling and pressing of clay, the application of the printed pattern onto the clay, and its pressing over a plaster mould must be done with extreme care so as not to cause problems later.

There are also problems associated with firing itself: porcelain shrinks markedly when fired – so a compensation must be planned for, as the slabs and bowls contract across the surface of the kiln batts. A layer of molochite on top of a waster of the same clay can often still not be sufficient to prevent a distortion. Despite these difficulties she has perfected a technique that makes the work unique in contemporary ceramics:

> The porcelain wall pieces are made from porcelain paper clay, screen printing and mono printing is carried out on leather-hard porcelain using coloured slips and underglaze colours. These are fired to 1250°C and further screen printing takes place to build up layers of underglaze colour and glaze to achieve a depth of colour and surface. The pieces undergo multiple firings, each time a greater depth and richness of surface is achieved.
> (Shaw, *Compositions*, p.10)

The inspiration for the pristine work is derived from its converse: distressed, old and weathered surfaces showing the evidence of the attrition of time, such as old buildings. In particular there is a love for the vernacular architecture of English allotment sheds, which 'are unique structures [constructed out] of a combination of materials that show signs of another use in a former life' (Shaw, *Compositions*, p.10). The sheds are used to store tools and are amateurishly built from a crazy juxtaposition of found materials – abandoned windows and old doors, bits of metal roofing (and none assembled in a manner obeying any fixed rule of perpendicularity that we might recognize). Yet outside the doors of these bizarre symbols of eccentric Englishness are precise and serried ranks of cultivated vegetables – neat rows of carefully tended parsnips and leeks; frothy mounds of arti-chokes and coriander – planted by the various peoples who have brought their own food culture with them to England, representing the fantastic diversity of cultures now living on this small island. The English allotments are large areas of people's gardens, once a place where the working classes could grow food after they had been lured to the new towns to work during the Industrial Revolution and which now have been adopted by the middle classes and recent migrants to these shores, who bring their exotic vegetables with them.

As might be expected Shaw is an enthusiastic gardener and cook, and the work focuses too on this passion: in her ceram-ics she deals with the repertoire of the domestic and the way that the paraphernalia of the kitchen juxtaposes itself. A ran-dom arrangement of cups and bowls and boards, of spoons and knives and other utensils, is ordered and presented, abstracted to a level of quiet finesse. They are slimmed till their three-dimensional presence is sucked away and there are just the subtlest inflections to tell us that the idea of this piece started out as a spoon or a cup. She has reached this understanding in the work through a complex developmen-tal process involving photography (which allows us to pull quite disparate elements together in one simple plane), further abstracting the image through drawing and then

creating complex patterns and grids onto a silk screen and applying the image to the pre-fired work by printing with slips and glazes. The slab of clay is fashioned into a three-dimensional form over plaster hump moulds.

The Englishness and understatement is also exemplified in Shaw's identification of the graphic drawing of Eric Rav-ilious and Victor Pasmore as major influences on her work. Her personal interest in the Japanese artistic past is not the enthusiasm of many of her contemporaries for the ceramic traditions of soft expressive throwing, the arcane Raku-fir-ing process or the accidental attachment of fly-ash to the surface of the work – instead it is the pattern-making of the Japanese textile designers. I think that she has also been fas-cinated by the modernist enterprise. She is inspired by the

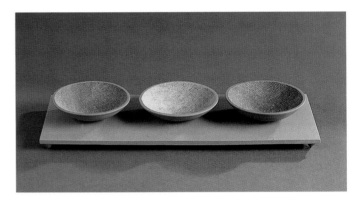

ABOVE: *Vicky Shaw composition, three bowls on grey.*

LEFT: *Vicky Shaw composition.*

BELOW: *Vicky Shaw composition.*

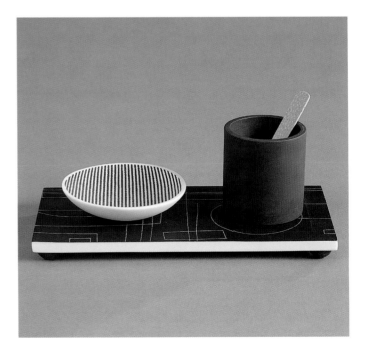

Nanako Kaji, porcelain construction.

simplification seen in the woodcuts of Utamaro, Hiroshige and Hokusai; it is the flattening of perspective and the celebration of the everyday and the ordinary as she weaves a series of lines that are a deracinated view of the thickness of reality. Everything is light and insubstantial, not earthbound; she is one of the pre-eminent potters making work that leaves the everyday, the sordid and the solid behind, searching 'to give to airy nothingness a local habitation and a name' (Shakespeare, *A Midsummer Night's Dream*).

Nanako Kaji

Nanako Kaji is a Japanese clay artist who utilizes the extreme control possible in an electric kiln firing to turn her very thick, uneven porcelain pieces into ceramic. They are based on collaborative improvisations with dancers and as such they are about movement made solid in clay through firing: lightness and grace given mass and density.

Nanako Kaji, porcelain construction.

Amy Cooper

Amy Cooper graduated from the ceramics course at the University of Wolverhampton engaged in two of the most contrasting expressions possible in clay and firing. She uses both porcelain and brick clay. The porcelain pieces are lights; they are cast very thin and high-fired to 1280°C to achieve great delicacy and translucence. The massive brick constructions are about the domestic – a suggestion of a familiar icon of the living room made in a quite alien material and turned into a rock-like substance at 1100°C.

Regina Heinz

Regina Heinz trained as a painter and cites Klee and Miro as important influences. She makes sealed slab forms that seem inflated; they are 'tailored' three-dimensional objects reminiscent of a landscape or of the human body.

She uses the extreme control afforded by an electric kiln to bring the glaze to a very precise point of only just starting to flux before using the computer control to switch the kiln

Regina Heinz Glaze Recipe	
Potash feldspar	10
Whiting	30
Lithium carbonate	10
China clay	30
Bisque fired to:	1100°C
Glaze temperature:	1035°C

LEFT: *Amy Cooper, 'Three Urchins', porcelain lights.*

BELOW: *Amy Cooper, 'Community seat with cat', brick clay.*

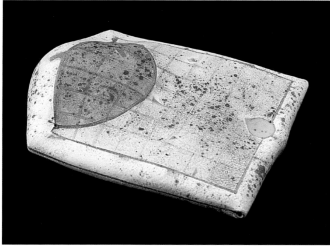

ABOVE: *Regina Heinz, 'Weathered' (detail), ceramic sculpture.*

LEFT: *Regina Heinz, 'Gravity', ceramic sculpture, 24 × 33 × 11 cm.*

off. She has developed a surface that is dependent on being slightly under-fired for its matt quality (any increase in temperature and the glaze will go shiny). She builds up cumulative layers of glaze, slip and washes of metal salts to achieve the final effect.

Chris Faller

Chris Faller was one of my post-graduate students at the University of Wolverhampton. His work focused on museum collections and 'museological culture', expressing a fascination with the growth of museums and the discourses that generate 'value'. Our discussions examined the ways in which ideas can influence practice. Like me he was fascinated by the way in which museum collections are full of ceramics – to me a source of enjoyment, to him as if nearly clogged with pottery. Of course much of it is broken, but some (like red and black figure-ware from Greece) is as pristine as the day it was interred.

His work begins with a philosophical position at its heart and then argues its direction away from that premise (as might be expected, the Heidegger position at its outset is quite close to my own standpoint):

My interest returns constantly to the clay Attic vases of the British Museum. It is as though the clay material records our human histories (questions arise such as, 'Who are we?' and 'Where are we going?'). I began to ask questions such as: 'What is history?' (Foucault); 'What were these objects for in terms of their use and aesthetic values?'; 'What are today's equivalents?'; 'How have objects changed, genealogically speaking?' and 'If archaeology is the source of museological study of what material and form would the archaeology of tomorrow consist?'

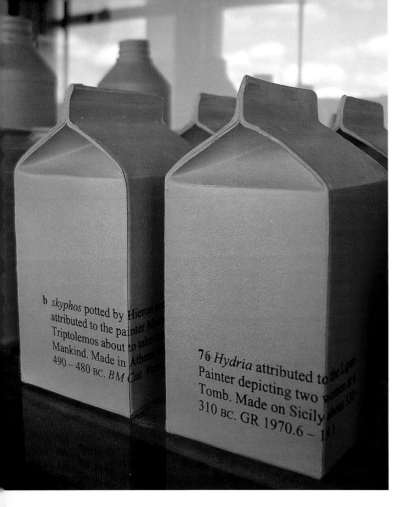

ABOVE: *Chris Faller, 'Genealogy of the Object' (detail), tetrapaks, slip-cast and finished with* terra sigillata. *Electric firing.*

BELOW: *Chris Faller, 'Genealogy of the Object', slip-cast and finished with* terra sigillata. *Electric firing.*

According to the German metaphysicist Martin Heidegger, the craft object reveals or discloses something of a synergy between human beings and their objects.* His argument, for me, overlooks postmodernity and the consumerist age (an era from which art forms consist largely of pastiches and parodies). Heidegger's arguments and investigations side completely with modernity ... it privileges the art (and *craft*) object, beauty, the role of the artist as the 'visionary' and canon (as myth-maker), craft traditions and preciousness. My manipulation of the clay material, therefore, needed to be informed by a practice that would free me from the *trappings* of modernity and the clay's material traditions ...

Faller is interesting in that his theoretical position then led him to make his work – a pastiche of Greek ceramics using the disposable vessels produced by our own culture as icons – utilizing a carefully researched application of *terra sigillata* to suggest a style of Greek firing from 2000 years ago. It is a style of work driven by ideas rather than passion – what Leach might have called 'Head over Heart'. Here is a clay artist dealing with the ramifications of firing and engaging with the legacy of Marcel Duchamp:

I consider my clay work as outside the spheres of current ceramic practices – the moulds can be made 'to order', after which 'anybody' could produce the work to/under my specific guidelines (a possible questioning toward the role and 'hand' of the artist?). In addition to this are the contexts with which I place my work, calling into question notions of how we view and classify objects and artefacts, clay traditions and museological practices.

Haico Nitzsche

The Platonist and the positivist share a reductionist view of metaphor: they think metaphors are either paraphrasable or useless for the one serious purpose that language has – namely representing reality. By contrast the Romantic has an expansionist view: he thinks metaphor is strange, mystic, wonderful. Romantics attribute metaphor to a mysterious faculty called the 'imagination', a faculty they suppose to be at the very centre of the self, the deep heart's core.

(Rorty, 1989, p.19)

---

* Farrell Krell, D. (ed.), *Basic Writings, Martin Heidegger* (Routledge, 2000).

Haico Nitzsche composition, silk-screened images, electric firing, 2.5 × 2m.

Haico Nitzsche is a Norwegian artist, known internationally for his pop art mimesis, which ranges from imitating clothes to newsprint, in ceramic. His work seems to be easily accessible, 'gettable', and yet he wants it to inhabit almost as mysterious an environment as the *anagama* firers. I was interested to ask him, someone who was not, apparently, besotted with kiln effect, 'What does the firing give the work?'

Shrinkage, a dead surface and eternal life. That is why glazes are required as a tool of expression. To begin with: one's acquaintance with raw clay is such a wonderful one, as it is so alive and responsive; that is why the change of character after firing is so disappointing … I use whatever firing technique necessary to obtain my wanted expression, colour, structure or surface … Ceramic material has a great tradition in faking other materials; as far as this can be called a tradition this is significant to me. In twisting reality and giving it another meaning I can express my meanings … The kiln and firing process is the point of no return …

One of the biggest advantages with clay is that it hardens when burnt and does not perish afterwards. The primitive force that fire has and so clearly radiates, is fascinating as well as frightening …

'Linear B' is a script used in Crete 3000 years ago for bookkeeping of groceries in the household. Tablets were made in raw clay, so that the script could be erased. However, when caught in a house fire they were hardened to ceramic and thus we can find examples of the earliest forms of writing.

Eva Kwong sculpture, 'Atomist energy', painted with slips and salt glazed, electric kiln firing.

His is an ironizing vision – using firing to fix the absurdity of human existence in a permanent state. The firing of ceramic takes the temporal and gives it an almost eternal dimension. These shopping lists can now be found in hallowed glass cases in the British Museum in London. Nitzsche has played the same game with contemporary newspapers; condemning the trivial to a place in eternity.

Eva Kwong

Eva Kwong works in a language of antimonies – opposites that seem mutually exclusive but which create a dynamic

experience. She uses the fixing of clay by fire to describe the wet and the moist. Her work references the fascination of her youth when she worked in a 'lending library' of plants and natural objects – it is a fascination that has never gone away. She talks of her Chinese grandmother folding a leaf into a grasshopper form – a memory of changing one material into another. Now she performs such transformations on sea creatures and corals and they become succulent forms evocative of that underwater world and of the erotic, where, if we are lucky, fire also burns. She speaks also of her delight in watching her daughter dancing – of her 'soft, young body' – qualities that can be very hard to realize in hard ceramic. She is using the idea of the soft blush of the flame of wood-firing, as the flame caresses the surfaces of her work, to create multi-layered associations.

The scale of the work is also significant. These works are much larger than us and yet are composed of elements of an intimate scale. Much as the human is composed of a variety of parts working subtly together – the pieces work on a number of different levels simultaneously. The work is both enticing and yet also forbidding, like the invitation from a fire-coral to stroke its fronds, and there is something also repelling about the work. The critic Bill Busta has written:

Tantric Buddhist painting uses colour to evoke states of mind – to set the tone for things just like music can create an atmosphere. Eva Kwong utilizes this active sense of colour as a catalyst between the form of the art and the imagination of the audience. The result is detailed sensuous surfaces that invite you to touch even as their shimmer holds the hand back.

Eva Kwong, 'The Immortal Peach', wood-fired.

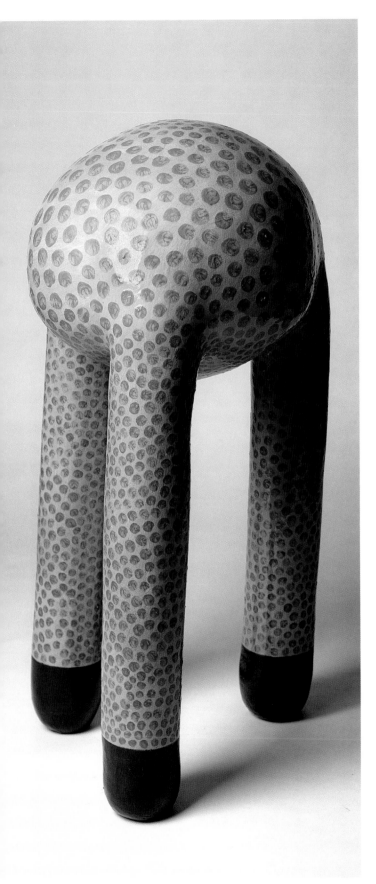

LEFT: *Eva Kwong, 'Acephaloid'.*

ABOVE: *Eva Kwong, 'Acephaloid 2', electric firing.*

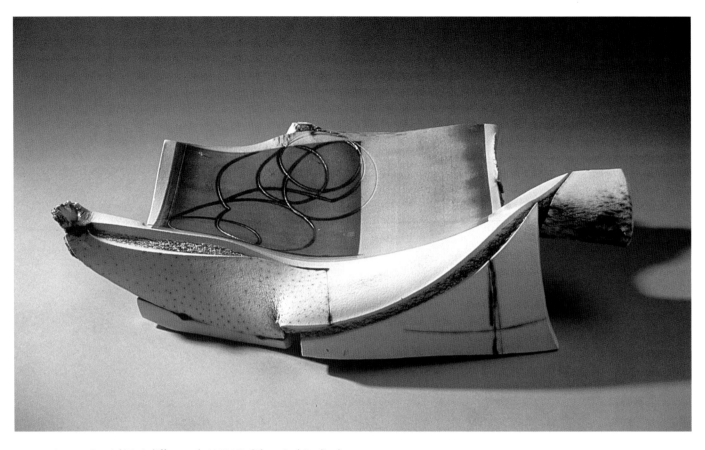

ABOVE & BELOW: *Daniel McAuliffe, vessel, 1160°C. (Photo Rod Dorling)*

Daniel McAuliffe

Daniel McAuliffe completed the MFA in Ceramics at the University of Wolverhampton. His parting comment (that he wished that he had learnt more about glazes from me) belied the fact that he understood quite enough to use materials in a highly innovative way. His work is about the precision, and the erosion, of both hope and surface, experienced in the urban environment. The forms are essentially three-dimensional paintings. They are inspired by contemporary architecture and the graphics associated with metropolitan life.

Clay is slab-rolled and geometric blocks of colour are silkscreen-printed using pure under-glaze pigments, defined by paper templates. Each form is produced from one large slab of clay; this is folded, cut and assembled in response to the composition of the print. Cutting, tearing and pulling produces rims and edges with varying layers and textures, reflecting the torn contours of city experience. The clay is rolled up into a form that can describe a vessel. Raw edges and visible seams are exposed, exposing structure. Breaks and tears represent the fragmentation of lives, buildings and the domestic.

The process of construction mirrors that of architecture; it utilizes hard clay material; and the pieces are assembled like the walls of prefabricated buildings. Like skyscrapers built on narrow bases there has to be consideration of weight distribution; the structural balance of the vessel has to be carefully monitored as the feet and legs are torn out. The vessels are bisque-fired to 900°C and then the edges are sanded smooth.

A copper carbonate wash is applied over the vessel then removed, leaving traces in the cuts and tears. A semi-matt transparent glaze is then sprayed over the surface and applied more generously to certain areas. It is then deliberately *over-fired* and the glaze blisters and bubbles. These areas are then sanded back, creating a subtle texture; a smoothing over of rough, distressed surfaces. The blistered glaze stands eloquently for the passage of time and the degradation of our urban environment. 'Over-fired' as a concept seems to imply that all is not quite well with the world.

Daniel McAuliffe vessel, commercial colours, electric-fired.
(Photo: Rod Dorling)

12

Experimental Kilns

Ian Gregory

Ian Gregory makes kilns and figures. This simple statement obscures the work of a lifetime and also reveals his deep involvement with structure and form. Both are completed with an honesty and bravado that, possibly, stems from his first career as an actor. He is certainly at home performing in front of the crowd, tantalizing us with the immediacy of his actions. I have acted as master of ceremonies for two demonstrations – one where he fired the 'Rocket Kiln' and the other where he built a dog in forty-five minutes.

The Rocket Kiln is a roll of ceramic fibre with a hole for a burner, and a tall chimney on top. Most of the demo involved chatting to the crowd as the kiln reached stoneware temperature in fifteen minutes. After half an hour we could go home with a finished, glazed pot. It is all about the demystification of an ancient process and showing that every rule (the length of firing, downdraught, and so on) is only there to be broken.

The speed of the building by hand exhibits another facet of the value of spontaneity. Every gestural mark captures the character and personality of the dog and the artist. (Sometimes a roughness of treatment is a sign of extreme care.) There is an energy captured in the work that stems from the long familiarity with animals, people, materials and processes – the knowledge of just how much risk can be taken before the piece collapses on its thin legs. There is an analyst's understanding of animals and people. There is a sense of the theatrical in the figures: humans, able to be objective and to understand the roles that they play, and the clothes (or not) that they wear, contrast with the honest directness of animals. Unlike humans the animals do not stand outside themselves and observe – they just *are* – lazily by the fire, menacing, oblivious to the world, or on a constant and undistractable guard.

OPPOSITE PAGE: *David Jones Raku firing.*
(Photo: Rod Dorling)

RIGHT: *Ian Gregory, Rocket Kiln.*

LEFT: *Ian Gregory, 'Trolley Kiln'.*

BELOW LEFT: *Ian Gregory, 'one dog and two birds', salt-glaze firing, 1250°C.*

BELOW RIGHT: *Ian Gregory, 'Which way?', salt-glaze firing, 1250°C.*

David Herrold

American clay artist David Herrold was artist-in-residence at the University of Wolverhampton. He wanted to test the limits and the possibilities of using the computer for kiln design. He drew a kiln using a CAD (computer-aided design) program, printed out the drawings and built it with the students.

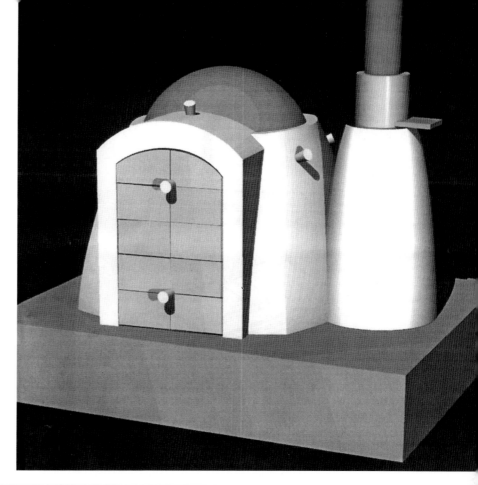

RIGHT: *David Herrold, sculpture kiln CAD design: 'Hotface' on paper.*

BELOW: *David Herrold, sculpture kiln building: 'Hotface' – laying the foundations.*

ABOVE LEFT: *David Herrold, sculpture kiln building: 'Hotface' – cutting the polystyrene form.*

ABOVE: *David Herrold, sculpture kiln building: 'Hotface' – polystyrene form.*

LEFT: *David Herrold, sculpture kiln building: 'Hotface' – applying the castable mix (ciment fondue, grog and clay).*

BELOW: *David Herrold, sculpture kiln building: 'Hotface' – the finished outer form.*

ABOVE: David Herrold, sculpture kiln building: 'Hotface', removing the polystyrene core by cutting it out.

RIGHT: David Herrold, sculpture kiln building: 'Hotface' – first firing with ash introduced over the gas burners in the flamepaths, to give a wood-kiln effect of blown ash.

BELOW RIGHT: David Herrold, sculpture kiln: 'Hotface' – products of first firing (wood-ash glazed vessels).

13

Fire and the Vessel

Variations in Firing Methods for Creative Effect

Categories of ceramic objects that are created to exploit the effects of glaze and firing are of course limited and artificial. Hollow forms that deal with containment and that do not have obvious figurative reference can be loosely classed as 'vessels'. At their simplest they are pots that have sloughed off their immediate employment as utilitarian; but they also number amongst themselves some of the most complex metaphoric pieces in the ceramic canon, dealing with inchoate levels of meaning that are there to be decoded.

The teapot that is priced so expensively that one dare not use it for everyday beverage preparation is already a non-utilitarian item. It is a short step to realizing that most of our works are priced many times higher than their utilitarian equivalents, so that though we may intend our pots for use the collector has paid for something that will adorn a shelf and never be brought into the kitchen. Then there are the pieces that are considered solely for display – in the collector's home or in the museum. They have been (derogatorily) classified as (merely) 'Decorative', or have had the (honorific) appellation 'Sculptural' applied to them. Separating the uses of language can be problematic (Aage Birck, the Danish potter, once asked in a symposium why it was that many a teapot-maker wanted to describe their product as 'sculpture', but no sculptor he knew wanted to describe their product as a 'teapot').

The firers of *anagama* kilns are often caught in this cleft stick – many have a profound commitment to being potters, not sculptors, and they wish to produce utilitarian items, but the firing actually pushes their work away from the functional towards a denial of that intention. Other potters have a clear sense that they are not making everyday items. Even if the work looks as if it could be used it is fired in such a way as to make it very problematic. Low-firing, for example, is a way of ensuring that the public will deal with the work in a different way – it produces ceramic that is more fragile and porous than higher-fired equivalents and, in the case of Raku, it is often glazed with fairly toxic materials.

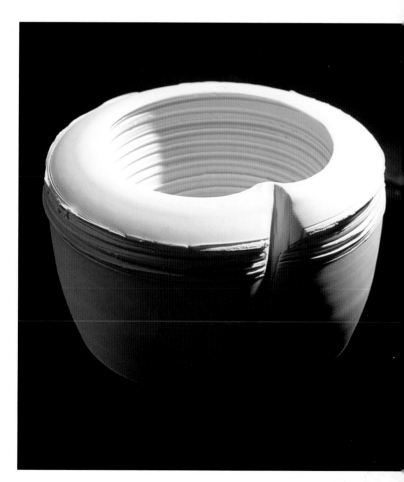

OPPOSITE PAGE: John Leach kiln, reduction back-pressure. (Photo: Rod Dorling)

RIGHT: David Jones, porcelain double-walled vessel. Electric kiln firing, 1260°C. (Photo: Rod Dorling)

Jane Perryman

Jane Perryman is a potter and the author of three important books on ceramics. Writing about her own work and that of others has enabled her to reach an understanding of her own thinking about clay and fire, and how it is informed by her own combination of East–West dialogue. She configures her thinking in terms of opposites. She clearly articulates the complementary ideas of *yin* and *yang*, and of the physical and the spiritual that is enhanced in the vocabulary of contrasts. This she achieves in her ceramics by smoke-firing (in a saggar): black (smoke-reduced areas) and white (unsmoked) surfaces create a dialogue in the black and white of the surfaces.

Her first visit to India was as a student of Iyengar yoga. India has a culture where there is still a vibrant handmade pottery tradition. It is directly related to domestic use and also to ritual observance. Perryman has taken both of these strands and knitted them into a range of expression that demonstrates a high level of critical understanding of her own work. She has said:

> During the last few years I have been working with a form influenced by the traditional, wide, round-bottomed cooking vessel used throughout India. It is either made from clay for use on a domestic scale, or from beaten metal to feed large groups of temple worshippers. Although it balances on a tiny point, it is impossible to knock over, but will happily rock. Expressing qualities of security and of being well grounded, it is the antithesis of the flared forms, a metaphor

for the opposing characteristics of the human psyche … The vessel represents the universal symbol for containing and offering, whether as nourishment for the physical body or the spiritual soul … I find it satisfying to be working with the opposite dynamics of slow control (coil building and burnishing) and fast, relatively uncontrolled firing, where I have an idea of the potential for surface marking but not the intensity of colour.

André Von Martens

André Von Martens is a German potter who has researched and re-created 'Black Firing', a technique that has been used for over a thousand years. Some of the finest examples of this practice have been discovered in Neolithic grave sites in North Germany and Denmark. His work is low-fired to 1060°C; this makes the ware hard enough not to be too easily broken but receptive to smoke. He then clams up the kiln while still adding more combustible material. This cannot burn properly so the kiln belches smoke and the red-hot pots absorb the smoke (soot) in this heavy in-kiln reduction. The firing leaves them black – all the pores in the clay are filled with soot, and they and the kiln are covered in fine black dust. They are first washed to remove the surface deposit and then, to seal them, are soaked in melted beeswax (at approximately 250°C) and finally they are polished.

Jane Perryman, burnished saggar-fired vessels, 40cm. (Photo: Graham Murrell)

ABOVE: André Von Martens, vessels from 'Black Firing'.

BELOW: André Von Martens, kiln after firing, full of soot.

BELOW RIGHT: Ashraf Hanna, Raku-fired vessel with resist slip and wax polish.

Ashraf Hanna

Another potter using controlled areas of smoke and then a wax finish is Ashraf Hanna. He was born in Egypt and now lives and works in Wales. His work appears to reference some of the ancient ceramics of the Nile delta, which were also finished by smoke and burnish. His smoking process is more simple, more direct and more of today – he burns newspapers on top of the pots in a dustbin, or Raku-fires the pots and reduces them in sawdust.

Tony Franks

The work of Tony Franks is deeply embedded in the worlds of ceramic history and tradition, whilst addressing contemporary issues in fine art. Firing is significant in the way that it makes permanent (as ceramic) clay processes, mirroring the metamorphic geological changes in the Earth. He makes large bone-china vessels that speak of the history, geography and the sensual components of the site and then move the perceptions of the viewer to the cosmological realm as we enter his meditative space:

> In Iceland one can observe brand new rocks coming into being … The wind erodes rocks and clay forms and collects in puddles … The major theme of the work is the way in which material processes create the starting point for an idea.

As Franks says, 'The quality of clay is raw, but making is refined.' What he is trying to capture is the 'vigour of the landscape' and the 'vigour of the weather'. It is 'not trying to deal with major issues but small, intimate things … memories – a dialogue with the Highlands of Scotland'; in the work, *rims* can be read as mountains and firing is volcanic change.

The pieces involve a strategy of making that is intimately linked to site, by cutting a depression in the earth and filling it with bone china:

> Physical links between the reality and the image are established by mixing organic material from the sites with the clay. When fired there are bits of bracken and heather, leaves and minerals – all are fired and coloured with salts and oxides. The bone china is alkaline so the copper sulphate goes blue when fired, the rutile orange. The firing must be slow and careful and is conducted in an electric kiln. On firing memories of these materials remain, sometimes being exposed by sandblasting, cutting and grinding.

OPPOSITE PAGE:
Tony Franks, 'Monega Hill', 2006, 35cm diameter. Bone China with organic materials and gravels collected locally in Scotland. (Photo: Shannon Tofts)

THIS PAGE:
ABOVE: Tony Franks, detail of wave bowl. (Photo: Shannon Tofts)

RIGHT: Tony Franks vessel. (Photo: Shannon Tofts)

These processes contain close analogies to geological weathering:

> The way the work is made reflects the way the land is made; processes of time, pressure and heat, accumulation and degradation, all echoing geological concerns of deep time, slow shift, constant renewal and the fundamental relationship between structure and landscape. Unsuccessful pieces are often broken down and the waste fragments are re-fired – 'fusing the loose granules together to form a kind of *Paté de Verre*'. The broken rims are reminiscent of walking on the edge of an *arête*. The best pieces convey the sense that 'I have walked up here'.

We can apply to his work a statement that Linda Weintraub has written concerning the photographs of Thomaś Joshua Cooper: 'People absorb the energy of the land but they also demonstrate that the land absorbs the energy of the people' (Weintraub, 2003, p.190).

Steve Heinemann

Steve Heinemann, from Canada, wished to take issue with the concept of the modern, and particularly with modernism; he has engaged in this debate using arguments constructed from slip-cast clay. His endeavour is to reclaim 'decoration' from the pejorative dismissal that the critics of 'high art' have bestowed upon it. The insight is that modern art and its explicators have defined it by contradistinction to Craft and thereby given the latter a very bad press.

Heinemann's take on 'modern clay' is a very sophisticated recapitulation of geological process. Like Tony Franks' work it is of clay and about clay. Heinemann likens the slip-casting process (where clay exists in its liquid form) to the geological process of sedimentation, and by combining this with sandblasting his methodology is an investigation of 'what Nature does'. Some of the pieces are massive forms and these very large, fragile shells of clay must be loaded into the kiln with extreme care.

Heinemann expresses the desire to talk about 'Pattern and Patterning', a 'core level where Science and Art come from'. He maintains that his 'doodles' investigating form come from the 'same place as', and therefore have the same significance as, the sketches examining pattern and decoration. His fellow Canadian, novelist Margaret Atwood, when discussing poetry and the novel, believes that the former comes from the same place in the brain as music and mathematics, while novel-writing is much closer to the everyday. I would speculate that pattern-making is possibly downgraded as an activity, as it is perhaps closer to the everyday. This psychological questioning parallels discussions within modernism, particularly those regarding the unconscious driving of creativity, at the turn of the previous century.

LEFT: Tony Franks vessel. (Photo: Shannon Tofts)

BELOW LEFT: Tony Franks vessel. (Photo: Shannon Tofts)

BELOW: Tony Franks vessel. (Photo: Shannon Tofts)

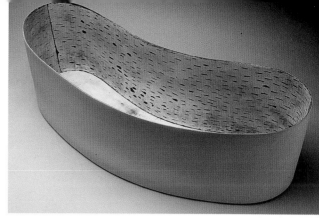

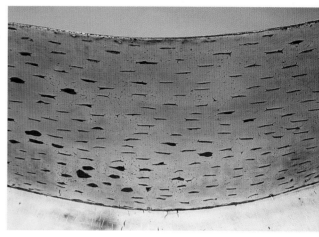

ABOVE: *Steve Heinemann, large vessel.*

ABOVE RIGHT: *Steve Heinemann, large vessel.*

RIGHT: *Steve Heinemann, large vessel (detail).*

BELOW: *Steve Heinemann, large vessel being loaded into kiln.*

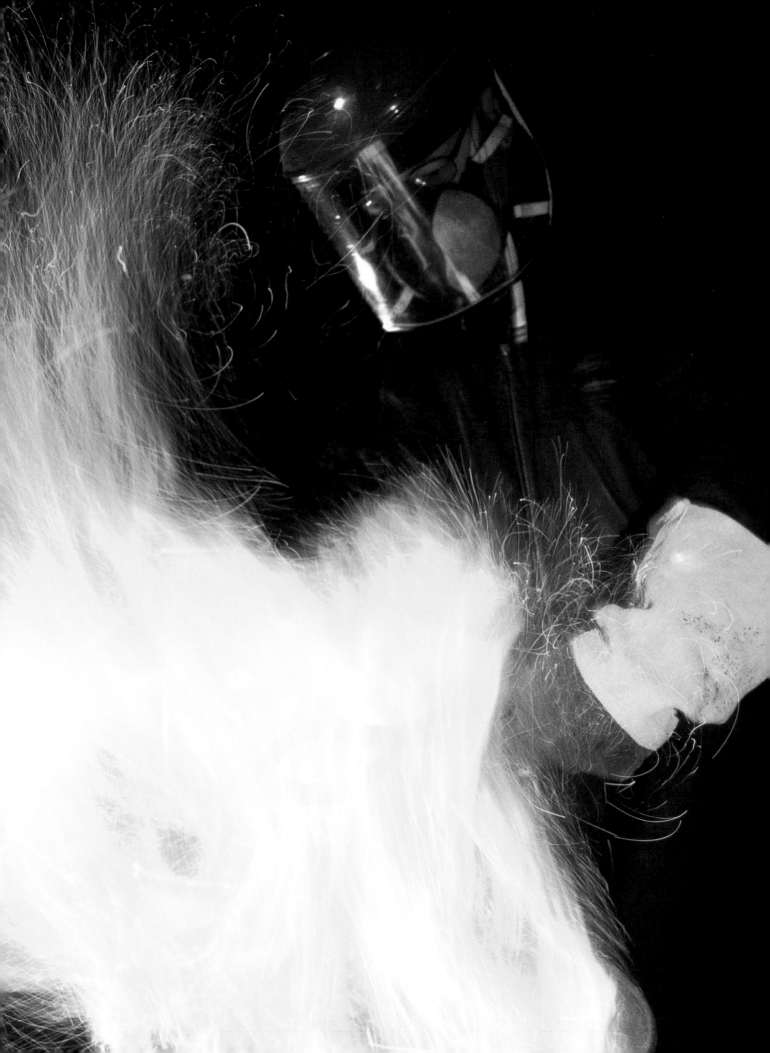

14

Firing as Metaphor

Emma Summers

Emma was a student at Wolverhampton University in the 1990s and did postgraduate studies in Cardiff. She writes movingly of the way that firing and its effects on clay can create a dialogue with the viewer that has profound political resonance.

'Anatomy of Exiles'

There is little doubt that ceramics, like any other visual art form, can be used to convey and interpret images and stories. Yet can the ceramic medium have an impact on contemporary social, political and human issues? Can the ceramic media affect a viewer in a similar way to that of a photojournalist or a documentary filmmaker? Is there a place for the ceramic artist to add something new to the debate of social injustices in the current media climate? Do the ideas, responses and methods of communication that an artist brings shed a different light on a story than that which a reporter may bring?

In 1999 I travelled to Thailand. Whilst there I became aware of the growing refugee crisis both inside Burma and on the border of Thailand because of the mass exodus of refugees from Burma. I witnessed first-hand the effects of a brutal regime on an innocent people and saw with my own eyes the terrible evidence of human suffering. It is difficult to comprehend such suffering and it is only when one witnesses it directly that it begins to affect one.

The importance of discovering and using familiar objects in the construction of the physical narrative became over-whelming. Food tins, baby clothes, bags and houses were chosen because of both their universal resonance and their direct relationship to the specific story of one child's life. They are also all elements of a wider, historical heritage of associative imagery. By using the object and through the making and firing processes, a narrative began to unfold. The Asian food tin was adopted both for its referencing to a geographical place and for its direct connection to the story. Through a series of trials, the tin was altered. The object was initially slip cast twenty-one times; a photographic image of a child was applied to each of the tins, which slowly faded to black through the series. In the second set of pieces the tin was physically altered during both the casting and the firing process. The finished tins slowly disintegrated through the series to create delicate and decayed-looking pieces.

Expanding these adopted processes, the objects began to reveal their own peculiar stories. Baby clothes were chosen for the universality of the image and for their direct, specific reference to the child's story. The same process of investigation, selection and construction was applied to other objects, including the bag and the house. When altered through a series of processes including mould-making, slip-casting and Raku-firing, the objects began to reveal a series of delicate remnants of the original object. By altering the surface, the glaze, the treatment and finally the environment in which they were placed, one was able to affect the way in which they read. Through the firing process the objects were burnt away revealing a remnant of the original material, a fragile residue of the original object. The work began to reveal and divulge its inherent narrative, its concealed story, whereby the pieces could be understood.

French installation artist Christian Boltanksi often refers to the need for art to be 'open' and 'unfocused', so that everyone can recognize something of his or her own self when viewing it. My work, even at this embryonic stage, began to reveal a myriad of reading possibilities held in a single narrative. The goal of this exhibition is to develop further a body of installation work that engages the viewer and encourages debate about both the subject of the individual story and also the wider issues of that subject in contemporary society.

OPPOSITE PAGE: *David Jones Raku firing.*
(Photo: Rod Dorling)

Christian Boltanksi often referred to the need to create a beginning and an end in an installation; by taking the participants on a physical journey one was able to impart a tension or suspense within the work, which is often more naturally created in film, theatre, literature or music:

'In films, novels and music there is always this issue of time, when you're looking at a static image there isn't that progression … I think one of the reasons we cry when watching a film or a play is because of the suspense … it shocks us, we never know exactly what is going to happen next.'

(Semin *et al.*, 2000, p.23)

Daphne Corregan

The archetype of 'the Shadow', and its suggestion of darkness, hovers over the work of Daphne Corregan. Jung propounded this concept, in order to talk about all that was not expressed in the everyday conscious life, and of a psychic need to access this otherness in order to achieve 'wholeness'.

Daphne was born in America and now resides in France. She fires her work very (Shadow-) black indeed; in order to get the hue of a raven's wing she seals up the kiln at high red heat (approximately 1050°C) and introduces bits of rubber inner tube – the pitch-black smoke permeates the pores in the clay and totally changes the colour of the body. The darkness can be viewed as a reflection on the subject matter, as well as the idea of the Heart of Darkness, in real and imagined research trips to the African continent: 'The 1994 world events, particularly the Yugoslavian and Rwanda wars, emotionally affected me and had an

LEFT: *Emma Summers, 'Summerhouse and Slide Projection', Raku-fired.*

BELOW: *Emma Summers, 'Food Tins', Raku-fired.*

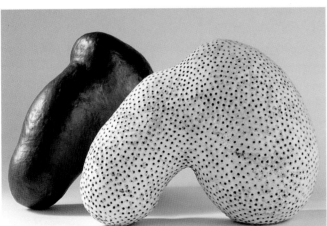

immediate effect on my work.' In Corregan's work there is a real sense of a European/American artist coming upon some of the horrors of post-colonial Africa, and also balancing it with the wonders of African art and being genuinely awe-struck.

The work has a strongly introspective quality and a complex relationship is developed between *inner* and *outer*; the surfaces connected by the many pierced holes:

> My travels to West Africa, and observations while there of some of their primitive methods of building mud houses, bronze and aluminium casting and the tools they use, have inspired me to use many of these techniques or materials for my own objects. I've become interested in the mould and some of the

ABOVE LEFT: *Daphne Corregan, 'Communicating Vessels', 1160°C gas firing.*

MIDDLE LEFT: *Daphne Corregan, 'Skulls', Raku black-fired, 1160°C gas firing.*

BELOW LEFT: *Daphne Corregan, 'Communicating Vases', Raku black-fired.*

BELOW: *Daphne Corregan, 'Two White Pots', 1160°C gas firing.*

ideas it conveys. Negative/positive, presence/absence of what was, contrast between the mould and the moulded ... Moulds used to cast bronze in Africa are made of a mixture of clay, dung and charcoal, very much like their architecture and resembling fetishes, and mosques as well as their homes.

Hers is an art composed of a dialogue between opposites – it is a duality of surfaces and also juxtaposition, often, of two forms that together make the piece:

different surface treatments between the inside space and the outside walls have been inspirational and highly connected to different reflections on contents, decoration, the unseen or hidden space and what is within. My recent work deals with communication and cultural exchanges (or non-exchanges). This interests me on an individual or broader level. My work is also fed by the idea of human displacements, voluntary or not, and how we deal with the consequential changes in our modes of thinking, eating, dressing, and so on ... My travels to Western Africa and recently to China have also left a strong impact on my work ... The new body of work, developed while in China, is gas-fired to 1160°C and white! The solution I found to maintain the feeling of depth in my surfaces was to wash the work in a black stain before covering the surface with a white engobe and to finally draw into that surface to reveal the black lines. The black bleeds into the white, giving it a used feeling equivalent to the quality I obtain with the blacks I'm used to working with – but without the same feeling of intensity.

The contrast between black and white is one of the oldest oppositions in art and culture. At the end of empire it is the job of the artist to re-examine its legacies and to try to reincorporate some of the antagonisms that were developed in the exploitation of those lands and, through the reconciliation of opposites, to forge a new synthesis. Through her new explorations in firing technologies Corregan may be finding new ways to reincorporate the Shadow into her work and life.

Jiansheng Li

Jiansheng (Jackson) Li is one of the great travellers of the world ceramics circuit. He says, 'I have always been away from home wandering around, stopping here and there, not knowing how far from spring. I love to have boiling water and tea, green tea from last year, smelling my home in China.' His work is nostalgia. He lives between Jingdezhen in China and Canada, stopping off everywhere en route. From afar his work reminds one of the strange scholar rocks collected by Confucian writers and artists as a symbol of the wonder of nature.

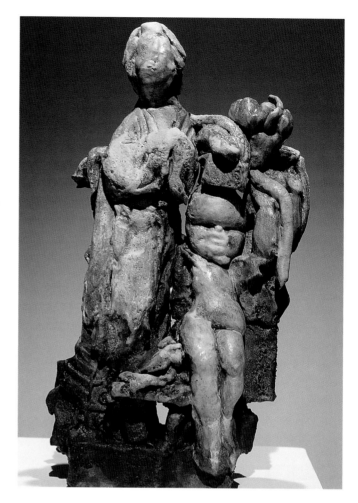

ABOVE: *Jiansheng Li, 'Dickingsing' sculpture.*

BELOW: *Jiansheng Li sculpture.*

Jiansheng Li sculptures.

On detailed examination they reveal a reference to Song dynasty figurines, apparently trapped in rocky ectoplasm – a fitting symbol for the re-emergence of Chinese ceramics once again as a world leader in style. The contemplative aura of those ancient forms is shattered in an expressive, Pollock-like pouring of glaze on these expressionistic sculptures. Li uses fired glaze to tell a story of the recurrence of the classical past in a new guise.

Marcio Mattos

Marcio Mattos is fluent in many languages. Born in Brazil, he lives between Britain, Brazil and Spain and moves effortlessly between their languages in conversation. He also has command of the language of science, having trained as an electrical engineer, and thus has also cultivated a very technical understanding of the chemistry and processes of firing. He is known internationally as much for being a free-improvising cello and bass player as for being a potter.

For us to speak of a 'philosophy of firing' requires the ability to translate one vocabulary (that of fire and clay) into another (the medium of words). Mattos modulates that translation with the analogy of music; this is a move that both helps, and hinders, my own investigation into the philosophical nature of firing. He sees ceramics and music

as not merely emotionally, but also as physically, connected. They both have a tactile dimension (the pressure of the finger pushing the strings down and the marking of the clay with the hand). His music is improvised – not written – and it is so with the clay: there is a framework, but one that evolves, and thus the final outcome is different every time in both processes. There is a creative impulse manifesting itself through freedom in two different modes of expression. In ceramics the potter goes from making, to glazing, to brushwork, to firing and it is impossible to identify which has the final say: 'There is something at the end which is ceramics or music, and can be the staring point for the next work.'

Next there is the need to play the kiln, as Mattos describes:

It can be like an instrument. You listen to the burners and watch the flame in order to control the firing. Each firing is so slightly different from the last, as the level of moisture in the atmosphere will require a subtly different response. Rather than just turning the kiln on and leaving it to be controlled by a computer you must be constantly attentive to the kiln – adjusting the burners in a very sensitive manner. And of course wood is even more extreme in the way that you must respond closely to changes within the kiln.

As a free improviser (someone who responds to what has just been played rather than from a score or even the simple outlines of a jazz standard as the ground for series of variations)

Marcio Mattos vessel.

ceramic makes itself solid and apparently permanent in the world. Mattos paraphrases Eric Dolphy in saying that music is like the wind – once it has gone you can never catch it again. In composition or in recording, 'when you have a finished piece you have congealed a moment in time'. It is an immediate product (but actually in music to make a recording as a product can take a year of post-production).

One of the most influential artists in Britain in the field of musical improvisation and aleatory music (based on chance) was, incidentally, Cornelius Cardew, the son of Bernard Leach's first and most influential apprentice, Michael Cardew. Cornelius Cardew was fascinated by the way in which music (like a firing) was a process, not an end in itself (an object). For him improvisation was a taking of the tradition and subverting it. He took performance – the means to realizing written musical scores – and made it into the end point. There is a strong similarity here with the thinking that informs many of the creators of self-firing structures and examining the process rather than the end point.

One of Cardew's most important pieces of music is called 'Treatise', named after *The Tractatus Logico-Philosphicus* (meaning, for Cardew, a thorough investigation) by Wittgenstein. *The Tractatus* is a very interesting document for, although Wittgenstein later disavowed most of his conclusions, it divides up the world in a way that artists might find very useful: that is, into things that can be said – namely propositions about things in the world – and things about which one can only show (ethics, the soul, aesthetics, and so on). Wittgenstein opens *The Tractatus* with an apparent puzzle concerning the world: 'The world is everything that is the case' – a curious pronouncement that concerns everything about which we can make a (linguistic) statement. He places a terrific emphasis on language to have the power to circumscribe the world – normally we would want to say that the world is made up of objects, whether we can directly apprehend them or not. As artists we might prefer to say that there are many ways of encountering the world; one of them is language but visual and tactile qualities also tell us much that words and language cannot. We need just think of the ways in which drawing and pots 'speak' to us.

there is no final or finished music/sound. The next performance responds to the make-up of the band and audience – much as the potter responds to the contents of the kiln and the prevailing weather in controlling the firing. The working life of the free improviser takes Mattos frequently to Germany where there is a strong following for the avant-guard and, interestingly, he has observed that in German the word ton means both 'sound' and 'clay'.

Mattos observes that 'A recording of an improvisation is a final statement; it is analogous to the finished ceramic'. Yet of course it is never final – the potter is always searching for that next effect, despite the ways in which the presence of

Wittgenstein later developed a system of thinking about the world in terms of 'Language Games' (in the 'Philosophical Investigations'), finding a different echo in the writings of another avant-guard composer John Cage, who took many ideas from Zen Buddhism under the umbrella of 'purposeless play'. He described music in this way:

> this play is an affirmation of life – not an attempt to bring order out of chaos, nor to suggest improvements in creation, but simply to wake up to the very life we are living, which is so excellent once one gets one's mind and desires out the way and lets it act of its own accord. 1967

One of the extraordinary aspects of firing is that, like music, it can be said to allow the participants to enter a 'Zen space'. The focus of the firing is all-absorbing – there really can be nothing else. There is the careful adjustment and attunement of the burners, or stoking with wood to keep the firing going just as it should, and there is no room for extraneous thoughts. It is not possible to put this concentration into words yet it is a state of being that is one of the most satisfying aspects of ceramics for many practitioners. It allows for a combination of freedom and control, a dichotomy on which Cornelius Cardew reflected in his meditations on the nature of improvisation in a diary entry of 1967:

> I compose systems. Sounds and potential sounds are around us all the time – they're all over. What you can do is to insert your logical construct into this seething mass – a system that enables some of it to become audible. That's why it's such an orgiastic experience to improvise – instead of composing a system to project into all this chaotic potential, you simply put yourself in there (you too are a system of sorts after all) and see what action that suicidal deed precipitates.
>
> (*Contact* magazine no. 26, spring 1983)

Or in our case let us focus just on the act of firing and see where that takes us.

Marcio Mattos vessel.

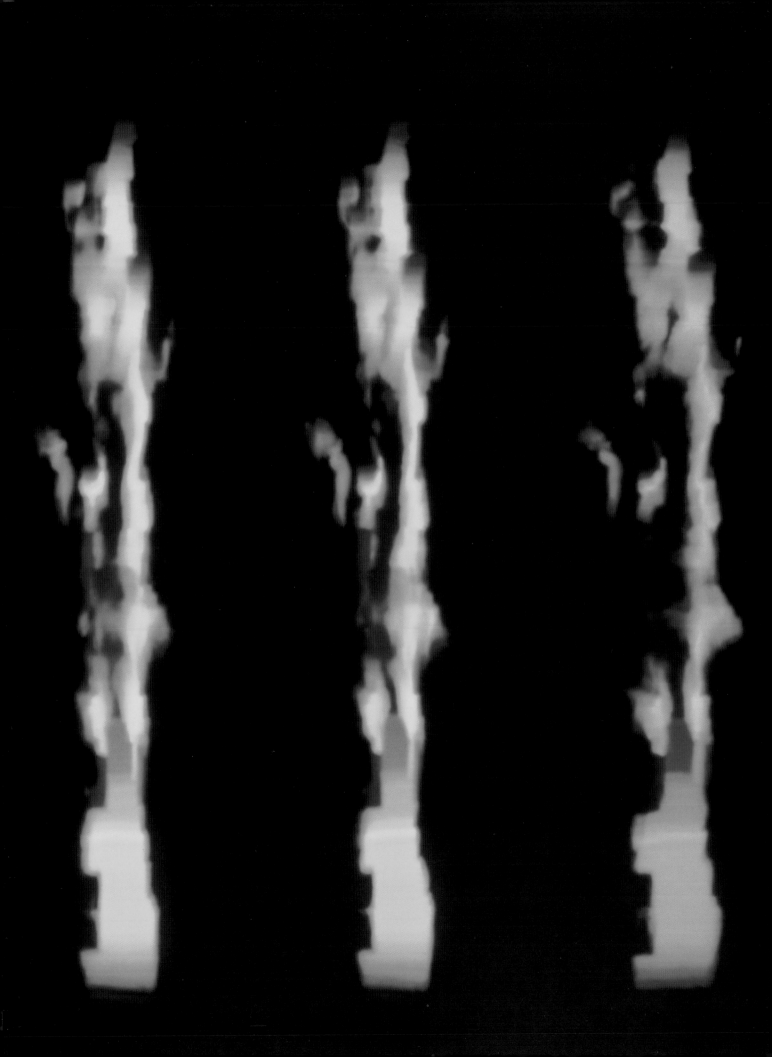

15

Sculpture and Site

ABOVE: *Robert Harrison, 'Celestial Alignments'. Bricks, steel, pre-fired ceramic.*

OPPOSITE PAGE:
Heat haze in gas kiln at Ibstock brickworks. (Photo: Rod Dorling)

Robert Harrison

Robert Harrison is renowned as a maker of large-scale architectural ceramics. He lives and works by the Archie Bray (one of the most famous sites for the creation of ceramic art in the world) and some of his most significant work has been made and inspired by the site. He is one of the leading artists of his generation working in architectural brick, using the material that the Bray was originally built to manufacture. His work is large, bold and quintessentially American. Inspired by the painting of Stella and Rauschenburg, and the nearly absurd scale of Claes Oldenburg's sculpture, he embarked on a series of projects, which were also informed by the 'Land Art' of Robert Smithson, with whom he shares a fascination for the spiral and a conception of the vastness of possible reaction in the environment.

His work has been elegantly described by his friend and critic Rick Newby:

'Celestial Alignments' represents the culmination of this aspect of Harrison's work. Incorporating his usual mix of materials, surrounded by four spiralling wooden columns and dramatically lit from above, the central 'stack', at 9½ft tall, stretches to the heavens. The stack, with its ziggurat crown of cut steel, is constructed of culvert pipe and enshrouded in galvanized wire fencing. The shroud, in turn, is wrapped with television cable sheathed in pliable aluminium and filled with multicoloured shards of locally manufactured tile, a tribute to ceramics and to hard-working western farmers who pile rocks in the corners of their stony fields.

Despite the obstacles, Harrison brought his project brilliantly to completion. Both social and spiritual space, 'A Potter's Shrine' truly resonates with its site. In its brickwork, it echoes the original studio buildings built in the early 1950s by Rudy Autio, Peter Voulkos and other Bray pioneers, and it mimics in its circular form (and acoustical qualities) the brickyard's crumbling but elegant beehive kilns, constructed before 1916. As unofficial curator of the shrine, Harrison asked Bray residents to contribute to what he saw more and more as a collaboration, and many Bray residents past and present have complied, placing (imperfect) examples of their works on the shrine's walls, ledges, benches and floor. Finally, the Bray's board asked Harrison to place Rudy Autio's bust of Archie Bray, founder of the foundation and its guardian angel, within the shrine. Deeply honoured by the request, Harrison placed the bust, sculpted by Autio in the early 1950s, facing west, 'at eye level in a position where he could oversee "future developments"'.

(*www.robertharrison.com*, used with permission)

The grandiose statements in brick have also been reconsidered in an intimate series of memorials that represent the antithesis of such large-scale expression in relation to one of the defining moments in recent American history; he chose to work with the most delicate of clays and to use burning to symbolize the change that had occurred in our consciousnesses. The use of a child's direct response to clay is a striving to regain that Romantic sense of lost innocence. Harrison writes:

ABOVE: *Robert Harrison, 'A Potter's Shrine'.*

LEFT: *Robert Harrison, 'Celestial Alignments' (detail).*

BELOW: *Robert Harrison, 'light radiator', wood-fired (1300°C) with lustres added afterwards and fired at 800°C.*

Robert Harrison, 'A Potter's Shrine' (detail).

Robert Harrison, 'light radiator', wood-fired (1300°C) with lustres added afterwards and fired at 800°C.

After the tragic events of 9/11 my attention turned to completing this new body of work. Reflecting on the relevance of the healing power of art, I was struck with the presence of 'inner light' emanating from the new pieces. A year ago my six-year-old daughter Hanna created a small ceramic piece that had a tremendous presence, subsequently inspiring the *clay windows* series. These new works strive to get to an essence of expression in form, through an architectural language. The juxtaposition of rough and refined surfaces continues to be a hallmark of the work. During the summer of 2001 I had the opportunity to work with high-temperature clays (porcelain and porcelanous stoneware) and fire the pieces in a variety of atmospheric kilns (wood, salt and soda). The surfaces remained unglazed and the only alteration to the form is the single incised line, which delineates the interior space of the piece. Gold lustre is fired onto the interior space to create the highly reflective *light radiator* series.

ABOVE: Gwen Heeney, 'Shadow Stack' disassembled. (Photo: Gwen Heeney)

RIGHT: Gwen Heeney, 'Shadow Stack'. (Photo: Gwen Heeney)

BELOW: Gwen Heeney, 'Shadow'. Photograph of shadow on the floor of the Archie Bray. (Photo: Gwen Heeney)

Gwen Heeney

In Europe, and throughout much of the rest of the world, a majority of people live in homes that have been fired – constructed of brick – that is, large modules of clay that are stuck together once they have been turned to ceramic. A house becomes a home once the hearth fire is set – and there is something of the idea about site and home that is evident in the work of many of the ceramic artists using brick whom I have met.

Heeney's world is framed by an unconscious knowledge that the material of her work is also that which is used for making houses. Bricks and blocks of clay can be sourced from the massive extruders of the brick industry and supplied to site for the rapid creation of a structure of clay that can be carved and returned to the factory to be fired.

> For the real houses of memory, the houses to which we return in dreams, the houses that are rich in unalterable oneirism, do not readily lend themselves to description. To describe them would be like showing them to visitors.' [*oneirism* is a word from psychoanalytic texts that describes a mental state of dream-likeness, experienced while awake]
>
> (Bachelard, 1994, p.12)

Gwen Heeney is one of the leading clay artists in the world; she focuses on brick and the industry not just as the source of her material, but also as a source of ideas for her sculpture. Her work references house and home in the way that many clay artists use the icons of the utilitarian world (such as cups and teapots) to weave their fantasies. She teaches on the BA and MA ceramics courses at the University of Wolverhampton, so I have had many years in which to observe the maturation and development of her work.

She has innovated techniques of working with brick and large, extruded, preformed clay blocks, which she carves when they are raw. She roughs out a three-dimensional form and then cuts out from that structure to reveal the (normally solid) form within (conceptually similar to Michelangelo's ideas about the mystic nature of stone-carving by an artist, to reveal the form hidden within). Most of her work can only be made to commission, as it is too large, time-consuming and expensive to work speculatively. Certainly maquettes are one way forward – but the thinking is also about structures that are greater than human size and one needs the experience of sketching in clay at these extremes in order to get a feel for magnitude.

Heeney's most recent sculpture has been made in America. It is a philosophical reflection on the practice that has brought her to the forefront of her field. It is a speculative piece that will be sited where it is made. She was the guest of the Archie Bray Foundation for the Ceramic Arts in Montana. This time the venue for the workshop was very important to her, as it was the site of a disused brickworks. Thus it already contained some of the narrative of her specialism. It is one of the most famous studios in America; Peter Voulkos, one of the most influential artists to emerge from the field of ceramics in the twentieth century, was the first resident artist. He went there to work at the beginning of his career and it has since become synonymous with the openness and experimentation that has defined the best of American ceramics for the last half-century.

In the piece 'Shadow Stack' Heeney is wishing to convey a self-reflective autobiography – it deals with her own innovations in establishing brick as a creative art medium and taking it into new forms of expression, particularly through treating brick as an ordinary studio ceramic medium and subjecting it to the standard range of firing possibilities available to potters. She aimed to evoke that past of the place as a factory that once manufactured her raw material – brick – and also to celebrate the new creative life it has discovered as a centre for the arts.

This time instead of accumulating mass to trim away, Heeney has cut down into the ground and built a piece of work in the large hole. It is a piece made of stepped brick, and thus defines a hollowness, a container in the traditional sense of a pot. It is inspired by photographs taken of the disintegration of the buildings and the shadows and light cast by the decrepit roof of the brickworks. The actual shapes of the individual elements in the sculpture derive from another trick of deconstruction. It arises like the Phoenix out of the ashes of her most recent sculpture.

The piece derived from an observation made over some time about the methodology of her practice. In order to make a piece she stacks raw clay blocks fresh from the brickworks and carves them. When dry it is disassembled and fired and then all the sections are returned to her to build. They are laid out for building and this randomized pattern is the starting point for the current work. It is a response to the deconstruction of an idea, a process, where that deconstruction becomes a methodology in its own right. In a workshop she made a collaborative piece with students. It was reminiscent of her own past work, in a style that she was employing when she published her definitive book *Brickworks*. It was disassembled and fired, then removed from the kiln and stacked (a process that she always follows before reassembling the final sculpture). However, what she was searching for this time was the effects of light and shadow; the wire-cut sections were lined up and left for the morning sun to illuminate them, creating a 'scaffolding', a pattern of black lines (of shadow) in the photograph, which echoed the photographs of the disintegrating roof. These images provide the visual stimulus for the construction of the brick form and for the light towers. And so she has made a site-sensitive installation, which uses the material and sources of inspiration derived from the material and related to the site itself.

Gail Nichols' Recipe for Soda-Firing Mix

Light soda ash (sodium carbonate)	25
Sodium bicarbonate	25
Whiting (calcium carbonate)	50

Wet with water and introduce into the kiln on an angle iron.

The companion piece created at the Bray seemingly makes even greater play with 'the idea of house'. 'Fossil Pit' is dug down into the ground and is a womb-like structure that could seemingly enclose. It is about the history of the human, represented by our dwellings:

dwelling places of the past remain in us for all time … the house is one of the greatest powers of the imagination for the thoughts, memories and dreams of mankind … It is the human being's first world … life begins well, it begins enclosed, protected, all warm in the bosom of the house.

(Bachelard, 1994, pp.6–7)

Working in the freedom provided by the Archie Bray Foundation she investigated new possibilities offered by firing. One of the other resident artists was the renowned soda firer Gail Nichols from Australia, and together they set about testing Gwen's bricks in soda- and salt-firing kilns. (The majority of work that is made from bricks is fired in the kilns of the brick factories, and it is generally orange to dark red to blue-black depending both on what materials are added to the iron-oxide coloured brick (mainly manganese) and the degree of reduction and temperature to which the kiln is fired.) The soda firing adds a new dimension to the work of richness through colour. Firing the bricks in a 'studio kiln' is a new departure for Gwen and represents the way in which brick and large-scale production is becoming part of the whole studio ceramics movement.

LEFT: *Gwen Heeney 'Fossil Pit'. (Photo: Gwen Heeney)*

BELOW LEFT: *Gwen Heeney building 'Fossil Pit'. (Photo: Gwen Heeney)*

BELOW: *Gwen Heeney 'Fossil Pit' (detail). (Photo: Gwen Heeney)*

Vigdis Øien

In Tae Kwon Do, as in the firing of ceramics, one is looking towards a focus on an instant in time, when all is in balance, and all the energies are directed in the right direction. Vigdis Øien, a clay artist from Norway, completed her MFA at the University of Wolverhampton having already represented her country at international level in this martial art. She also recognizes that the speed and force of the carving tools through the clay is another echo, for her, of the 'Way of hand and foot'. She sees it as the lightening speed of action or reaction, in a state of total awareness, to capture her energy in the physicality of clay.

In Tae Kwon Do, when one makes a move towards an opponent they make a response; likewise in ceramics clay responds to the pushing of hand and idea. In both martial art and sculpting there is a necessary mindfulness, an awareness, a transformation of energy – which in ceramics is made permanent through firing. The sinuous lines of Øien's forms relate both to the land and to the movements involved in the Tae Kwon Do pattern.

It is also as if the artist, who sculpted the work when she was pregnant, had lain and pressed her own body into the clay, creating a 'negative space' of female forms, a vocabulary of curves and undulations. They may also be interpreted as the moorings of boats, another of the motifs expressed in her work – another sort of vessel carrying ideas

LEFT: *Vigdis Øien, 'Still Standing Still'. (Photo: Synlig)*

BELOW: *Vigdis Øien, brick sculpture, manganese brick, 1100°C. (Photo: Synlig)*

Vigdis Øien, brick sculpture, 'Inside Outside' (detail), manganese brick, 1100°C. (see also page 16). (Photo: Synlig)

Ruth Gibson

Ruth Gibson was one of our students on the ceramics degree course at the University of Wolverhampton. She was interested to engage in the possibilities of utilizing firing and clay to effect a 'creative response to a sixteenth-century Tudor mansion house in Shrewsbury, prior to its redevelopment into apartments'. It can also stand as an investigation of our own pasts and histories:

> To confront a person with his shadow is to show him his own light. Once one has experienced a few times what it is like to stand judgingly between the opposites, one begins to understand what is meant by the self. Anyone who perceives his shadow and his light simultaneously sees himself from two sides and thus gets in the middle

> (Jung, 1959, p.872)

in the way that a woman's body carries the unborn child. The lines do not just need to be read in this way: they seem also to be a tracing, following the U-shaped hanging valleys, now a fjord, running to the sea; soft lines marking the hardness of the rock; a road snaking its way around the margins of the water.

Vigdis Øien lives and works in the heart of a glaciated landscape on the west coast of Norway, where she was brought up. At the summer cottage, where she used to come with her fisherman grandfather, one can see the rocks scoured ten thousand years ago by gigantic ice floes. From the boathouse below the cabin she retrieved his boat-building tools after his death and they were refashioned by her sculptor husband into the carving tools she now uses in her work, carving brick into monumental structures.

When she works, she says, 'it is as if I put my whole body into the process'; it is a controlled fight with, rather than against, the clay. It is not merely a journey through the Norwegian environment, but also a sense of 'the flow of music' in her creation of the massiveness of the land. In the grandeur of the large ceramics can be read the ancient stories of the Norse Sagas – the female and male principles have become a central motif in the work as principles of opposites. Simultaneously with the sculpted form 'Ups and Downs' she made an upright totemic piece called 'Still Standing Still', which related, in an unconscious way, to the pre-Christian grave markers of the Nordic past. Thus there are numerous references to sources of power, ancient and modern, with the unglazed clay reading like skin, bringing ancient and contemporary, Eastern and Western energies together in firing.

Ruth Gibson, 'Whitehall Installation' view. Floor piece in manganese-stained brick clay, porcelain inlay, 1100°C.

Gibson endeavoured to record a slice of the past, through photography and ceramics, and to create an installation: 'a body of work that is directly related to the building'. As she said in her statement accompanying her degree exhibition: 'I am fascinated by "time" and "history" and the different ways we document and record our lives.' The objects are marked by the footsteps of the past; clay proved to be an ideal way to take impressions of surfaces and to create interplay between heavily worn floorboards and the effect of time, symbolized by the evanescent movement of light and shadow from a barred window across the floor: 'Once fired,

these imprints freeze this moment in the history of the building.' They exposed qualities that will be:

> hidden away behind new walls and fitted carpets … Using sheets of porcelain paper clay laid onto the floor in the pattern of the light, I then pressed blocks of brick clay on top to take a large pressing. This pressing of the floor not only creates an illusion of light, capturing a transient moment with the permanence of fired clay, but also records the scale and texture of the 400-year-old oak floorboards.

To complete the installation, black and white images of the building were printed onto porcelain slabs and hung above the floor pressing, creating a division of space. Using the translucent and fragile qualities of porcelain, this curtain of torn and cracked hangings reflects the decaying surfaces of the walls of the rooms worn by the passage of time. Images of the buildings hang in shreds like memories frozen in time, adding another dimension to the sense of fragility and the ephemeral nature of the work, and creating a narrative of melancholy using the mnemonic qualities of clays enhanced by firing. The work was installed in the building as an exhibition piece, thus juxtaposing a new positioning for the old and unconscious history of place.

LEFT: Ruth Gibson, 'Whitehall' detail. Porcelain hangings, 1270°C firing.

BELOW: Ruth Gibson, 'Illusion of Light', 'Whitehall' detail. Manganese bricks, 1100°C firing.

Ruth Gibson, 'Linley Standing Stones', ash-glazed sculpture, 1260°C.

Historically it was a short step from seeing the effects of the fall of ash onto the pots in a kiln as they stood in the flame path to using the ash – particularly the finest fraction as a glaze. After washing to remove the most soluble alkalis the ash is dried and used as a glaze component. As a student Ruth Gibson did a series of tests in order to determine the best surface for a body of work. This demonstrates how even a very traditional exercise like a line blend of wood ash and clay can attain a metaphysical dimension:

A site-related project based at Linley Beech Tree Avenue, South Shropshire. Ideas were developed from historical research of the area, and inspired by the beautiful ancient landscape, and man's impact and relationship with it over thousands of years. A series of large ceramic standing stones were created by gathering clay textures taken directly from the beech trees. These incorporated graffiti and marks made by man, which had altered over time with the growth of the trees, becoming distorted, almost abstract. Glazing them with wood-ash glazes, made from fallen beech tree branches gathered from the site, enhanced the site-related nature of the standing stones. This project is also concerned with documentation and preservation of the marks on the trees that will soon be lost as the trees are coming to the end of their natural lives. The stones themselves make reference to ancient times, resembling the standing stones of this ancient landscape, and are a homage to this outstanding Shropshire landmark.

'There is always left
When bereft or uneasy
The comfort of trees'
Bob Gibson

Emma Fenelon

Of course once one has considered the possibility of wood ash as a component in glazes it is but a short step to testing other materials. I want to illustrate the work of Emma Fenelon, as she has developed a carefully articulated rationale for the use of human ash from cremations.

Emma graduated from the ceramics degree course at the London Institute, Camberwell. She achieved some notoriety for this body of work, which dealt with 'firing' in extremis.

Standing next to my tall ceramic 'trees' at my degree show and answering questions about how and why I had glazed my work with the cremated remains of Lily, John and Kathleen, I realized that exploring my work's origins is like one of those dot-to-dot pictures, where joining the points slowly reveals the image and I am only part of the way through!

One layer of the picture came when I volunteered to write an article under the title 'Is ceramics a dying art?' Playing with ideas, I juxtaposed the words and came up with 'the art of dying' and 'ceramics' and knew I had the solution to my quest for significant materials to add to my ceramics: I would use human ash.

I loved the way the brick clay I was using for my trees handled, but I hated the orange fired colour. My search for materials to change the colour and surface of the clay meshed somewhere on route with a theme I was exploring: how what we know (or think we know) changes what we see. Looking for things that would change my work in physical and metaphysical ways, I tried making an ash glaze from my divorce papers, which worked well, but I wanted to find something that would be significant and personal to any viewer; human ash was the perfect answer.

The next obstacle was getting the ash. I was told that some crematoriums simply pour the excess ashes onto the grass, but I did not want anonymous ashes and to feel like Burke and Hare, so I wrote to my local newspaper's letter page. I asked if anyone would like to donate their loved one's ashes. One thing led to another and I soon found I had a small queue of people offering me ashes. The college panicked and ran the idea past their ethics committee, who could not come up with any reasons why I couldn't proceed. People arrived at college clutching urns, only too happy to have something special to do with them. I left time for people to change their minds but no one did.

The next stage was to create glazes using the ash. I eventually found a standardized analysis of human cremated remains (at *www.potters.org*):

P_2O_5	50.15
CaO	38.96
K_2O	4.80
Na_2O	3.79
SiO_2	1.10
MgO	0.90
Fe_2O_3	0.21
ZnO	0.10

I also learnt a great deal about cremation during my search: how the body is incinerated to about 800°C, leaving the bones, and after all the bits like artificial hips joints are removed the rest is put through a pulverizer called a cremulator, leaving an ash that is fairly gritty. Not having a grinder I experimented with sieving the ashes to get a finer grade. I also fired the ashes in a small saggar to 1260°C and they turned into pretty grains of pink and turquoise. Human ash melts at around 3000°C, but using the low-firing brick clay meant I had an upper firing temperature of 1080–1100°C. I tried some line blends. In the end the best results came from adding the ash in increasing amounts to a high-alkaline glaze I had already used, creating a volcanic glaze that changed from turquoise to green depending on the concentration of added ash.

I didn't have many problems using the ash; a few students were squeamish and didn't want their work fired in the same kiln as mine. The technician wondered about putting a votive 'Our Lady' on the kiln but was unsure of 'their' faith. Mostly I had a queue of people wanting to see what human ashes actually look like.

For the final pieces I used combination of stains, biscuit slips and glazes with from 10 per cent to 50 per cent cremains added. Each tree had a varied surface unlike the others. I used ashes from one person per tree, which set people speculating that the differences between the trees were due to the individuality of the ashes. I think it was because I added the glazes on in slightly different combinations and thicknesses!

In the final analysis I feel that using human ash is no different to using any other unwashed impure bone ash, except that this type comes with a story and history attached, imbuing it with significances that bone ash from cows and horses has lost or never had.

Emma Fenelon

LEFT: *Emma Fenelon, 'Two trees', human-ash glaze.*

BELOW: *Emma Fenelon, 'Installation of Trees', coated with human-ash glaze.*

ABOVE: *Yo Akiyama using a flame to dry the surface of the clay. (Photo: Courtesy of Frank Steyaert Gallery, Ghent, Belgium)*

BELOW: *Yo Akiyama turning the skin of the clay inside out. (Photo: Courtesy of Frank Steyaert Gallery, Ghent, Belgium)*

Yo Akiyama

Yo Akiyama is a Japanese artist working in clay who has brought a new expression to the medium with his giant clay works. It is a monumentality, which also works on a small scale. Fire and firing is an essential part of his expression. Firstly the 'skin' of the clay is caused to peel back by heating the surface with a blowtorch, and then the pieces are finished black during a long firing with very heavy reduction, which leaves the surfaces a deep, dark black:

In ceramics as a medium of expression there intrinsically inheres an element of metamorphosis. Artists progress their work always confronting the qualitative change of clay itself or its metamorphosis into ceramic. It is also a process of killing something and giving birth to another thing. It is to contemplate the substance of this 'something'; to try to consider every material and every phenomenon in the context of the mechanism of ceramics.

Isn't is possible to see a tool called a kiln as 'earthenware burnt from within'? Inside its artificial small space the material's metamorphosis is accelerated, and time is compressed. Thus, two kinds of time different in speed simultaneously exist inside and outside the kiln.

Recently, it seems to me that somehow there is a similarity between a jet engine and a 'vessel'. Suppose that 'air and combustible gas' are replaced by 'space'. Then, the 'vessel' absorbs the external space, compresses it, transforms it and finally releases it to the outside.

The boundary between the inside and the outside is perceived by a viewer as a surface. A gaze on this surface from the inside (or from the other side). Just like, for example, when we imagine the overhead earth's surface while staying in a limestone cave, or the inside stalactitic walls while standing on the earth's surface.

Provided that poetry transcends words by the use of words, we can say that plastic art uses forms, colours and the logics and ideas that back them up to grasp something that transcends all of them.

I once happened to witness a talk of a young musician with his professor over his career change from pianist to composer. The professor said, 'If you can write your own song, you will be all right. Your study will take care of the rest.' Even John Cage's music can make us feel his own song. Picturing some composers to myself, I was giving consent to the professor's words. And I found myself starting to think, 'What about my own song?'

Sometimes I am just fascinated with a situation where order tries to conquer disorder, or disorder tries to invade order. Probably it is because I respond to a struggling tension between the two or a sign of transition.

I cannot use easily the word 'tradition', because tradition is profoundly related to my own identity. What really concerns me is, 'What values make me recognize a certain matter as tradition?' Or, 'At what point will tradition be able to take part in a creative activity?'

I read *The Notebooks of Malte Laurids Brigge* by Rainer Maria Rilke before starting to pursue the path of fine art, when only my inward longing for fine art seemed to support my life. I cannot even remember if I read through to the end this somewhat gloomy story of Malte's wandering soul, but my young heart was surely captured by a passage which is as follows:

For the sake of a single verse, one must see many cities, men and things, one must know the animals … the gesture with which the little flowers open in the morning. One must be able to think back to roads in unknown regions … to the sea itself, to seas, to nights of travel that rushed along on high and flew with all the stars…

He says that not till these various experiences have turned to blood within us, 'not till then can it happen that in a most rare hour the first word of a verse arises…'. This made me feel that my first and yet invisible creative work would be extremely far, and at the same time my longing for it was furthermore intensified.

Strangely enough, this longing occasionally springs to life again. Then I think that one day I might get my authentic 'first word of a verse'.

Yo Akiyama

PHOTOS THIS PAGE:
Yo Akiyama. (Photo: Courtesy of Frank Steyaert Gallery, Ghent, Belgium)

ABOVE: Bai Ming, 'Form and Process', reduction-fired porcelain, 2004, each 23cm high.

TOP RIGHT: Bai Ming, Compendium Series, reduction-fired porcelain, 2003, 58cm.

ABOVE RIGHT: Bai Ming, 'Between Ceramics and Stone', reduction-fired porcelain, 2004, 22 × 15 × 14cm.

Bai Ming

The Chinese clay artist Bai Ming works with the awareness of the many thousands of years of Chinese ceramic history on his shoulders. Yet although his work is embedded in Chinese tradition, it is not weighed down by it. In his search for meaning in clay and firing he says: 'Just like the Chinese characters, the different structures composed of different strokes embody quite different meanings'. The piece 'Appliance Form and Process' makes the equivalence between the traditional Chinese bottle form and the human figure. They are similar objects stretching back through history and yet individually different, like the multitudinous Chinese polity. He also deals with the tradition of the 'scholar rock' – a found object that suggests the grandeur and creativity of nature, making with his firing a new surface and a new meaning for a traditional form.

Wenzhi Zhang

Wenzhi Zhang is a Chinese artist who is making work of a colossal scale – creating free-standing figurative pieces that impress with their connotation of China as the next world super-power. These are contrasted with the murals which hearken back to a more idyllic world, of peasant calm, before China had engaged with globalized capitalism.

RIGHT: Wenzhi Zhang, mural. Dongping river drawing, stoneware firing.

BELOW: Wenzhi Zhang, 'a new mankind', reduction-fired stoneware, China.

BELOW RIGHT: Wenzhi Zhang, mural. Wood-fired stoneware, 'Dragon and Horse', China.

Richard Hirsch

Over the past forty years the name of Richard Hirsch has, like that of Paul Soldner, become synonymous with the word 'Raku'. Yet, for the objects that Hirsch has been making for the past ten years, the idea of Raku as a mode of firing has had very little part to play. I have dealt with his Raku work in my other book; in this new work 'Raku' is not merely a practical technique involving the fast firing of ceramics, and a very enjoyable participation sport involving fire, but more profoundly it can be considered a way in which a process and its associations can come to be a way of thinking. This has lead Hirsch away from a focus on this sole form of firing to embracing the entire vocabulary of fire.

Raku ware was traditionally produced for *Cha-no-Yu*. This Japanese concept is better translated as 'The Way of Tea' than the phrase 'Tea Ceremony'. It is informed by the Zen Buddhist and Taoist attitude to life and implies an emphasis on a state of being or a state of mind that the terms 'Ceremony' or 'Ritual' do not. This refinement of a difficult translation of a foreign cultural concept that has occurred in the West is a process that has also informed Hirsch's own recent thinking in his creation of objects.

It is quite extraordinary that the Americans could have hit on a ceramic process so close to the most elevated notion of the soul of Japan in its role in *Cha-no-yu*, creating a new philosophy of firing and making. The reinvention of Raku in the 1960s and 1970s perfectly complemented that period of freedom and experimentation. The new (American) Raku derives not from the quietude of the contemplative soul, which was a feature of Japanese tradition, but the energy and dynamism of the New World – a synthesis of abstract expressionism and the spontaneous enthusiastic vitality of America. But there was also an interest in Eastern philosophies – particularly Zen – amongst the Abstract Expressionist artists and the Raku potters. In the spirit of the times artists working in ceramics also demonstrated an interest in meaning, introspection and synchronicity (the word that Jung used to describe an apparently meaningful coincidence). One of its most powerful expressions was found in the search for 'kiln gifts'; the search for 'accidental blessings' given by the fire became an intimate part of the equation. There developed a focused awareness shown by potters not just to accept the accidental chance happenings thrown up by process but actually to plan for them – a phenomenon seen very clearly amongst contemporary *anagama* firers.

Hirsch's ceramic work is touched with traces of alchemy. The majority of the objects made over the past three decades have been 'Tripods' – three-legged bowls that conjure a memory of the retorts and alembics of the medieval scientist. (For further discussion of Raku and Hirsch's early work, *see* Jones, 1999.)

Hirsch has titled his personal workshop 'The Vessel Research Centre'. Here experiments are performed: the idea of a once useful object is pushed far into the background as the bowl section becomes almost incidental; the supports grow longer into spider-legged fantasies of containment and then metamorphose into ploughshares or knives or the cutting tools of ceremony.

For the past few years Hirsch has collected and re-presented the artisanal objects to be found in the local antique shops and flea markets by re-interpreting them in fired material as well as letting them stand for themselves, repositioned anew in his work. No longer is the doyen of Raku using solely ceramic, but he has extended his repertoire to include glass, bronze and any number of multiple-fired ceramics – from wood to salt, but still including Raku. Some of the objects are painted and eroded, an aspect that refers back to the tripods; they convey the impression of having been dug from the ground, scoured by centuries of exposure to humic acid.

Hirsch is a master of the illusion of ageing – using layers of copper and iron sprayed onto the hot surfaces of his work to evoke rust and bronze ageing, creating a dynamic within the work that allows it to be contemporary, whilst at the same time to 'smell of the past'.

The new works seem to be about pestle and mortars, the primitive crushers used in farmhouses over many generations; they are another symbol of the domestic. In his most recent work it is not just the use of stained *terra sigillata* that is used to age the work, but paint, as well as other firing techniques. The pieces are still about that lost world of use, now that 'function' has been appropriated by the industrial manufacturer. Metaphoric representation is also still at the centre of this work – he has left the three-legged tripod bowl form (inspired by Chinese bronzes) behind and is now working with a new concept inspired by another collecting 'addiction' – that of the Chinese Scholar Rock. The new work is composed of a number of elements, which are interchangeable so that one pestle may live with another, on a variety of stands; as we walked around the studio he explained that, for him, the assemblages are not instant unions and 'can be composed of parts that are up to ten yeas old … Once they are given to the photographer that is the marriage'. Thus the deliberations and experimentations end with 'the wedding photo'.

Hirsch assembles the ceramic in a method analogous to the way that the Chinese rocks are positioned in their wooden sockets for contemplation. The Scholar Rocks deal with issues of scale; they evoke mountains and entire landscapes in a microcosm. Though Richard's work is considerably larger than most of the Chinese Scholar Rocks, both seem to want to suggest much larger panoramas than the small objects that they are in reality.

The work deals in contrasts: bits of clay are savagely gouged out of some parts of the pieces, and in others the clay ends in an abstract interpretation of a stone axe. The tools lying across them are reminiscent of a tool used to remove the flesh from a lemon, but there are also hints of the sacrificial stone knives used to extract the heart of a victim; in his hands they very often suggest (ambiguously) the darker, more sinister use. When the pestles are made from glass we recall objects from anthropological collections, made by craftsmen in cultures where pure quartz crystal was either the sharpest material known at that time, or used solely for its ritual brilliance. Hirsch talks of 'the marks of use' found on many of the objects in the collection; it is these qualities that are searched out in the multiplicity of firings to which his work is subjected. The new pieces can be read as a disaggregation of the 'Tripods'; the individual legs and bowls are dismembered from the piece and assembled as individual units to create new, composite wholes.

The new work, such as 'Altar Bowl', which Hirsch describes as 'using new materials with a Raku sensibility', are about alchemical change. (This has, incidentally, often stood, loosely, as a metaphor for personal growth and development.) Hirsch has commented that: 'if you work long enough with Raku then the individual is the final product; you are changed by Raku.' He goes on to elucidate his attitude to materials and their interrelationship: 'Wood is treated as I would clay, the cohesion between the parts is my Raku sensibility.' There are elements that are electric-fired, for example bronze glaze etched by acid, wood-fired, salted, and so on. The introduction of new types of firing and other materials into the work brings a baggage of associations

ABOVE: *Richard Hirsch sculpture. Multiple-fired ceramics.*

BELOW LEFT: *Richard Hirsch sculpture, ceramic and wood.*

BELOW: *Richard Hirsch sculpture. Ceramic and glass.*

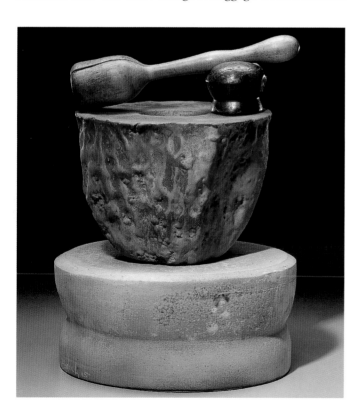

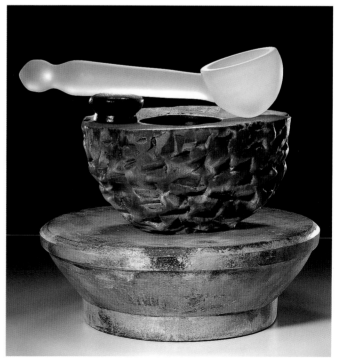

Ching-Yuan Chang, 'A Gift for the Hunter', wood-fired reduction.

gleaned from our innate knowledge of material culture. The stoneware firing changes the soft clay to a hard, dense, tight substance, which thereby carries a sense of formality. This now plays against the idea of the soft, open, casual structures made and fired in Raku, and can be read to represent uncharted territory.

There are many parallels between *Cha-no-Yu* (the Tea Ceremony) and Hirsch's work, particularly in the use and combination of a multiplicity of materials. The composite new forms represent a new way of working whereby disparate elements are handled with a unified sensibility, similar to that provided by the teaching of Sen-no-Rikyu – an influential Tea Master. The work has strong symbolic and metaphoric resonances; in this way it parallels what happens in *Cha-no-Yu* where the tea bowl and its contents 'stand for' refreshment and drinking, whilst simultaneously being the conveyors of a real drink. This theme of sustenance and its 'metaphorizing' appears again in Hirsch's pestle and mortar pieces. The 'ladles' are made of glass – a supercooled liquid – and as such are literally (scientifically) fluid and therefore embody the implication that they are not to be used. Finally there is the coming together that matches objects of an oriental past and sensibility with an American past and culture, all deriving from ideas generated by Raku – the youngest of the firing disciplines.

Ching-Yuan Chang

Ching-Yuan Chang is one of Taiwan's foremost artists. He studied ceramics in the USA and his friend and teacher Richard Hirsch has said of him: 'America is his hometown and Taiwan is his country' (author's personal communication). His work deals with this feeling of displacement – a very common theme in modernist narratives. It has a very classical feel, yet many of the forms of expression deal with a postmodern sensibility.

Deleuze and Guatteri, in their book *A Thousand Plateaus: Capitalism and Schizophrenia* (1987), talk of 'deterritorialized nomads', a concept originally drawn to describe the situation of so many people in a globalized economy who do not belong to any one time or place. It can also be stretched to describe people away from their homeland, who are forced to converse and create in a new language. In Ching-Yuan's case both his studies and early professional life involved learning an American voice with which to speak and to make.

He now resides once more in Taiwan, in Tainan, the old capital. In our discussions he described his dislocation in terms of 'feeling to be an alien, even in your own country'. For, of course, now his sensibilities are also Western. He uses this dynamic as a source of energy for the work. His ceramics use a fantastic range of fired surface together in one piece: 'Because everything is new; it is not a connection to history, but to use.' Of course Taiwan has a compromised history and relation to tradition. The territory is disputed with mainland China, and the Chinese Emperor's collection from the Imperial Palace is now in the National Museum, in Taipei. Ching-Yuan feels that his work speaks of this sense of disputed land as well as of himself. He talks of the work being like an umbilical cord that ties him to Taiwan and to America. He employs his astonishing command of fired surface, but is not using it in a referential postmodern idiom – instead he is using fired surface like a painter, choosing the glazes and kilns to give the precise nuance to the work that is required. Thus one can find elements of porcelain with a celadon glaze conjoined to a sawdust-smoked element, and earthenware juxtaposed with wood-fired grogged clay. There is an evident facility with his manipulations of such materials, in manners of such complexity, which does not quite obscure the essential dislocation, and sadness, embodied in his expression in fired clay.

Frank Steyaert

'And this also,' said Marlow suddenly, 'has been one of the dark places of the earth.'

(Conrad, 1995, p.1)

Joseph Conrad wrote *Heart of Darkness* about a journey into the vast jungle of the Belgian Congo. It is the story of an inner journey into the very centre of the African continent. As Marlow travels on his boat upriver so he gets closer to the demonic figure of Kurtz whom a reader of Jung might identify as a 'Shadow' symbol – the story being also an inner psychological journey.

Frank Steyaert is a vessel maker, and he has his studio on the banks of the Dender River in Belgium. Like Conrad he journeys down into the world, on the sails of his imagination. The vessels made by Steyaert are not pots, as such, but boats. These are boats but not boats; their material is clay and their function is not to carry cargoes but ideas. These boats are all derelict; they carried once but now, broken and useless, they

Ching-Yuan Chang, untitled. Wood-fired and celadon-glazed, 102 × 73 × 45cm.

function only as symbols. They are not inhabited, there are no figurines but some of the detail is perfect and exact – the trappings of humanity are there. They are painted with a variety of engobes and slips and fired to emphasize this aura of ruin, weathering and age; it is a *trompe l'oeil* effect employed so that the imagination can roam far beyond the piece. They suggest that maritime past when a shipwreck was a much more common occurrence and then our minds travel to the eventual, and inevitable, foundering of our own bodily vessels on the shoals of time: 'In his studio lies a shard of Jomon ceramics. It is 7,000 years old, but it still bears a fingerprint from its maker, and the nuances of grey, caused by heating a moment of the past, eternally legible' (Mayer, 1999).

A ship should be a protective container for the 'souls who travel in her'. When it becomes derelict it tells a new narrative of the fragility of hopes and existences.

In and out of rivers, streams of death in life, whose banks were rotting into mud, whose waters, thickened with slime, invaded the contorted mangroves, that seemed to writhe at us in the extremity of an impotent despair. Nowhere did we stop long enough to get a particularized impression, but the general sense of vague and oppressive wonder grew upon me. It was like a weary pilgrimage amongst hints for nightmares.

(Conrad, 1995)

The fired form is fixed forever, but new discourses can continue to accrete around the work.

TOP LEFT: *Frank Steyaert sculpture, derelict vessel, 2005. 79 × 95 × 26cm.*

LEFT: *Frank Steyaert sculpture, derelict vessel, 1997. 46 × 125 × 54cm.*

Steven Montgomery

Vanity of vanities, saith the preacher, all is vanity.

(Ecclesiastes 12:8)

Firing occurs somewhere in the middle of my process and never determines a conclusion. I regard my electric kiln without romance and no more significant than my drill press, belt sander or hacksaw. Any suggestion of process is antithetical to my intent and any lingering sentiment I may attach to the fact that my work is handmade must be balanced with the needs of my subject. The modernist tenet that heralded the importance of honesty in materials ended with modernism and no longer seems applicable. I don't really give a damn about ceramics! That categorization has no real significance for me and functions only as a public relations anecdote and historical footnote. (Steven Montgomery, 5 November 2004)

Despite this iconoclastic statement, Montgomery is one of the most skilled contemporary artists working in clay. The symbol of Fire (implying the 'life' inherent in the internal combustion engine) and its absence (reflecting the demise of carbon-based technologies and perhaps implicitly America itself) resides at the heart of some of his most profound work. He trained as a painter and finishes much of the work with non-fired surfaces, but his work is about combustion. The subject matter has been dominated by the associations of his upbringing in Detroit – home of the American automotive industry and a manufacturing centre of the internal combustion engine. However, Montgomery says: "I'm terrified of technology and machinery; in 1979 an automobile I was driving caught fire on the freeway and burned up on me. It was engulfed in flames in a minute and a half."

Montgomery escaped unscathed, and never drove again. Now he uses fired clay to enter a different narrative, which is not merely an exercise in *Trompe l'oeil* mimesis, replicating engines. In our conversations he has stated, 'I'm commenting on my mistrust of technology.' The pieces suggest engines and have a quite uncanny similarity to their metal counterparts but have an ironic thrust. They are not part of the hyperreal, as described by Umberto Eco, or the postmodern simulacra of Baudrillard, which are exercises in recreating an object, precisely, in another material: they are imaginary assemblages that resemble (very closely) the working parts of a car. They echo pipes and hydraulics mediated by the urban decay one passes through on the way to Montgomery's studio in Brooklyn, away from his home in downtown Manhattan. They comment on oxidation and decay (metal fatigue, rusting and ageing); they work as a metaphor for the breakdown in the promise of the American Dream, suggesting a post-Armageddon society; in their isolation the pipes and motor of a car remind us of our own (all too frail) bodies. The idea of the body as a machine invested with life by spirit or mind has been an ongoing trope of philosophy, particularly since Descartes. The alchemy of vitalization by fire or spark in the Frankenstein story by Mary Shelley is now absent in Montgomery's pieces. The simulation of decay in the work serves to remind us of the impermanence of human pleasures and the transient nature of life.

RIGHT: Steven Montgomery, 'Static Fuel', multiple firing, 2001.

BELOW: Steven Montgomery, 'Static Fuel', multiple firing, 1998.

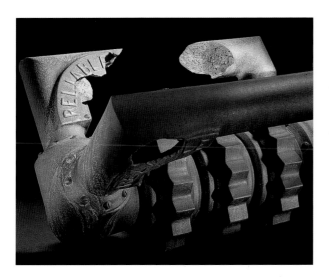

Steven Montgomery, 'Security Breach', 2004, multiple firing.

Thus the pieces work in a similar way to the *Vanitas* paintings of the sixteenth century – they were a comment on the brevity of human life (symbolized by a skull, a mirror, *broken pottery* and smoke). Death has scorched its way into the creative consciousness of many of us post 9/11: the *mirror* apparently reflects the truth of the world (and Montgomery's work disrupts that appearance); he has *broken* the mould of pottery – yet uses all of the language of ceramics

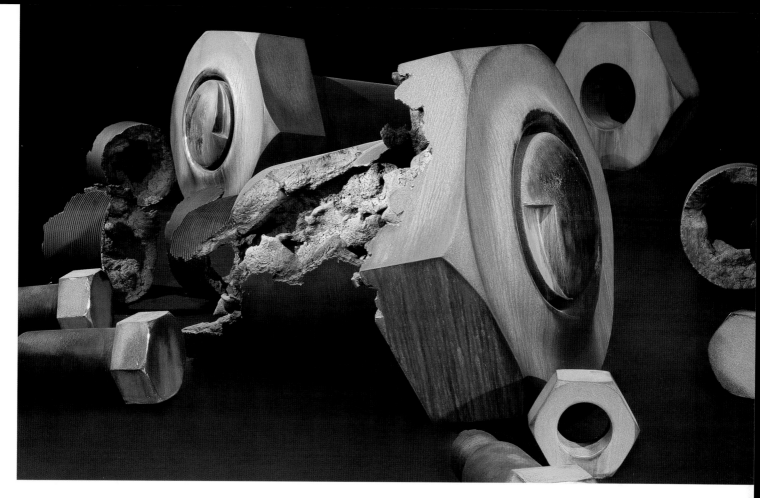

Steven Montgomery, nut and bolt, ceramic with fired and non-fired surfaces.

to convey his message; and the *smoke* has cleared and is long gone from the engines and the giant 'Twin Towers'. In the machine-age the machine was worshipped as a god. Montgomery's bleak pieces without vital fire represent the death of that otherness and seem to 'Be' only in their materiality. His is a language of fire and fired ceramic that visually denies its inception and yet the knowledge of clay and its firing is so

Steven Montgomery, 'Yellow Hazard', multiple firing and non-ceramic media, 2004.

powerfully extant that it serves to subvert its subject matter. The clay literally breaks through the apparent metalness of the surfaces, and takes us into the realm that Freud refers to as the *unheimlich* (the uncanny), as it disrupts our perceptions.

Montgomery points out the gap in the skyline from his rooftop vantage point in Manhattan where he had watched the destruction of the Twin Towers on 9/11. He says that the nuts and bolts that held the building together did not withstand the extraordinary heat of the fire – the buildings crumpled. His most recent body of work includes giant ceramic simulacra of rotten bank vault doors with hazard tape – as if to warn us that the very things that were designed to protect Capital (perhaps the defining image of America and the Thing to be most protected in the 'War on Terror') can no longer be relied upon to keep us safe.

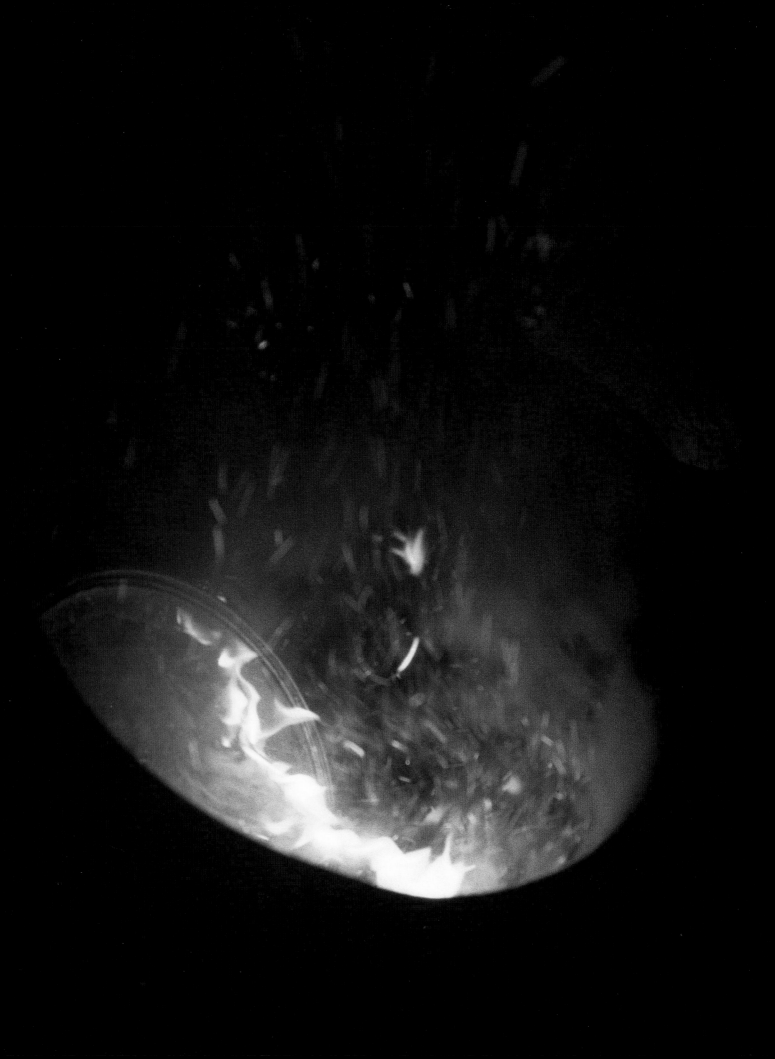

16

Fire and Site

Neil Brownsword

Neil Brownsword makes work that appears humorous and is even more than a little indecorous, but it is informed by the tragedy that seemingly lurks behind every funny man. He comments not just on the demise of 'the Potteries' as a viable 'site' of industry in Staffordshire, England (he still lives in Stoke-on-Trent), but also on the human condition. A Samuel Beckett of ceramics, he adopts the guise of a cheeky little boy who cannot help but be naughty. For instance, by presenting some of the exhibition materials for his major show at the Potteries Museum and Art Gallery, Stoke in 2005 with the same scatological wit he demonstrated in his earlier figurative pieces – utilizing all manner of pottery processes to a sublimely vulgar end. Like the great British comic George Formby his world of double entendre thinly veils a sharply observed sadness at the folly of the world.

This ultimately tragic vision has come to the fore much more strongly in recent years. The early figurative work is composed of carefully articulated surfaces that demonstrate an almost obsessive interest in and knowledge of ceramic history, firing and glaze. He utilizes the processes to reference past ceramic traditions and to be rude – I would say essentially human – though many wish to consign the body and its peculiarities to the 'animal' or 'base' instincts.

It is ironic that Stoke, the symbol of an industrialized attitude to ceramics (which has been demonized by writers from Ruskin and Leach to the craft potters of today), could suddenly cease to exist as a viable force in the modern globalized economy and cease major production within such a short time. It is the elegiac pieces of Neil Brownsword that sing the lament for this culture of skill, born of a division of labour more severe than that of the Lancashire fabric industry commented on by Marx and Engels. Brownsword has created a physical postmodern commentary on that world of skill, manifested in the factories of Stoke. He takes the detritus of the ceramic industry and refashions found objects by reprocessing them wet and then re-firing. The materials derive both from history – he scavenges the waste heaps of Staffordshire, even under his own Stoke garden – and also from the ceramic industry of today (in the form of waste material from forming processes).

OPPOSITE PAGE:
David Jones Raku firing. (Photo: Rod Dorling)

RIGHT: *Neil Brownsword, 'Something so Pure'.*

ABOVE: *Neil Brownsword, 'Salvage Series' (detail). Multi-fired found objects and 'new scrap'.*

BELOW: *Neil Brownsword, 'Salvage Series' (general view). Multi-fired found objects and 'new scrap'.*

His work represents the absence of the worker. It seems to me to be a comment in clay on the 'Unknown Craftsman'. Bernard Leach and his friend Soetsu Yanagi revered the ceramics of the feudal past, in an age before Art and the signing of work, and the associated cult of the artist. Brownsword is drawing attention to the fantastic skills and complexities of creativity in a highly industrialized output. (Wedgwood's factory was the model for 'progress' – the division of labour and exploitation of the worker in the formative Industrial Revolution.) The objects he finds are traces of real human lives; they might be an old teacup lived out in the same soil on which he now lives. By re-firing them, or casting them and re-firing them, Brownsword transforms them into tiny monuments to a lost culture. They become objects that symbolically represent the decay of a once great industry, caused by a lack of investment and the neglect of factory owners and governments.

A placement at the European Ceramic Work Centre in Holland gave the required distance to reflect on home, site and place:

On my return to Holland the poignant impact of these experiences remained omnipresent but difficult to express through making. Whilst unconnected pursuits of material investigations prevailed, this unconscious 'store of knowledge, of place', as critic Pam Johnson suggests, 'was conceptualized through crafting'. Chaotic arrangements of demolished detritus and the discarded began to be externalized through chance forming extraneous waste materials that occurred inadvertently following various periods of making. Flotsam that evolved from transitory moments of deconstruction and disintegration began to be consciously utilized as visual analogies to express the realities of the Potteries' economic and social deterioration.*

---

* Johnson, P., '3Up Close', *Crafts* (November–December 2000, p.54).

David Jones

Fixing Light – Fixing Fire

A biography of longing. This is how one becomes undone –
by a word, a place, the photos of a mountain of shoes.
Anne Michaels, *Fugitive Pieces*.

Throughout my time engaged in research for this book I have created two touring exhibitions that deal with some of the concepts developed here, in an attempt to make an equivalence between theoretical writing and practice. In 2001, after the publication of *Raku – Investigations into Fire*, I created a collaborative, installed exhibition entitled 'Fixing Light – Fixing Fire' with the photographer from the book, Rod Dorling, and designer John Bell. It was based on the idea of Raku, and the associated 'Tea Ceremony'.

In the creation of the show we started by searching for a concept on which to 'hang' the complexities of the physical ceramic world and the in-between world of appearance contributed by the photographs. The bridge/footpath is an essential part of the Zen garden (leading to the Tea House) and joined one part of the garden to another, connecting one idea about nature to the next. It was a powerful image that we employed to suggest a bridge between cultures – a visual and experiential expression of correspondences. It is a symbol that stands for the meeting of three disparate individuals, each employing a separate discipline; it builds associations between histories and cultures. Some links are made to the deep past, to the geology of clay; other images reference the latest inventions of mankind – from the most recent developments in digital photography to the space-age materials employed in kiln design. A bridge carries; for us it became a significant metaphor for the holding together of cultures and ideas – a figurative bridge between concepts.

In the exhibition there are pots that are actually held and supported, floating; there are photographs, hanging beside them, not nailed to the wall but occupying physical space and having volume in the same way as the material ceramics that some of them represent. The bridge concept represents a bringing together of a series of antimonies: East and West, Japan and England, Old World and New World, Europe and America (where Raku was reinvented in the twentieth century), cold and hot, dark and light, physical and the spiritual and *wabi-sabi* (an aesthetic from Zen teaching that suggests value in a beauty that is imperfect, impermanent, or incomplete) as opposed to extreme opulence. For me the bridge aspires to take us from oppositions generated by the particular to more philosophical generalizations.

By suspending the ceramic in the air its essential mass and the sense of the weight, of clay, are denied. It was important to us that we moved away from a conventional plinth-based exhibition and yet maintained the possibility of viewing the pots from all sides. The floating of the vessels on pierced metal plates, strung up with metal wires, emphasizes the total form of the pieces, and suggests a suspension in air. They are there to be grasped and yet their fragility denies this option. (A separate handling area of work was provided for the audience to satisfy this essential urge to clutch, possess and experience the work with the nerves of the fingers.)

The exhibition only floats because it is anchored. This fundamental underpinning to the show is provided by a weighted metal tray suggesting, and echoing, the footpath through the grass in a Japanese Zen garden. It must be of a sufficient weight (nearly 1 ton) in order to hold the wire frame in tension and to keep the pot-holding metal plates under taut control. We used discarded kiln slabs from Ibstock Brick Company, inches thick and burnt brown through repeated firing and excessive build-up of sintered clays. These brought memory traces of firing in the burnt-in colour and worked as a perfect paving slab for our suggested 'Zen Pathway to the Tea House' – a fertile metaphor linking us to the history of Raku in the sand gardens of temples in medieval Japan. The history of Zen is full of journeys – Basho the great *haiku* poet made an extended perambulation to the far north of Japan; it was an actual physical journey but one that he recast as mythopoetic experience. (It was an evocation of the astringency and deserted feel of a lake in winter – *wabi*.) The pathway of kiln slabs leads one through the installation; they lie under the floating pierced metal plates and echo their transparent weightlessness like a dense physical shadow. The rectangular format is also employed by the photographs, which surround the central bridge structure; they enclose it, but allow the gaze to penetrate the large hanging images.

These floating images are arranged to suggest the screen in a cathedral around an altar. The images are taken from a variety of firings. There are images that suggest extreme heat, and these were arranged to hang facing inwards, encircling the ceramics with burning reddish tones; backed onto them were pictures of smoke and Raku firing that were printed to give cooler, bluer hues, suggesting the outer face of the chamber.

The photographs are not in their natural milieu – attached to a wall; instead they are reconsidered as three-dimensional entities (of which they are a representation), though they are actually two-dimensional. In the installation they also create a physical framing device for the ceramic. As we developed the inner circle of coloured photographs it became apparent that the ceramics that I had developed to the point of being a clear signature would not sit comfortably with the images, as they were too colourful. So over the duration of the developmental period of the exhibition I created an evolving series of ceramic wares, each one becoming tonally darker and more sombre as the colour was bled from them, leaving only patches of lustre on the burnt surface. I also developed a treatment with *terra sigillata* that glistened a shiny black when fired with a heavy Raku reduction in dense sawdust.

David Jones, 'Fixing Light – Fixing Fire'
installation. (Photo: Rod Dorling)

ABOVE: *David Jones, 'Fixing Light – Fixing Fire' installation. (Photo: Rod Dorling)*

LEFT: *David Jones, 'Like Skin', Raku-fired. (Photo: Rod Dorling)*

BELOW: *David Jones, double-walled pot, Raku-fired. (Photo: Rod Dorling)*

The interactions with John Bell, the exhibition designer, also induced us to re-evaluate certain outcomes. John's CAD drawings had always had a horizon line so that one could orient oneself in the virtual space. The metaphysical horizon became a real horizon line only as the show took shape. We used an image of the vast man-made hole that is Wheal Martin china clay mines in Cornwall in the UK. This image encircles the dais of pots, which are themselves framed by the screen of hanging pictures. This is profoundly relevant to the installation as the china clay that was extracted from the pit is both a material link and ideational conjunction between my clay and photographic paper, for it is a major constituent of both. The image tries to dislocate any sense of scale experienced within the exhibition – it is the largest object presented to the visitors at the experience of the installation yet is the narrowest in its execution (at only 10in high). It is a 360-degree panorama (created in Adobe Photoshop®) from a number of images; it continues the ceramic reference for it is as if the viewer is standing within a vast

bowl (made of clay) looking out. In its use of the natural environment as metaphor it mirrors the use in the Zen gardens of Japan of elements from their surroundings (like Mt Fuji, imagined in sand). We attempted to subvert this natural association by linking the clay pit to the industrial extraction of clay; in its form the vast hole can also be read as the 'negative space' occupied by Mt Fuji.

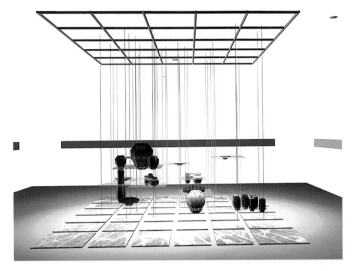

RIGHT: David Jones, 'Durch das Feuer Gehen' installation design, drawn as a CAD image by John Bell.

BELOW: David Jones, large Raku-fired bowl. (Photo: Rod Dorling)

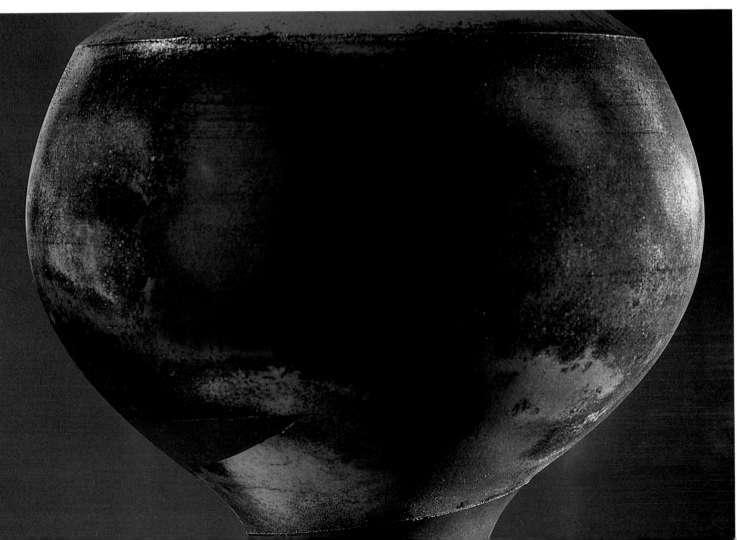

David Jones, 'Durch das Feuer Gehen' installation: ceramics, photographic frieze, video projection. (Photo: John William Bell)

In the material processes of the finishing of the works there are still deeper associations. Rod used silver in the photographic emulsions in the film and I used silver in my glazes. The photograph becomes a permanent image when the finger presses the shutter and exposes the film to light. Raku is about freezing an instant in a firing when the pot is removed from the kiln red-hot, and plunged into sawdust to reduce the oxide in the glaze to pure silver and make the body go black: Fixing Light–Fixing Fire.

Durch das Feuer Gehen

I wished to continue this train of thought and reflection through exhibition and in 2006, with my collaborative team, we presented the next conceptual investigation: *'Durch das Feuer Gehen'* ('Trial by Fire'). This was conceived for a quite different venue – the Keramikmuseum Westerwald –

an enormous ceramics museum in Germany that charts the history of fired clay and provided an opportunity for us to comment on the history and archaeology of ceramics.

I have chosen to use an edited version of a specially commissioned essay by Catherine Bates to provide another perspective on my work – so that in a sense I too stand outside the book and am critically examined. It also shows another way in which language can be used to weave a philosophical and poetic spell and to give an insight into the nature of fire and firing:

It's the difference that you notice first, a way of showing that changes your way of seeing – your way of being, even – for this is an exhibition that takes you back to first principles. Everywhere else in this museum (an entire space dedicated to the showing of ceramics – the dream of potters everywhere) pieces are presented in what has long become the accepted vernacular of ceramic display: spotlights, glass cases, plinths. But in this exhibition the pedestals and vitrines are gone and

ABOVE: *David Jones, Raku-fired vessel, 'Durch das Feuer Gehen'. (Photo: Rod Dorling)*

BELOW: *David Jones, two Raku-fired vessels, 'Durch das Feuer Gehen'. (Photo: Rod Dorling)*

instead the pots hang suspended, heavy yet strangely aerial, held up, supported – cradled, almost – by industrial steel mesh that is strong yet light, the individual pieces not kept apart in pristine isolation but clustered, huddled together as if for warmth (maternal metaphors come to mind). Conspicuous by their absence, the white plinths (that, in their bare minimality, were trying their hardest to disappear, to shrink from your sights and to focus your wandering eyes exclusively on what's on show) are, you now realize, anything but neutral. Laden surfaces, rather; sacrificial altars that offer up their contents to view. And, once turned over to your directed gaze, the pieces that are presented to you thus are conceived of in a very particular way: as exquisite, inviting, seductive, feminine, but at the same time as finished, stilled, cold, closed, frozen in time. As objects. As objects, moreover, that inevitably set you up, that invariably position you as the subject, as the solid bourgeois citizen who is possessed of an appraising, appreciative, and, possibly, an acquiring eye.

How break up that sordid contract? How put viewer and viewed into a different relation? How display pots without the deadness of the reliquary? By turning, this exhibition seems to suggest, to theatre. Or rather – since, pooled in their spots of light, the pieces otherwise conventionally displayed could still be thought of as 'theatrical' – by turning to dramaturgy, a distinction that exhibition designer John Bell, with a background in designing for the stage, insists that we make. For it's not just that the bulbs that illuminate the pieces in this show are never still, the pots constantly moving in and out of the shadows like characters on the stage: we too are drawn in – active participants. Eschewing the balconies and stalls that the museum's multi-levelled, mezzanined space allows for – vantage points from which you might have viewed the exhibits distantly, as through a proscenium arch – the exhibition design rather leads you, guides you in. A photographic frieze on the horizon line – the black-and-white panorama of a Cornish clay pit – takes you down a ramp, round a corner, so that you are no longer the settled subject, complacently looking on, but now a player, or more, perhaps, a neophyte – like the uncertain initiate whose rite of passage it was once the job of the Greek temple to enact, to dramatize, to event: its mystic architecture leading you up its steps, down shafts, along passageways, through labyrinths, confronting you now with dead corners, now with blind walls, until bringing you, disconcerted and blinking, into a bright courtyard lit only by the sky. Revelation.

The very approach to this exhibition is thus experiential, ritualized; and if you've come this far you will already encounter the pots in a different way. With their supports gone, their habitual props kicked away, they hover and float, suspended from above, held up from below, their gravity now made visible and their connection with the ground the question that is newly posed. For that is what this exhibition is really about. Clay cut wet from the soil and fashioned into shape … in myth the world over a metaphor for humankind:

a scoop of soil, a little spit, the breath of the god infused and lo! a creation. Perhaps every potter lives with that legend, but philosophically trained David Jones does so quite consciously, his material malleable, mouldable to the fingers, yet with a wayward grain that still resists and insists on going its own way: a whole theology there. So clay has a familiar feel about it, a deep chthonic connection in which we recognize our bodies and ourselves, a creatureliness, a fleshliness. But it possesses at the same time an otherness, an elemental quality that remains alien and strange – the more so, perhaps, for its ancient familiarity. For when you dig down, deep and dark, you don't know what you are going to drag up, any more than you know what's at the end of the umbilicus, what prodigy or monster is going to be dragged from the womb. As Freud pointed out in a famous essay, the *'Heimliche'* – that which is homely, cosy, warm – also shades off, weirdly, into the *Unheimliche*, into that which is uncanny and sinister, dangerous because hidden away or secreted from view: something once all too familiar but now frightening and strange because forgotten and repressed long ago.

So the potter's material (symbolically extracted from the soil) and the potter's art (his flesh on that flesh, his act of creation, the process by which he brings something to completion, into the light): these will bring with them the shock of discovery, the uncertain experience of finding something that he didn't know but which, strangely, he finds he already knew. These pots, then – Raku-black, austere, matt (against iridescent gleams), their surfaces pitted, and often deliberately cut, gouged, slashed – strain mutely to be understood. But not until the pertinent questioning of an Israeli student would understanding dawn in the maker's mind and the process finally be complete. Not until then would the connection be made with a darker past; between these blackened pots, bearing the imprint of the potter's hands, the last thing to touch them before the fire … and other hands, blackened by fire, bodies damaged beyond repair, unceremoniously piled beside murderous ovens, German–Jewish grandparents, a flight to England, a life of exile, survival, guilt. All known about, and yet not until now known with that uncanny certitude, the unmistakable shock of recognition: the truth embedded in surprise. A finding out that only the act of making made possible, the business of going forward blindly, of not really knowing what your motivation is nor what you are going to unearth. 'No one kneads us again out of earth and clay', wrote Paul Celan, his own identity irreparably broken, traumatized by war: 'no one incants our dust. No one.' Yet this clay speaks, incants on a generation's behalf – and the more piercingly for not being intentionally or consciously voiced.

This exhibition represents, then, a very personal trial by fire, and one that has a particular resonance – a homeliness, indeed – in finding itself housed here in Germany, a country with which the artist is connected now not only by that past but by experiences that are quite different: a conscious, happy, current present of holidays, of a new German family, of professional connections, of a long career as a successful artist in clay. The enigma of survival. And something literal, perhaps, to be found in the prefix of that word … suggesting that we live on but not only in time – living beyond our predecessors, continuing the family line forward – but also in space: as if to survive were necessarily to live on, that is to say to live on top of or over and above what came before, to tread upon a layer of earth that supervenes between ourselves and history, to walk on the bones of the past. That is our ground. And the pots in this exhibition demonstrate our profound connectedness with it. A geological stratum in which embedded memories – collective as well as personal – are brought up from below, specimens that confront us with the past (archaeology was Freud's favourite metaphor for psycho-analysis; and the exhibition's grids and tessellations allude consciously to the techniques used in recording archaeological sites); but a living ground, as well – breathing soil from

which that clay is cut and from which those creatural vessels are shaped, speaking to us in a language that we may not be able to recognize at first but which we can still, in this exhibition at least, strive to understand.

Catherine Bates
(Essay in *Durch das Feuer Gehen* catalogue, Höhr-Grenzhausen, Germany: Neue Keramik, 2006.)

Sebastian Blackie

Sebastian Blackie is profoundly interested in the idea of fire, and things changed by fire, as a means of marking place. He is the author of *Dear Mr Leach*, and his ideas about fire and firing range through Western and Eastern histories.

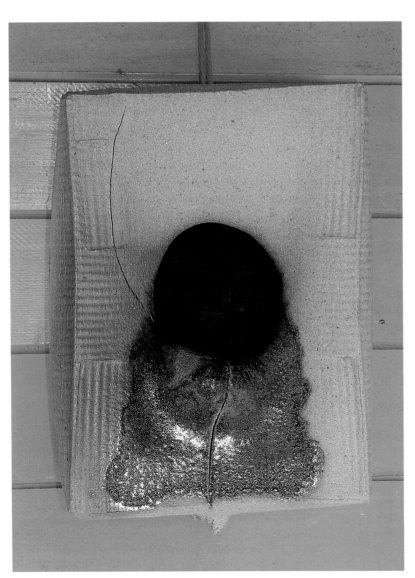

Ceramic artefacts in addition to their more obvious function can be interpreted as signifiers of locus. The Devon harvest jug, for example: its form, scale and decoration are not arbitrary but a function of late seventeenth- and eighteenth-century agricultural practices in that part of England. In due course the industrialization (or at least mechanization) of both agriculture and ceramics rendered their production and use redundant. These jugs reflect the geology of the area. A geology that influences both crops and pots. The combination of red Fremmington clay (apparently imported by an iceberg) and regional cream ball clays gave a contrast that made it possible for local potters to decorate their work with relatively complex graphic images. They are rich and generous as befits its association with harvest. The images of sun and corn celebrate the jug's function – to slake the harvester's thirst. The real and unromantic thirst of insecure back-breaking agricultural labour. A pot made in the same style today may have its value but it is about something else completely. The original jugs are a kind of map by which the past may be located and explored.

During the same period imported porcelain produced a very different ceramic map. A map that traces the values and aspirations of the wealthy. A map that starts in Europe with oriental-inspired designs, exotic fantasies, sent out to be made in China to return, years later as porcelain pots, including, on one infamous but thought-provoking

Sebastian Blackie, 'Urine', charcoal and nappy cleanser on mixed clay stoneware body, press-moulded, reduced, 1280°C, 30 × 23 × 16cm.

occasion, with all the designer's notes faithfully reproduced in the fired decoration. This is a map where the ceramics seem to have no direct relationship to the place in which they reside; nevertheless there is one, and it can give us insight into our contemporary understanding of space and identification.

I enjoy the challenge of working in the discomfort of our complex, often confusing, globalized culture. My current research takes the idea of ceramics as indicator of place and space, as map. The work is, I think, in a tradition by concept if not by appearance. By gathering objects, organic and inorganic, natural and manufactured, found or abandoned from a particular place, I begin to build a body of some kind of evidence. The juxtaposition of objects with one another and contextualization by location suggest narratives that can be intriguing and, at times, disturbing; however, it is the extraordinary transformation that takes place when these things are fired that is for me the fascinating focus. Hidden identities are revealed through fire, traces are left that can be more eloquent and evocative than the original. The horrific and repugnant can become sensually attractive when the evidence is fabricated by heat. It intrigues me that a discarded condom will imprint itself on clay or that shrimps will leave their ghost-like, calcium shells surrounded by a halo of salt glaze when fired. Copper wire will become unstable under heat, volatilizing to draw a beautiful purple loop across the clay's surface, but it is a disturbing beauty when one realizes that the wire had been used as a ligature. Our sense of security is challenged when materials that may seem innocuous before firing such as pleasantly scented nappy cleanser turn into dramatic corrosive glazes.

This approach rejects the traditional use of kilns to complete the process of turning clay into product, controlling the firing to achieve a predetermined result. Here the firing is engaged in partnership to explore an idea. It is the means of asking questions, not a way to give answers. Knowledge of kiln technology and control is required but old habits must be questioned and speed of firing, atmosphere and final temperature are not a given. An understanding of ceramic chemistry will help anticipate how materials behave and may assist in analysing the fired results but the outcome is usually unexpected and thought provoking at a number of levels.

We live in, what may prove to be, a brief period of time where the differences between places seem ever diminished and the vernacular is something of the past. The same technology that

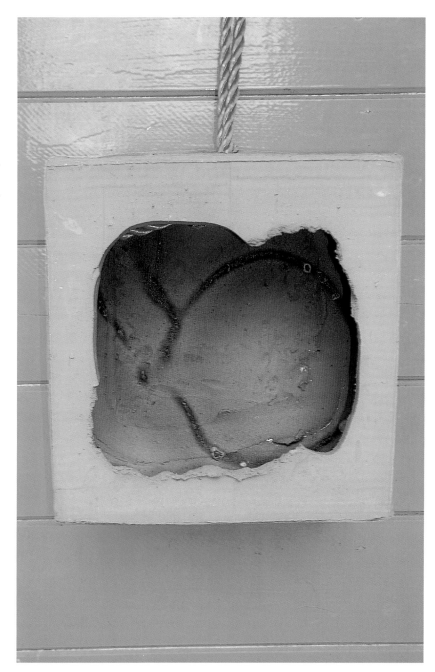

Sebastian Blackie, 'Ligature', electric flex on Sussex brick clay, press-moulded, oxidized, 1000°C, 24 × 24 × 15cm.

allows us to travel to different places transports materials and goods that reduce the contrasts we seek. My research, however, demonstrates that this is too simplistic and that it is the way we look that needs to be different. Under heat, places reveal that particular and distinct identities are sustained. That when the ordinary and overlooked are converted by fire psychological as well as physical space is described. The kiln gives material form to the intangible, it literally fires the imagination.

Sebastian Blackie

17

Site and Fire

*… bonfires and torches of the fire-festivals are to be regarded primarily
as weapons directed against witches and wizards.*

(J.G. Fraser, *The Golden Bough*, ch. 63/3)

The Space and Place
of Fire and Firing

There have been many artists in the last few years who have
identified the possibility of firing to emancipate itself from
ceramics and to become an essential end in itself – sometimes with fired clay objects as a by-product, sometimes
solely with fire at its centre. The knowledge of fire and firing
developed by a potter can be put to other uses, which start
to profoundly question the nature of our contemporary
lives – but also function as pure spectacle in their atavistic
re-creation of primal fire.

The idea of 'place' or 'site' is very important in this context. With the creation of a self-firing structure something
happens once and uniquely. It is an echo of a more 'primitive' 'site' in a society, a sacred space involving a privileged
form of behaviour or a forbidden activity. This is what
Michel Foucault called a heterotopia, to distinguish it from
a utopia (an imaginary site that does not exist):

Heterotopias and heterochronies are structured and distrib-
uted in a relatively complex fashion. First of all, there are heterotopias of indefinitely accumulating time, for example
museums and libraries. Museums and libraries have become
heterotopias in which time never stops building up and
topping its own summit, whereas in the seventeenth century,

even at the end of the century, museums and libraries were
the expression of an individual choice. By contrast, the idea
of accumulating everything, of establishing a sort of general
archive, the will to enclose in one place all times, all epochs,
all forms, all tastes, the idea of constituting a place of all times
that is itself outside of time and inaccessible to its ravages, the
project of organizing in this way a sort of perpetual and indef-
inite accumulation of time in an immobile place, this whole
idea belongs to our modernity. The museum and the library
are heterotopias that are proper to Western culture of the
nineteenth century.

(Of Other Spaces, *Diacritics* 16, spring 1986, pp22–7)

Heterotopias are real places. They are the repositories of
knowledge and information, based on objects, about the
past. For Foucault they are alternative sites that are linked to
the temporal (*chronique*), not the eternal. Not merely are
there special places like museums that are outside of the normal social sphere, but we can also interpret the unique per-
formances, which occur as one-off events or at the festivals of
ceramics, that have developed in recent years in this way.

Playing with fire is fun, and not just a little bit dangerous
(it is quite, as we were warned when we were young). Some
heeded the warning and stayed well away from such a potentially deadly force, but to many of us it appears so very attractive. Allowed to sit up all night and next day and all next
night, when we fire an *anagama*, the stokers keep a roaring
bonfire (albeit a contained one) going for days or even weeks.
It is a wonderful self-indulgence and on an individual level
represents a serious squandering of scarce carbon resources.
If this does not seem slightly crazy in our world, conscious of
global warming and diminishing resources, then there are
still other artists for whom the nature of a result is perhaps

OPPOSITE PAGE: Petra Reynolds and Jeremy Steward firing.
(Photo: Rod Dorling)

Fire is more a social reality than a natural reality.

(Bachelard, *The Psychoanalysis of Fire*, p.10)

no longer seen in terms of a tangible, physical product, but of incandescence itself. They do not even justify themselves in terms of the beauty of the pots from a long firing. They have taken the idea of 'kiln' and expanded it so that it can be an end in itself. Even more atmospheric is the idea of firing as the end experience; this is firing as an aspect of 'Performance Art'.

The kiln as a destination in its own right is an important aspect of much contemporary ceramic activity. Within our ceramics community there is a considerable generosity regarding the sharing of knowledge of skills and experience through the various media of magazines, books, the Internet and workshop demonstrations. The growth and development of the festival aspect of ceramics, where anything between twenty and seven thousand (at the National Council for Education in the Ceramic Arts (NCECA)) individuals can attend a gathering has further stimulated interest in performance. Thus there are potters who have become expert in the articulating of situations, structures and audiences. Firing is now a 'happening'. Firing is an 'event'. These are manifestations that take their cues from sited sculpture (the permanent solid object left after the firing) or architecture (many of these pieces echo buildings with planned openings for the flame to escape). Some are literally windows; others allude to the openings that we traditionally find in homes or ritual buildings. Some of the earliest art created in this field left merely scorched earth when the piece was finished.

Wali Hawes

Wali Hawes was the first ceramic performance artist that I encountered – at a potters' camp in Sherborne in the UK about twenty years ago. I was there with my children while he built and fired a 'Fire Tree' that captivated our imaginations, and continues to be a source of family discussion to this day. It was the way that he generated a sense of involvement that made his work so appealing – a real openness that seemed unavowedly populist and all encompassing.

Hawes has described his work to me as follows:

Firetrees are large tree-like structures made from clay. By throwing wood into the large openings in the trunks and then lighting the fire, light and sparks would shoot out of the open holes of the branches. They created lovely spectacles of light and were a huge hit on the island of Réunion …

This style of performance clay unites several aspects inherent in the ceramic process: clay, forming and fire. Fire becomes part of the whole and is not only a tool to convert clay into ceramics. The kiln, too, becomes a ceramic object, a piece of sculpture totally true to the elements of which it is composed.

His is an art of demystification: all is possible – and permissible. Breaking through the rules of ceramics can be very difficult as there is so much to learn but his experiments with the 'Four Mobile' (the portable wood-fired kiln built in a disused shopping trolley) or the 'Mangagama' (a kiln made out of a pile of Japanese comics) shows how an irreverence of spirit can combine with a deep understanding and respect for the craft and the tradition.

Wali Hawes, fire trees, at Réunion.

Rina Kimche

Rina is a clay artist who has worked for many years in ceramics, not just to evolve a distinctive personal vocabulary, but also within the public sphere, to bring the opposing groups together in her strife-torn land. In her account one can see how the new collaborative actions of firing can work symbolically to create such a community:

The caskets are seen as an illusionary safe, protected, secure space. My first small pinched caskets were more like caves, wombs, very intimate. The later ones were more sophisticated and architectural. The inner void of the caskets is of deep and important meaning for me.

As for the 'Firings': there is a 'Fire for Peace' and a 'Fire for War'. Ceramics is usually, if not always, about Peace.

In 2003 we had, here in Israel, a one-week symposium – 'Fire for Peace'. It took place in the Arabic town of Um El Fahem and the participants were both Arab and Jewish ceramicists. Our guest artist was Nina Hole, from Denmark. We worked and lived together for a whole week. Nina was

conducting work on one of her special constructions to be fired at the end of that week with a big celebration of 'Fire for Peace'. Clay symposia really bring people together, with tolerance and acceptance. Some great friendships develop and good connections are made between communities who are so often portrayed as 'at war'.

Rina Kimche

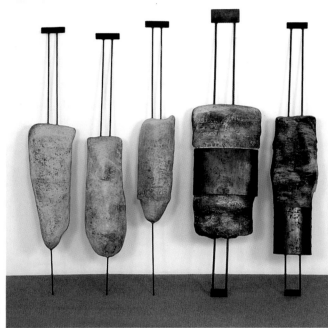

RIGHT: *Rina Kimche, 'Caskets'.*

BELOW: *Rina Kimche, 'Casket'.*

ABOVE: *Nina Hole, 'Fredonia', firing.*

BELOW: *Nina Hole, 'Fredonia', fired.*

Nina Hole

a reverie by the fireside, when the flame twists the frail birch branches, is sufficient to evoke the volcano and the funeral pyre ... the contemplation of fire brings us back to the very origins of philosophic thought.

(Bachelard, 1987, p.18)

Nina Hole is at the forefront of the new movement of building and firing site-specific 'sculpture kilns'. Her new work (that she has completed since I last wrote about her in *Raku – Investigations into Fire*) has moved the issue forward and involved many more public demonstrations and involved new participants in this exciting new departure in ceramics. Her work creates places for 'reverie' and reflection in a fast-moving world as we sit and watch the flames unfold.

John Roloff

A mould for fire, where the fire is cast.

(Roloff, 1990, statement for '51 million BTUs')

The vessels that we travel in, or drink from, can be beautifully designed receptacles for our bodies or our bodily needs; when they are made referentially, stripped of their immediate function, they can stand metaphorically for 'the journey', an allegory of our becoming as human individuals. The philosopher Plato writes of *Chora* – an imaginary space where the ultimate form of a cup, a boat, and so on, reside. *Chora* grounds itself in the ambiguous space between an idea and its material copy; it was Plato's rationale for how we recognize classes or concepts. *Chora* is also a word for receptacle and thus can be considered a metaphor for all containers that carry ideas. We have seen how pots, devoid of utility, can be apprehended as symbols, standing for a wide range of natural effect and human affect, or emotion. The ship, as a symbol for travel and exploration, can also serve this function. ('Humboldt Ship' is part of the series created by John Roloff at the end of the 1980s, and references the great nineteenth-century explorer.)

John Roloff was born in Oregon in the USA; Oregon was at the far end of the journey by Lewis and Clark in their mapping of the Louisiana Purchase for Jefferson in America, or indeed their midpoint – for it was here that they turned round and went home (having discovered and been nearly killed by the Rockies). Oregon stops at the ocean, like California, where Roloff trained and has subsequently lived. The seas of the world are still largely uncharted and imperfectly explored and Roloff's own first studies betrayed a fascination

ABOVE: *John Roloff, 'Earth Orchid', steel, propane, refractory materials, 10m long, 1988.*

RIGHT: *John Roloff, 'Earth Orchid', steel, altered refractory materials, 10m long, 1988.*

with the edge of the world where he had washed up; they were in marine geology, but he re-evaluated his path and graduated from Robert Arneson's ceramic sculpture programme. Water and the sea have been an equal preoccupation alongside fire for Roloff and have provided many of the themes for his improvisations. Roloff was one of the very first artists making fire pieces. He used the newly invented material of ceramic fibre in the creation of huge works.

Roloff understands the language and methodologies of ceramics, but his thinking comes out of a Fine Art/Action/Happening/Performance methodology. His audience is not necessarily that of potters, and his language, although apparently the same, addresses distinctly conceptual issues rather than 'just the making of a self-firing structure':

> The kilns are designed from a knowledge of principals about heat flow, from conceptual ideas, and from an intuitive point of view. The kiln's operation and results are only partially predictable and are allowed 'a mind of their own'. When successful, a firing can approach an irrational point, the verge of losing control, a metaphor is suggested of the unconscious in a primitive or vulnerable state where time becomes emotion, chemistry spirit and matter theatre.

> (Roloff, 1983, p.6)

ABOVE: *John Roloff, 'Humboldt Ship', steel, propane, refractory materials, 4.5m high, 1989.*

RIGHT: *John Roloff, 'Humboldt Ship', steel, altered refractory materials, 4.5m high, 1989.*

BELOW: *John Roloff, 'Oculus', steel, propane, brick, 3m diameter, 1989.*

He has stated that the oceanographic research is still ongoing; his interests reflect the balance between positivistic (scientific) thinking and artistic expression in life. It is an aspect of the way that much thinking proceeds through opposites: Nietzsche makes a distinction between Apollonian and Dionysiac modes of thinking, Jung between the Conscious and the Unconscious, Plato between Idea and Material object. These are dichotomies that are well illustrated in Roloff's work: there is an overlap of material thinking in the disciplines of geology and ceramics that has created a dialectical opposition that has fuelled much of his output. There is evidence of a strong ecological dimension to both enterprises; a scientific methodology cuts some of the flimsy romantic attachment to nature and can home in on the wanton exploitation of the Earth's resources.

The piece '51 million BTUs' is considered as a trilogy composed of three spatially distinct objects, reflecting on the exploitation of fossil fuel reserves by mankind – and by implication in art. It is a piece of Fire about fire and firing. The first 'act' is 'Untitled' (Earth Orchid). He says he was:

> relating to the fire from a geologic, predominantly volcanic, point of view … The firing is the catalyst; it activates the image. It is the culmination for the concept and construction of the piece … the firing creates a kind of memory, both as an intense image in the minds of the people who witness the event and in the alteration of the materials that come into contact with the heat … to get enough pressure for the firing the local gas company had to run a special line to a more remote underground source, the pipe was quite long and went right into the ground … This [botanical] form in both 'Untitled' (Earth Orchid), and in the tree-like flues of 'Humboldt Ship' refers to the original nature of the material in plant form in an ancient forest before it fell into the swamp and became transformed into fuel … [It is probably worth reminding ourselves that Humboldt was one of the great explorers and one of the last 'Renaissance men' who tried to know everything.]

There has always been an alchemical reference in working with flame and Roloff notices the apparent animation by fire: 'The firing reminded me of a lung that was breathing' (Roloff, 1990, statement for '51 million BTUs'). The second element is 'Humboldt Ship' and the third action, 'Oculus' (*see also* page 19), once again betrays an environmental concern 'with the source of heat (propane) used to fire the bathysphere images and its origin in the earth as a hydrocarbon-rich fuel' (ibid.). It represents the eye and the underwater exploration device used to prospect for petrochemical reserves.

The concerns of the artist regarding allegories of change have not shifted radically in recent output, but have developed away from fire as a presence in the artwork; yet fire and energy conversion into plant matter is still a preoccupation. His current work is an intervention in a quarry and focused on deposits of ancient clays, volcanic rocks and lavas.

Tom Barnett

Tom Barnett is a sculptor whose work has now pulled him in a new direction. We have had an ongoing discussion as this book progressed and in response to many of my questions he has written this piece that sums up the various pulls on a creative person as their work develops, influenced by fire.

Stories From the Hearth by Tom Barnett

> We shape our buildings; thereafter they shape us.
> Winston Churchill

In the year 2000 a number of artists, including myself, were invited by the artist–owners of The Islington Mill, Salford, Greater Manchester to look around their building and put forward proposals for site-specific artworks to be exhibited there. They had recently begun to redevelop the five-storey building as a gallery and artists' studio space. Much of it was still unkempt and damp. Many spaces were disused and quite atmospheric – full of junk and old equipment, relics of the varied history of the building. To me it was a wonderful space, rich with potential.

I had a number of initial thoughts for artwork to be installed within the building. I mentioned them to the gallery owners after our tour of the building. One of those suggestions was very specific: I proposed to build during the exhibition a sculpture resembling the Islington Mill building itself and fire it as a kiln for the closing party that had been planned at the end of the exhibition. On mentioning this, the gallery owner's eyes lit up. I elaborated on the idea and, essentially pending a proper written proposal and funding confirmation, I had the go-ahead. We agreed that a damp and enclosed space in a derelict roofless outbuilding was an ideal site. I went off to develop the proposal. It was immensely difficult but turned out to be very successful.

This project was the starting point for a series of firing events exploring similar themes. But what previous experiences and influences had inspired me to conceive this idea for the Islington Mill?

I had worked with performance artist Michael Mayhew. (He organized one-off events that were enigmatic, spectacular and magical.) I had also been in Japan and had helped fire *noborigamas*, and watched others firing *anagama* kilns. I had been entranced by the physicality of the kiln as an object/container. I found the sense of ritual, purpose and community within those people involved with the firing inspiring and warming. The ceramics that emerged from those kilns I respected but cared little for. But I loved this firing process, having previously always fired in an electric kiln. Finally, what perhaps gave me a solid idea of the format in which I wanted to work was seeing stunning images of Danish artist Nina Hole's artwork (*see* page 180 and Jones, 1999). I remember thinking her towering forms that lit up from within as if covered by windows were quite beautiful and unique.

A central element of these firing projects is architecture. I present an interpretation of architectural form (and context), determining the scale, the amount of detail, texture and colour. All of these things have an effect on how something is seen and understood as a sculpture. Too much detail and it becomes 'a doll's house'. Too little and it no longer resembles the building.

ABOVE LEFT: *Tom Barnett, 'Clay Body Incubator', Archie Bray, USA, 2005.*

ABOVE: *Tom Barnett, Bridport, removing ceramic fibre blanket.*

LEFT: *Tom Barnett, 'Energy Centre', Bracknell, 2006.*

BELOW: *Tom Barnett, Bridport, removing ceramic fibre blanket.*

Scale is decided in terms of how much I can physically achieve with however much help I might have and the time I have available. It is usually no taller than an adult. This functions to transform one's perception of the building from gigantic and encapsulating to a human-sized object. As an object it becomes more comprehensible as a physical symbol of the institution it represents. As a symbol it gains further potency when undergoing the firing process.

A number of the buildings that have been my subject matter in these firing projects were originally built during the era of the English Industrial Revolution. When an industrial building becomes a cultural space its function changes from that of producing things to producing ideas and inspiring reflection. The sculpture–kiln event echoes this change. The kiln, traditionally known in ceramics for producing wares, becomes instead a site for reflection and reverie.

This reverie is intended for the transformative creative energy (by analogy inherent in the heat of the kiln), which reflects the energy and life given to the real building when people occupy or use it. The kiln-building then becomes container and vessel and it is the fire that brings its unique form to life. To see a miniature version of the building being constructed – to see it being fired, to see it glowing bold and vivid orange-yellow in the darkness of night – is analogous to the birth and life of the building.

> Energy injects life, processes and transformation into the inanimate world of matter … And thus into the world of architecture. We are accustomed to thinking of the latter exclusively in terms of physical, mute, immutable objects … (yet) … architecture can … be thought of as a transformation of the material environment by changing living beings, an artifact continuously altered by use and circumstance, in constant degradation and repair before the aggression of time, permanently perishing and renewing itself.*
> (Luis Fernández-Galiano, 2000, p.4)

I am dealing with 'the building', 'the kiln' and 'the body'. Each is dependent upon energy to maintain their life. The building is brought to life by human activity. The kiln is brought to life by heat energy (and human activity). The body lives by use of 'endosomatic' energy (the metabolic transformation of food energy into muscle energy). Thermal energy and its maintenance is crucial in all three:

> The fire was the most life-like element of the house: it consumed food and left behind waste; it could grow and move seemingly by its own will; and it could exhaust itself and die. And most important it was warm, one of the most fundamental qualities that we associate with our lives. When

the fire dies, its remains become cold, just as the body becomes cold when a person dies. Drawing a parallel to the concept of the soul that animates the physical body of the person, the fire, then, is the animating spirit for the body of the house.**

Constructing a sculpture of a specific building (often in a very public place within a town or city) provides an opportunity to discuss the building with the public. These discussions often range from what the building was once used for, to what it could be used for, or whether it is being used effectively, who uses it, how it looks, or how it could be used. In other words the sculpture becomes a site for discussion. Quite often stories are told, memories brought out, opinions aired. This may or may not lead on to the science or the poetics of the firing but it delineates a space for reflection and conversation.

It is these 'non-art' communities that are really interesting to meet because those engaged by the piece might not ever have stepped into a gallery, perhaps having specific opinions about art and artists. It is an opportunity to dispel myths, to engage, and to create. In some projects I have taken this engagement to its next logical step and invited people to make something to be fired with the kiln. The firing process and ritual event becomes a group activity – and the 'belonging' of the artwork stretches beyond my own hands.

The drawing together of people to witness the event is echoed on a smaller scale with the gathering of people's artworks to be fired within the kiln. Some people take away memories. Others take their artworks. The kiln acts as a terminal for creative exchange. For me this is where the real creative energies of kiln-artworks lie.

Tom Barnett

Neville Assad Salha

> All really inhabited space bears the essence of the notion of home … the sheltered being gives perceptible limits to his shelter. He experiences the house in its reality and in its virtuality, by means of thought and dreams.
> (Bachelard, G., *The Poetics of Space*, trans. Maria Jolas (Beacon Press, 1994, p.5)

Neville Assad Salha was born in Australia; his parents were born in Lebanon. The concepts of 'place' and 'space' are

---

* Interestingly, Luis Fernández-Galiano goes on to state that that fire itself can be seen as architectural in that it defines a thermal space with its heat.

** Lisa Heschong, *Thermal Delight in Architecture* (MIT Press, 1979), p.72.

central to an understanding of his work. His work utilizes vessels (references to containers traditionally used for food), buildings (containers traditionally inhabited by live bodies) and coffins (containers inhabited by dead bodies):

> My work over the past twenty years has placed a strong emphasis on cultural exchange and diversification between the Middle East and Australia. Many of my concerns appear in the tension between a first-generation Middle Eastern living in an anglicized country.
>
> Works produced over this period of time have covered a broad spectrum in the use of clay – from the functional to the more conceptual with the interest of understanding space and the use of it, becoming a diagram not of what space is, but what it represents. This then takes me to looking at the outer perimeter of the objects produced and the outline that they can represent (crossover of cultural exchange).
>
> Many of these forms end up representing dwellings of some sort – places of birth, living and death. At this stage, transferring my place of living to the Middle East (to take up a post teaching ceramics at the American University in Beirut) may change the scale and representation of the architectural forms that I will make.

The detail of his work is Australian: 'The Australian landscape holds much of my attention as it gives a sense of strong tonal qualities along with the mark-making and shadows recorded from this landscape'. The forms of his ceramics

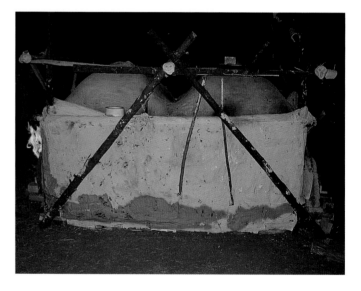

draw on the oriental part of his psyche – they are reminiscent of objects that enclose space for transformation that we might consider to be a dwelling for the afterlife; he titles them: 'Cocoon, Mummy, Sarcophagus' and they also include vessels like the 'Middle Eastern water-carrying forms, along with funery containers'. The work is very attentive to the architectural environment and his pieces manifest a sense of scale, whether they are of human size or small objects. He has often used an icon of architecture in order to mediate his ceramics, and is particularly fond of the religious building with a double cupola, which he has constructed both at large scale and for a plinth. Such a building is a space for reflection and for contacting the infinite, it is 'the container of thought' and as such the pieces work as a 'visual diary to memory'.

His work is a meditation on dualism and duality; it is a reflection on here and there, the two sides of 'The Green Line' (dividing areas of Beirut), this life and the next, caterpillar and butterfly. These twin-domed pieces also have the comforting appearance of breasts; they appear to be a nurturing form, a feeling that is fundamental to Assad Salha's

work. The large self-fired structure, made and assembled for the Clay Modern Symposium at Gulgong in Australia, is a piece about a building containing fire: the flames suggests inspiration and the word of God; it suggests fire acting as comforter and as a transformative force. In 2006, with Lebanon again a site not of home but of conflagration, the piece, symbolic of Middle Eastern shrines, made and fired with joy, good humour and mutual understanding in Australia, seems sadly prophetic.

Jørgenn Hansen

Jørgenn Hansen started his work creating self-firing structures in collaboration with his fellow Dane, Nina Hole. He now works with teams drawn from the locality and builds and fires structures in many countries; he is particularly concerned to elicit the historical and social resonance of the works:

> I use the firing to make the strength and the story in the piece come out. The firing can give life to the piece and the variations and traces add to its story. A work is like a shot of a camera. It needs developing – and only the right choice of technique can make the work visible … My sculptures often relate to modern buildings.
>
> (Hansen, statement for '*Verwandlungskreis*' ('Circle of Transformation'), Berlin, 2002)

ABOVE: *Jørgenn Hansen firing 'Verwandlungskreis'.*

BELOW: *Jørgenn Hansen, 'Verwandlungskreis' firing.*

RIGHT: *Jørgenn Hansen, 'Verwandlungskreis' after firing.*

The conjunction of ancient and modern are important aspects in the work, easily understandable and attracting the viewer's interest because of the obvious relation to the surroundings and its history.

In Berlin my work was juxtaposed with three building sites with big cranes and scaffolding all around us. The Springer building was behind, square and glassy; it has for years been the symbol of German conservatism (Morgenposten and Bild)! My work in front was like a gypsy thing happening at the building's foot – on the other side of the former Wall. They did not like the project. The newspaper *Morgenposten* three times had journalists talk with me and take photos, only they never made an article. But the morning after the glowing, on the night of the open museums in Berlin, there was a very beautiful picture on the front page of the *Berliner Zeitung*.

The name '*Verwandlungskreis*' refers to the history of the site and to its future. Berlin is fast changing. The sculpture was a metaphor in the way, that time, life, is a ring. The outer ring is more open and not at all solid, as the inner is. When the outer ring breaks down, the inner will still stand unbroken as a symbol that some things are stable. It was ordinary, simple, primitive, and elementary in its form and in its construction methods. I wanted something extremely simple to be able to relate to the complex reality.

A lot of fire was here during the war. From pictures I knew what it looked like. And I knew that not long after being made my sculpture would also be in ruins. But at the same time I wanted to show that through fire, transformation is achieved – that I know from my kilns and we know it from history. The flames bring a new story like the bird Phoenix. I like the picture of a scarred eucalyptus tree amid completely new green trees in an Australian forest. That's what my projects are about: time and change.

The firing is particularly spectacular – and easy to understand for the audience. I like the movement there is in the fire. You feed the wood, you wait, smoke, smoke disappears, the temperature rises, you feed again, and so on. The fire is demanding that you follow its rhythm, like the clay demands that you do not pile more than a certain amount up, and that you do not fire too fast and so on. The audience feels these demands and it adds to the intensity of the play. And I use the look of the flames in the picture of the burning sculpture. In '*Verwandlungskreis*' I had eleven fireboxes and eleven holes on the top. With certain intervals first smoke then red flames appeared and then disappeared. The audience follows this closely. Also, with the work with the wood, the preparation and the splitting and the carrying, I make part of the spectacle. I am making a drama out of the creation of a play and a sculpture. In my last work 'Displacement' in Reykjavik in August 2006, I used the melting of clay to intensify the drama of the performance and to affect the shape of the work.

Jørgenn Hansen

Peter Lange

Peter Lange goes through life tangentially. He has approached the firing of ceramics with a slight disregard for traditional kiln structures. But underneath the showman's jolly smile there exists the sort of teacher who you always wanted in school, who communicates a lesson in such a mad and enjoyable way that you were never aware that you were learning. Peter teaches that anything is possible and everything should be risked in crazy endeavour. When the medicine show swings into town and disgorges him to an assembled audience there is a palpable feeling of excitement – for he knows how to play us and our emotions as well as having a brilliant understanding of kilns such that he can totally subvert those conventions. I have met him at potters' gatherings in the UK and Australia, and he has delighted the audiences with his reverentially irreverent attitude to clay and firing.

I was so impressed at watching his 'Mazdagama' that we emailed for months and he finally sent this document, which answers all my carefully considered general set of questions (which I had posed as a set of headings to all contributors, point by point).

Kiln/Firing

This method of firing produces random effects, similar to a pit-firing but with the added surprises that result from the pots being placed in places like the glove box, on the spare wheel and so on. Repeated firings may well establish which part of a Mercedes (and which model) will give the best effects. With the wood, sawdust, fireworks, salt, electric wiring, upholstery and stuff that's fallen down the back of the seat all having an effect, it is a bit of a lottery as to which pots will be blessed by the kiln gods and/or St Christopher.

The interior reaches about 800°C. It is certainly hot enough to cause the windscreen to melt and run all over the steering wheel and when the tyres burst (over-inflating the tyres is helpful here) you know that the firing's pretty much done. The atmospheric conditions vary wildly but it became clear, after the first carload came out a little pallid, that to maintain the reduction so carefully nurtured during the firing there needed to be a bit of effort put into reduction cooling, so at the end of the firing the interior of the car was filled with grass picked on the spot from the paddock and the windows covered with fibre.

The spectacle, so often seen on telly, of a car bursting into flames and burning out in minutes is to be avoided. It will produce only oxidized and broken pots. The best firing will take a couple of hours, and progression from the rear hatch

ABOVE: *Peter Lange, 'Mercedes Mazdagama', loading.*

BELOW: *Peter Lange, 'Mercedes Mazdagama', the firing.*

ABOVE: Peter Lange, 'Mercedes Mazdagama', the 'kiln' after firing.

BELOW: Peter Lange, 'Mercedes Mazdagama', 'The fired driver'.

through to the front of the kiln will be slow; windows should explode at decent intervals to keep the spectators on their toes, and carefully-placed rockets will do the same.

The choice of kiln is based on the current market for used cars, and it may not always be possible to find a Mercedes, but it must be said the quality of the fired pots was a lot higher than with either the Mazda or the Holden. It might be best to avoid the models with airbags unless a way could be found to inflate them with LPG (liquefied petroleum gas).

Kiln Plan

Look in the glove box – the manual might be helpful here.

Tradition

This technique developed from a New Zealand tradition of local lads stealing your car on a Saturday night and torching it. It only requires the additional effort of filling it full of biscuited pots before leaving it outside your house.

Materials

The same as for any pit-firing: open-body robust clay, oxides, seaweed, old computers, but most important … fireworks.

Health and Safety Issues

Are any resulting fatalities to be registered against motor vehicle statistics or art and craft statistics?

The Ice Kiln

The Ice Kiln is designed for all of us who would like to see what is going on in a kiln in an increasingly absurd world.

Peter Lange

BELOW: *Peter Lange, 'The Ice Kiln', made from blocks of ice, ceramics and fireworks.*

BELOW LEFT: *Peter Lange, 'The Ice Kiln', made from blocks of ice, ceramics and fireworks. Firing.*

BOTTOM: *Peter Lange, 'The Ice Kiln', made from blocks of ice, ceramics and fireworks. The end.*

18

The Denial of Fire

While concluding the writing of this book I had the pleasure of visiting the installation 'Fragile Ecologies' by Elizabeth Stanek, Andrée Singer Thompson and Valerie Otani at the NCECA, Portland in the USA. I was fascinated by the concept that nothing was fixed through firing in their collaborative exhibition because of the absence of fire from the installation – they were adamant about the impermanence of the exhibit. This allows us to focus on our obsession with leaving a 'Grecian urn' long after we are dead, to memorialize ourselves, and starts to interrogate the nature of firing through its absence. Heating, as distinct from firing, was evident in the exhibit – but it allows clay to return to its former nature through physical as opposed to chemical transformation. Yet the idea of firing was never far from one's thoughts as the concept of 'global warming', brought about by the over-exploitation of petrochemical and other carbon reserves, was the focus of the installation, forcing us to focus on the nature of firing and the contributions of ceramicists to this problem, therefore a fitting reflection on this survey of firing.

'Dust to Mud – Mud to Dust'

The first question of course was, how to get dry again.
Lewis Carroll, *Alice in Wonderland* (ch. 3)

This story of the rising levels of a sea (of tears) received an answer, not merely in the frustration of leading environmental activists over a failure to engage with the dangers of global warming, nor just within the pages of *Alice in Wonderland*, but more recently in the installation exhibit 'Fragile Ecologies'.

In this exhibit clay enters as an active, mutable and changeable player. The voice of clay is heard initially within the ground as a result of millions of years of geology. It is a history that commenced in lava flows that cool and crystallize; this symmetry in the rocks is finally eaten by hot gases venting from the earth's core and they become feldspars (the major ingredient in glazes used to create the shiny coat worn by many stoneware pots). These feldspars are washed in the acid rain of the Earth's early ecosystem; as the soluble metal salts are washed out, clay remains.

In the 1960s chemist Graham Cairns-Smith of the University of Glasgow proposed the 'clay–life' theory, which challenged the long-favoured notion that life emerged from the primordial oceans after millions of years of chemical reactions between simple organic molecules. His theory suggested that life evolves with clay; that it forms a crystalline basis on which the 'primal soup' is catalysed and amino acids form, and it also occurs much more quickly as a result. (It was also suggested that the receptivity of the lung lining to silicates and clay structures is what creates their carcinogenic potential.) Stories that link us to clay of course predate these hypotheses; the mythic fashioning of humankind from clay can be found in stories from all over the world, testifying to clay's fluency in speaking form. Clay's own experience as an actor on its own stage is the focus of this exhibition.

Instead of resorting to the history of forms derived from millennia of use as containers, or to the imitation of the living world, clay is used to stand for itself, to stand for (the) Earth. The artists are dealing with a simple vocabulary of dryness and wetness, of form and its erosion, of a becoming and an annihilation. (But one in which the (informed ceramic) audience also knows that out of that destruction can arise new formations.) A mountain is represented by two conical heaps of dust – one of bentonite and one of ball clay, placed in a perspex vitrine. The piles are not isolated from the audience but are open at the top; as we approach the exhibit it jerks to life – we literally impinge on its fragile state of being.

OPPOSITE PAGE: David Jones Raku firing.
(Photo: Rod Dorling)

A photoelectric sensor, activated by our approach, triggers a valve that allows the ingress of water via transparent, plastic tubing into the environment, and slowly, through the short history of the exhibit, it transforms itself. The 'sea level' metaphorically rises and slakes the powdery deposits of clay. The first time that I saw the installation it was quite fresh and the water was just beginning to surround the 'clay castle', and, like a child's creation on the sea-shore, it was starting to be eroded until we could foresee that there would be nothing left but a pile of sludgy mud. However, in one corner of the piece, the mud (that had been wetted in testing) was now desiccated flaking platelets and was once more about to be inundated – a cycle like life. I saw powerful parallels with a hospital – the sick patient hooked up to juddering technology; Andrée Singer Thompson commented that it was one of the 'unexpected surprises' of the piece that it could throw up such an allusion.

The other elements of the installation followed a similar rule of display and activity and were in the classical vitrine of a gallery show, yet undercutting the assumptions of such a model through the denial of anything to take home or to enter a museum collection except experience. It was a spectacle born of the theatre, and the vitrines acted like a proscenium arch to separate spectators from the action. It was also reminiscent of the experiments of a surreal scientist – giant Petri dishes laid out for our examination, as bizarre tests took place. Elizabeth Stanek says, 'I don't see this as such as object-oriented work – it's more about setting up systems.' The script for the performance is written but instead of there being a strict time-based process we are party to 'an action'. As Lewis Carroll described it, 'they began running when they liked, and left off when they liked, so that it was not easy to know when the race was over' (Carroll, *Alice in Wonderland*, ch. 3).

Like Alice's Caucus Race in *Wonderland*, our experience of the exhibit starts just when we feel like intervening, by our presence in proximity to the 'experiments'. Just like Alice's race it is eventually 'very drying' and some of the pieces lose their wetness. Thus a clay slip is dried out, as we walk towards it, by our triggering an overhead heat lamp, and the clay curls (and the artists have noticed its affinity to a wet natural phenomenon; it is entitled 'uplifted wave'). All around the exhibit is a clicking and sighing as water trickles into the vitrines; fans whirr, creating drying winds; or the heat lamps switch on as someone starts another part of the race and gets too close, thus activating further 'ecological' change.

Thus clay in its many states is taken as the symbol of the material that is acted upon by human presence in the environment. We cease to be the actors, and, cleverly stage-managed by the artists, we become instead the audience, merely observing the effects of our presence within this microcosm of the Earth. Powerful parallels appear with the issues of global warming and climate change. In the context of the opening address at NCECA this exhibit provided a visceral, artistic and experiential counterpoint to the speech made by David Suzuki, urging an intelligent response to global warming (*see* www.davidsuzuki.org). Both speech and art exhibit were exhortations to action. The speech was a declamatory call to change human behaviours; the artists' response more measured and cooler than the impassioned address by the environmental warrior. As Stanek says of the work: 'It certainly makes no attempt to directly impact specific issues or

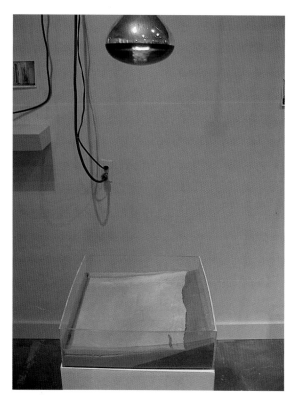

Elizabeth Stanek, Andrée Singer Thompson and Valerie Otani, heat lamp and drying clay.

Elizabeth Stanek, Andrée Singer Thompson and Valerie Otani installation. (Photo: David Jones)

Elizabeth Stanek, Andrée Singer Thompson and Valerie Otani, uplifted wave. (Photo: Elizabeth Stanek)

to have a political impact, but rather attempts to create an experience which might lead people to consider their responsibility in a very general way' (author's personal correspondence). Theirs is a very powerful statement made out of material rather than just ideas. It acts as a poetic corollary to Suzuki's analysis of an atmosphere overloaded with carbon dioxide and its implications not just for potters but for the entire human race.

As an exhibit it reversed the normal trope of art creating order out of chaos; the carefully fashioned and burnished balls of clay (representing the accretion of time and acculturated practice) slake down to amorphous, primordial sludge – mountains dissolve and rivers disappear. To compensate there were mechanically induced objects of beauty familiar from a thousand photographs of dried-up lake beds as the slip, under a heat lamp, dried to a shiny skin that curled as it contracted away from the coarser clay beneath. It acts as a physical and metaphorical correlate to underscore the nightmare description verbally evoked by Dr David Suzuki.

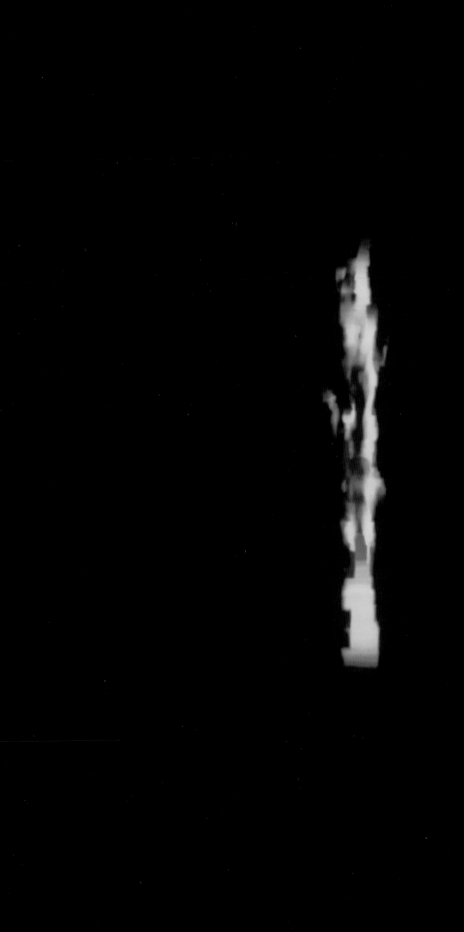

19

1887: A Conclusion

Fire and heat provide modes of explanation in the most varied domains, because they have been for us the occasion of unforgettable memories, for simple and decisive personal experiences.

(Bachelard, *The Psychoanalysis of Fire*, p.7)

Contemporary ceramics is now torn between the magnetic pull of two artistic giants of the last century (both incidentally born in the same year: 1887). Bernard Leach and Marcel Duchamp could not have represented more polar opposites in terms of their thinking. Yet we can use them to explore the modes of thinking that inform firing and to develop a philosophy of firing for the twenty-first century.

Leach's absolutist philosophy of ceramics was informed by his Eastern Baha'i faith (a belief system that recognizes all religions as having access to the one god). His writings encapsulated a belief in order, perfection and beauty; he proposed a hierarchical canon of quality, which saw Chinese Song dynasty ceramics as the zenith of creativity in clay. Duchamp, on the other hand, is renowned for his iconoclasm in the placement of a urinal in an art exhibition. It is also maintained that he was responsible for the postmodern egalitarianism/'dumbing down' in the art world, by shifting the emphasis to the spectator. Duchamp recognized the importance of the viewer, critic and audience in formulating assessments of value, and this position acts as a useful balance to Leach's zeal as a proselytizer for a very particular kind of ceramics.

Leach emphasized the improvement to the maker through doing, and the role of the potter as moral being, and by default he canonized himself in the role of the purveyor of wisdom (the philosopher–saint). Duchamp emphasized the

role of the artist as a privileged figure, able to make ascriptions of quality and definition that are as a philosopher dealing with language. In a lecture in America towards the end of his life Duchamp once more elucidated a position that can be seen to be very significant to us, as potters firing kilns – or indeed having kilns fired for us. In his lecture entitled 'The Creative Act', given at the Museum of Modern Art, New York on 19 October 1961, Marcel Duchamp states that, 'the personal "art coefficient" is like an arithmetical relation between the unexpressed, but intended, and the unintentionally expressed'.

As potters we talk at length about 'kiln gifts': accidental qualities, noticed and searched out, effects for which we try to plan but only rarely achieve. It is an awareness that sometimes the work can come out of the kiln better than it went in. We too are trying to effect a balance between intended results and unconscious and the unforeseen results that can make or mar a piece. And all of this can be in the eye of the beholder. The audience is the final arbiter that tells us whether the fall of ash on a rim was fortuitous or a disaster. Leach used the mysticism of his own religious beliefs to see the range of accidents as god-given blessings to the work; Duchamp perceives a more modern interpretation of phenomena and an interplay between conscious and unconscious manifestations.

The contrast is great between the product of fifteen days of hard personal endeavour in planning and executing a firing and the 'readymade' – the mass-produced item, removed from the warehouse shelves and turned into another object that will be fetishized by art audiences. Leach always recognized the importance of the moral dimension to labour and believed, indeed like the early Karl Marx, that work, at its

OPPOSITE PAGE: Heat seen down the length of Ibstock Brick tunnel kiln. (Photo: Rod Dorling)

best, could be ennobling. It is a sentiment that permeates much thinking in ceramics today as we listen to colleagues retelling their epic struggles with a massive kiln.

Duchamp's thinking is expressed in a highly poeticized form and might be seen to be very close to the position of Leach when he says: 'the artist acts like a mediumistic being who, from the labyrinth beyond time and space, seeks his way out to a clearing' ('The Creative Act' lecture, New York, 1961). We recognize the idea of the artist-as-shaman, acting as a go-between to enable the coming into being of something else – a new way of thinking about the everyday and enabling something magic to enter our consciousnesses. That sense of magic surrounding the act of firing and the fired, transformed object is at the heart of much of the everyday transactions concerning fired ceramic, and is a phrase that has been uttered by many of the contributors to my quest for a better understanding of the nature of 'the fired'.

Roland Barthes, in his examination of the everyday, demonstrates that signs can be seen to carry a rich nexus of meaning that was not conceived by the original maker of the image or text. We can read into objects, and the desire to possess them, a range of meanings that is hard to fathom on the surface but, on closer examination, reveal their true nature in establishing power relationships between the owner, the maker and the audience. What, then, is the significance, or importance, of the fired object? In it we can experience not merely the travails of the maker fashioning from 'base' clay but also the burning and transformation effected by the kiln. Our first experiences are those of sensual pleasure or disgust as our hands and eyes take in the surface of the pot. At an exhibition one can see many people placing a fired object that has no useful purpose to their lips, merely to expose it to the high concentration of nerve endings (or in an unconscious gesture governed by millennia of pottery usage).

Firing is a *liminal* activity – it sets a boundary that is crossed by the clay after being transformed in the kiln; it can no longer retrace its steps to mud and it has become part of our 'civilized world'. It can act as a metaphor for our own transition from one state of being, understanding or awareness, to another.

In the past pots always had *function* as an end point of reference. Contemporary non-utilitarian ceramics and fire structures are difficult to decipher, as many of the signs encoded in their form and surface do not have word-based equivalences. In the West ceramics has been a medium mainly of useful items, a low-status enterprise that has attracted few critics, and thus very few writers have emerged to understand the expressive nature of the object and to develop a language in which to do so.

The pristine surface of a porcelain bowl or the cracked and peeling exterior of a sited wood-fired sculpture bring a complex of associations with them that are not merely to do with a learned appreciation of ceramic technologies but are also to do with our reading of them as 'texts'. These interpretations can be more akin to a psychoanalytic reading. I have noted many reports of feelings associated with masculinity and the heroic – the endurance aspect of long, hard firing. Indeed, how many times have potters confided in me, almost misty-eyed, the pleasure of bending really high cones – and we buy into that celebration in our appreciation of the crusty brown and burnt surfaces, celebrating the macho values that hark back to a chivalric code where men pitted themselves against dragons.

This view of the heroic as earthy and natural goes back to the source of Leach's thinking in the British Arts and Crafts Movement, championed by John Ruskin. The latter's rejection of modernism, particularly as exemplified by the industrial age, sees itself recast in the dichotomy between town and country seen in mid-twentieth-century ceramics. The more recent return to truly archaic modes of firing (for example, using Japanese or African techniques of a thousand years ago) is seen by some as a Romantic excess. But we do really need this aspect of male heroism in present-day society. It represents a true link to the recent past in the industrialized West when most men in the population did 'real' manual labour. Furnace working, steel smelting, glassmaking, industrial ceramics – now (in the West) these are almost all a memory trace of lost generations. (Of course one of the great developments in recent ceramic practice is that it has opened up these worlds to women as well.) *Anagama*-firing recapitulates some of the excitement and danger of those lives and keeps the archetype of fire alive in a culture that no longer has very much connection to the primitive call of fire beyond the summer barbecue (which is, of course, also a haven for lost masculinity).

The concept of *chora*, an idea dealing with real and imaginary place or site and its ancillary meaning as receptacle, brings, as Kristeva has noted, overtones of the feminine into the philosophy of firing. She talks of a prelinguistic site inhabited only by the primitive drives that make us human. Buying a pot marked by real fire is a way of buying into that myth of an ancient past composed of polarities explained by the gods. There is a melancholy in this referencing of older worlds, of a power and fear exerted by fire, on our still primitive souls. At its most profound we are, when firing or holding a piece of ceramic, in contact with a primal history, and, in the words of Yeats:

changed, changed utterly:
A terrible beauty is born.

(W.B. Yeats, 'Easter 1916')

The poem [or pot] is thus the veil which makes the fire visible, which reveals it precisely by veiling and concealing it ... because it detains in the dark that which can only be revealed in the light of darkness and keeps this mystery dark, even in the light which the dark makes the first dawn of all.

(Blanchot, 1982, p.230)

Glossary

Absorbed: Taken in or soaked up by chemical or physical action.

Adsorbed: Held as a thin film on the surface of a material.

Anagama: Japanese word for a single-chambered kiln built on a slight incline.

Ash: The mineral left over after a material has burnt. It contains many alkaline (metal) materials that react with the silica in the clay to make a glaze.

Bag wall: A structure in the kiln to protect the ware from the direct impingement of the flame.

Bisque firing: First firing, which turns the clay to a 'biscuit-like' hardness. This is a compromise to changing clay to ceramic, making it hard enough to handle and glaze easily whilst remaining sufficiently porous to accept the glaze.

Carbon trap: A glaze that seals in soot, trapping it while the glaze is liquid.

Celadon: A stoneware glaze that fires green, grey or bluish. It commonly contains between a quarter and 2 per cent iron oxide.

Ceramic fibre: A low-density material made by extruding alumina- and silica-based compounds into a vacuum, used as an insulating material in kilns.

Conduction: The process by which heat is directly transmitted through the material of a substance when there is a difference of temperature between adjoining regions, without movement of the material.

Cone: A mix of materials that always melts at a given temperature, formed into a pyramid and placed in the kiln to measure the heat-work. The cone always bends once it has experienced a specified level of heat-work.

Convection: The movement caused within a fluid or gas by the tendency of hotter and therefore less dense material to rise, and colder, denser material to sink, resulting in the transfer of heat.

Crash cooling: Where a sudden drop in temperature from the highest temperature is achieved – by removing spyhole covers or opening the damper, stoke holes, and so on. Useful for creating a sudden late oxidation for the ceramics in order to give a clear glaze surface.

Damper: A movable item (a brick, a kiln shelf, a piece of metal or similar) in the base of the chimney to restrict flow of gases out of the kiln. The damper is pushed in to achieve reduction.

Dunting: Cracking in the clay body occurring on rapid cooling in a kiln.

Earthenware: Pottery fired at low temperatures to a porous state that can be made impervious to liquids by the use of a glaze.

Element: A term used by both chemists and ceramicists. The chemist defines an element as the simplest, most pure and indivisible material capable of participating in a chemical reaction. A potter will use the word to refer to the electrical heating wire or rod within a kiln.

Engobe: A semi-vitreous slip (in composition between a slip and a glaze, it can be considered to be clay with some glaze materials added).

Flame path: The direction taken by the fire through the pack in a fuel-burning kiln.

Flashing: The halo effect on ceramic from where the flame has passed.

Flashpoint: The temperature at which a particular organic compound gives off sufficient vapour to ignite in air.

Flux: A substance mixed with a solid to lower its melting point, used to promote vitrification in ceramics.

Fly ash: The very finest component of inorganic material produced by burning wood, which deposits furthest through the pack of ware in the kiln.

Glaze: a glassy layer fused onto the surface of the ceramic.

Grog: Crushed unglazed pottery or brick.

Heat sink: A device or substance that absorbs excess heat.

Heat-work: The word used to describe the measurement of the changes that have been effected on a clay or a glaze. It is a function of a combination of effects: temperature, duration of the firing, kiln atmosphere, volatiles in the kiln, and so on.

Low-temperature salt firing: Firing at approximately 1100 °C with sawdust, salts and reactives around the ware (*see* Jones, 1999).

Neutral firing: the atmospheric condition in an electric kiln that is neither oxidizing nor reducing.

Noborigama: Japanese word used to describe a multi-chambered climbing kiln.

Oxidation: A chemical reaction with oxygen/burning.

Phases: A term that implies different physical characteristics of the same chemical.

Plastic memory: The strange quality of violently deformed clay to move itself back to that position after firing even if the damage looks like it has been undone.

Porcelain: A clay body that is formulated to be white and translucent after firing at temperatures in the range of 1250 °C to 1400 °C.

Radiation: The emission of heat/energy as electromagnetic waves or as moving subatomic particles.

Raku firing: A firing process involving the removal of the red-hot ware from the kiln and subjecting it to a variety of treatments (*see* Jones, 1999).

Reduction: A reaction taking place in the absence of oxygen.

Refractory: Having a high melting point, resistant to heat.

Saggar: A fire-proof container to exclude or contain vapours that will mark the body of the clay.

Salt: Sodium chloride.

Salts: A product of reaction by a metal and an acid. (In ceramics we tend to use soluble versions of metals for creating vapours, such as cobalt nitrate for example.)

Sawdust firing: Setting the ware in a pile of sawdust and burning it to effect a surface pattern of black and natural clay colour (*see* Jones, 1999).

Slip: an homogenous mix of clay and water.

Soak: Maintain a temperature in the kiln without deviation in order to smooth-glaze or to burn out carbonaceous materials.

Stoke hole: Aperture for feeding in wood to a kiln.

Stoneware: Pottery fired at high temperature, which is impermeable and partly vitrified but opaque.

Temmoku: A stoneware glaze that fires black, brown or purplish. It commonly contains 10–20 per cent iron oxide.

Temperature: The measurement recorded by the pyrometer.

Bibliography and Further Reading

Ceramics

Barley, N., *Smashing Pots. Feats of Clay from Africa* (London: British Museum Press, 1994)

Blackie, S., *Dear Mr. Leach* (London: A&C Black, 2004)

Caiger-Smith, A., *Lustre Pottery* (New York: New Amsterdam Books, 1991)

Cardew, M., *Pioneer Pottery* (London: Longman, 1969)

Duchamp, M., 'The Creative Act', *Art and Artists* (July 1966)

Fernández-Galiano, L., *Fire and Memory (On Architecture and Memory)*, trans. Gina Cariño (Cambridge, MA: MIT Press, 2000)

Gregory, I., *Kilnbuilding* (London: A&C Black, 1977)

Gregory, I., *Alternative Kilns* (London: A&C Black, 2005)

Hamer, F. and Hamer, J., *The Potter's Illustrated Dictionary of Materials and Techniques* (London: A&C Black, 2004)

Heeney, G., *Brickworks* (London: A&C Black, 2003)

Jones, D., *Durch das Feuer Gehen* (Höhr-Grenzhausen, Germany: Neue Keramik, 2006)

Jones, D., *Raku – Investigations into Fire* (Marlborough: Crowood Press, 1999)

Koyama, F., *The Heritage of Japanese Ceramics* (New York: Weatherhill, 1973)

Leach, B., *A Potter's Book* (London: Faber, 1977)

Mayer, Conrad, *In/Out-Side (Catalogue of Frank Steyaert)* (Frank Steyaert Gallery, 1999)

Meanley, P., *An Investigation into the Philosophical, Technical and Aesthetic Possibilities of Salt-Glazing, using the Teapot as a Model* (University of Ulster Press, 1998)

Olsen, F., *The Kiln Book* (London: A&C Black, 1983)

Roloff, J., 'Kiln Projects', *Artery* (February–March 1983, p.6)

Semin, D., Garb, T., Kuspit, D. and Perec, G., *Christian Boltanski* (London: Phaidon, 2000)

Shaw, V., *Compositions* (Hohenberg a. d. Eger: Deutsches Porzellanmuseum, 2005)

Troy, J., *Wood Fired Stoneware and Porcelain* (Krause Publications, 1995)

Philosophy and Literature

Bachelard, G., *The Psychoanalysis of Fire* (London: Quartet Books, 1987)

Bachelard, G., *The Poetics of Space* (Boston, MA: Beacon Press, 1994)

Barthes, R., 'The Death of the Author' in R. Barthes, *The Death of the Author* (New York: Noonday Press, 1977)

Barthes, R., *Mythologies* (London: Paladin, 1989)

Baudrillard, J., *Simulations* (New York: Semiotext(e), 1983)

Benjamin, W., *Illuminations*, trans. Hannah Arendt (Orlando, FL: Harcourt Brace, 1968)

Blanchot, M., *The Space of Literature* (Lincoln: University of Nebraska Press, 1982)

Boltanski, C., *Christian Boltanski* (London: Phaidon, 1997)

Brophy, B.A., *Mozart the Dramatist: A New View of Mozart, His Operas and His Age* (New York: Da Capo, 1990)

Cage, John, *A Year from Monday* (Middletown CT: Western University Press, 1967)

Conrad, J., *Heart of Darkness* (London: Penguin, 1995)

Cummings, K., 'Craft: Risk, Certainty and Opportunity', *Point Magazine* (No. 3)

Dante, *The Divine Comedy* (London: Penguin, 1971)

Deleuze, G. and Guatteri, F., *A Thousand Plateaus: Capitalism and Schizophrenia* (Minneapolis, MN: University of Minnesota Press, 1987)

Derrida, J., *Of Grammatology* (Baltimore, MD: John Hopkins University Press, 1997)

Eco, U., *Travels in Hyperreality* (London: Pan Books, 1987)

Eliot, T.S., 'Four Quartets' in *The Complete Poems and Plays of T.S. Eliot* (London: Faber and Faber, 1969)

Eliot, T.S., 'The Wasteland' in *The Complete Poems and Plays of T.S. Eliot* (London: Faber and Faber, 1969)

Foucault, M., Of Other Spaces (1967) Heterotopias, *Diacritics* 16, Spring 1986, 22–27

Freud, S., *The Interpretation of Dreams* (London: Penguin, 1972)

Gleeson, J., *The Arcanum* (Bantam Press, 1998)

Heidegger, M., *Being and Time* (Oxford: Blackwell, 1962)

Heidegger, M., *Poetry, Language, Truth* (New York: Harper Row, 1975)

Jung, C.G., 'Good and Evil in Analytical Psychology' in *Civilization in Transition*, Collected Works Vol.10 (Princeton University Press, 1959)

Jung, C.G., *Four Psychological Types* (New York: Routledge, 1972)

Jung, C.G., *Man and his Symbols* (New York: Routledge, 1972)

Levi-Strauss, C., *The Raw and the Cooked* (University of Chicago Press, 1969)

Merleau-Ponty, M., *The Phenomenology of Perception* (New York: Routledge, 1962)

Michaels, A., *Fugitive Pieces* (London: Bloomsbury, 1997)

Milton, J., *Paradise Lost* (Oxford World Classics, 2004)

Naylor, G., *The Arts and Crafts Movement: A Study of Its Sources, Ideals, and Influence on Design Theory* (Cambridge, MA: MIT Press, 1971)

Pye, D., *The Nature and Art of Workmanship* (London: A&C Black, 1995)

Pyne, S., *Fire: A Brief History* (London: British Museum Press, 2001)

Rawson, P., *Ceramics* (Philadelphia: University of Pennsylvania Press, 1984)

Rorty, R., *Contingency, Irony, and Solidarity* (New York: Cambridge University Press, 1989)

Rye, O., The Art of Uncertainty, *Ceramic Art and Perception*, 1992.

Tilbury, J., 'Cornelius Cardew', *Contact* (Spring 1983), pp.4–12 (at www.users.waitrose.com/~chobbs/tilburycardew.html)

Weintraub, L., *Making Contemporary Art* (London: Thames and Hudson, 2003)

Wimsatt, W. and Beardsley, M., *The Intentional Fallacy*, reprinted in Margolis, J., *Philosophy Looks at the Arts* (New York: Scribners, 1962)

Wittgenstein, L., *Philosophical Investigations* (Oxford: Blackwell, 1953)

Wittgenstein, L., *Tractatus Logico-Philosophicus* (London: Routledge & Kegan Paul, 1953)

Wood, D., *Philosophy at the Limit* (London: Unwin Hayman, 1990)

Journals

American Ceramics
Ceramic Review
Ceramics Art and Perception
Ceramics Monthly
Neue Keramik
New Ceramics
Studio Potter

Suppliers

UK

Bath Potters' Supplies
Unit 18
Fourth Avenue
Westfield Trading Estate
Radstock
Bath
Somerset BA3 4XE
Tel: 01761 411 077
Fax: 01761 414 115
Email:
enquiries@bathpotters.demon.co.uk

Craftline
Cairneycroft
133 Draycott Old Road
Forsbrook
Stoke-on-Trent ST11 9AJ
Tel: 01782 393222
(Visits by appointment only, other-
wise materials delivered.)

Potclays Ltd
Brickkiln Lane
Etruria
Stoke-on-Trent
Staffordshire ST4 7BP
Tel: 01782 219816
Email: potclays@btinternet.com

Potterycrafts Ltd
Campbell Road
Stoke-on-Trent
Staffordshire ST4 4ET
Tel: 01782 745000
Fax: 01782 746000
Email: Sales@potterycrafts.co.uk
Website: www.potterycrafts.co.uk

Valentine's Clay Products
The Sliphouse
Birches Head Road
Hanley
Stoke-on-Trent
Staffordshire ST1 6LH
Tel: 01782 271200

Germany

Nabertherm GmbH
28865
Lilienthal
Bremen
Tel: +49 (4298) 922-0

Australia

Ceramic Supply Co.
17–19 Paves Street
Guildford, NSW 2161
Tel: 612 9892 1566
Email: csco@bigpond.com

Clayworks Australia
6 Johnstone Court
Dandenong
Victoria 3175
Tel: 613 9791 6749

Pottery Supplies
South Castlemain St
Paddington
Queensland 4064
Tel: 617 3368 2877

Walker Ceramics
Boronia Road
Wantirna
Victoria 3125
Tel: 613 9725 7255

USA and Canada

AFTOSA
1032 Ohio Avenue
Richmond
CA 94804
Tel: 800 2310397
Website: www.aftosa.com

American Art Clay Co.
W 16th Street,
Indianapolis
IN 46222
Tel: 317 244 6871
Website: www.amaco.com

Laguna Clay Co.
1440 Lomitas Avenue
City of Industry
CA 91746
Tel: 800 452 4862
Fax: (626) 333 7694
Website: www.lagunaclay.com

Minnesota Clay Co.
8001 Grand Avenue South
Bloomington
MN 55420
Tel: 612 884 9101

Tuckers Pottery Supplies Inc.
15 West Pearce St
Richmond Hill
Ontario
Canada L4B1 H6
Tel: 800 304 6185
Email: Tuckers@passport.ca
Website: www.tuckerspottery.com

Index